The New
FLOWER ARRANGING
FROM YOUR GARDEN

Acclaimed as 'the First Lady of Flower Arranging', Sheila Macqueen was for many years chief demonstrator and decorator for the Constance Spry Organisation. She has written a number of books and countless articles on her subject and travelled throughout Britain and Europe, Australia and North America lecturing and demonstrating flower arranging. Mrs Macqueen has enjoyed the distinction of arranging flowers for a host of Royal occasions, including the two recent Royal Weddings.

also by Sheila Macqueen

COMPLETE FLOWER ARRANGING

The New
FLOWER ARRANGING
FROM YOUR GARDEN
Sheila Macqueen

GUILD PUBLISHING LONDON

To Sophie Leaning and Netta Statham
whose gardening knowledge has helped me
so much through the years.

First published in Great Britain 1977 by Ward Lock Limited
in association with Peter Crawley

This edition 1988 by
Guild Publishing by arrangement with
Macmillan London Ltd.

Typeset by Wyvern Typesetting Limited, Bristol

Printed in Hong Kong

CONTENTS

Preface

THE FLOWER ARRANGER'S GARDEN   5
CALENDAR OF MATERIALS   16
PRINCIPLES OF ARRANGING AND CONDITIONING   20
SMALL AND MINIATURE FLOWER ARRANGEMENTS   24
DRIED FLOWERS: PRESERVING AND ARRANGING   29
A–Z OF PLANTS TO GROW   33

Index   123

Preface

It is wonderful for me that the continued success of *Flower Arranging From Your Garden* has resulted in a further edition *plus* my greatest delight – to have a greatly increased number of colour photographs showing more of the flowers I find best for arranging. Colour really brings a book to life and this added bonus should help everyone to have a better idea of what they are going to grow and subsequently arrange.

I have added further plants and some new varieties, and have also included the new rose 'Sheila Macqueen' – naturally terribly exciting! It will be shown for the first time at Chelsea in 1988. I have known Jack Harkness for many years and when he suggested that I should come and choose a rose out of an acre of new roses it was unbelievable; I felt like a child let loose in a toy shop at Christmas time! It was one of the most difficult things I have ever had to do. Having first spotted the green cross I really felt so drawn to it that I went back time and time again. I picked it on three different occasions and it always lasted beautifully in water and seemed disease-free, as far as one could tell.

I hope so much that this book will encourage more people to want to grow flowers in their gardens, and then to arrange them – there is no greater thrill than seeing flowers you have grown yourself in a lovely arrangement in your home.

Sheila Macqueen
June, 1987

THE FLOWER ARRANGER'S GARDEN

Starting a garden from scratch

If you are starting right at the beginning, with virtually a piece of waste ground, the layout you plan is most important. Assuming it is feasible and you have the time, it is best to start by clearing the area completely of stones and stumps, weeds and rough grass, using a rotary cultivator or, if the weeds are really vicious, by applying a powerful weed-killer which any good garden centre will recommend. Time spent in preparation at this early stage will be invaluable in the future, but the first objective of this initial clearing is to show you the basic shape of the ground and any noticeable features in or near it.

Making your plan

I suggest the best way of going about this is to begin *inside* your house. Walk from room to room, deciding which room you will be sitting in most, and go to the window in that room from which you get the best view of the garden. If you really feel you will not see very much from the house, decide on the sitting area you will use most outside. Then take paper and pencil and make rough sketches of what you would like to see from these positions. I know most books will tell you to start with a layout on graph paper, but I feel this comes later, for after all you don't look down on trees, paths and lawns and I think it is important to try first of all to visualize your garden as you would eventually like to see it in its maturity.

Study the problems, such as an ugly shed to be hidden, or a cold prevailing wind; draw in the features you want to emphasize, such as a fine tree or a natural slope, and remember practical considerations. Ask all your friends for advice: everyone loves to give advice, though you may not want to take it all. Often you will find that something will strike one person and something else another, and you will be given quite a lot of useful ideas. For example, we had decided to make a path between the house and a wall, and some sensible friend said 'Make it wide enough for the barrow.' I have never ceased to be grateful for the enormous amount of walking that advice saved me.

Practical points to remember

I shall not attempt to advise you on every aspect of garden design, but I would like to suggest that the following points should always be kept in mind.

The cost of upkeep steadily increases all the time and there is always a limit to the time you can spend on your garden. For example, grass paths look attractive, but make for a lot of work, and, especially in the vegetable garden, some form of concrete or stone path will save effort in the future.

When you are thinking about your lawn, remember that bold sweeping curves not only look better, but will save you hours of manoeuvring the mower around fiddly sharp corners.

Never plant a flower border too near a hedge: make a path at the back, which makes for easy working and prevents weeds from beyond and under the hedge from encroaching into the garden.

Always make borders wider than you think they should be, and try to place at least some so that you can look along them: you can get a wonderful effect from a wide flower border, whereas narrow borders seen straight on are often disappointing.

Don't make too many small flower beds: they look fussy and take up a lot of time.

A paved area can be a lovely feature in a garden with either sink gardens or just paving and sweet-smelling plants such as pinks, lavender and honeysuckle growing from small areas left clear between the paving stones. Best of all, if you can design your paved area so that it is close by the house, slightly sunken or sheltered by wall and hedge, you have a perfect 'sitting-out' place.

Rock gardens also need to be near the house. The whole pattern of our lives has changed; when it was relatively easy to get help it was pleasant to wander round a garden and enjoy one surprise after another, walking from hedged rose garden to lily pool to rock garden: now I feel envy for those of my friends who had the foresight to place a rock pool or rock garden as a feature easily seen from the house or perhaps next to the sun loggia. Even on a chill spring evening or damp summer night you can then sit and enjoy the garden – with a little ingenious use of lighting, and maybe a drink in your hand, what could make a more attractive view! The Americans are past masters at this, and I have sat in some of the smallest gardens, where lovely walls festooned with colourful plants and hidden lighting make you feel they are twice or three times the size they really are.

The first year – take your time!

If you have to tackle an overgrown garden, in some ways it can be difficult – but at least there will be some trees or shrubs that will give the garden a furnished look, and this does help. I strongly recommend you should not make many changes until you have had a chance to see the garden right through one season. So often there are hidden treasures that can easily be destroyed, never to be found again. If you live with the garden for a year, you may find there is a good reason for some of the earlier planting. In a garden near me, for instance, the new owner cut down all the polygonum (knotweed or Russian vine) covering a fence, only to find it had covered the most unsightly and makeshift structure, which of course was exactly why it had been put there in the first place. I had an old plum tree cut down when we first moved in, but it was not until the following autumn that I bitterly regretted it; as soon as all the leaves were off the other trees, I had an uninterrupted view of the next-door-neighbour's house, and pleasant as it is, I would really much have preferred the old tree. These are just two warnings against being over-hasty.

The first year will not be wasted – whilst you are thinking about ways and means of re-planning the parts you find unattractive, the better sections can be improved. Laurel and rhododendrons, for instance, are shrubs that can stand being cut back really hard, allowing new growth to appear which is often such an improvement. Prune a little at a time or maybe cut back every other one. I know exactly what can happen when one has a pair of secateurs in the hand – there is a strong urge to make a clean sweep, but this may have the effect of killing, not curing, overgrown shrubs.

Whether your garden is one you have created yourself or one you have taken over, it is a good idea occasionally to ask someone else to look at it with a fresh eye. A great friend who is an excellent gardener came to help me once, and every now and then would say something like 'Why do you keep that old rose when it never really does anything?' How right she was, but somehow I had never thought of getting rid of it and replacing it with a more attractive plant. This can often happen and is just one way in which you can improve your garden.

Now, a five-year plan

When you have decided on the basic layout, it is time to get out the squared paper and carefully plot out the area each plant will need when it is fully grown. But don't attempt to buy and plant all of the flowers in one season. I find it best to have a five-year plan and work outwards, concentrating first on the area near the house. If you are lucky enough to have a pleasant view, you need do no more at first than plant for a little colour and flowers to pick, but even in later years, remember not to interrupt the view.

One of the loveliest gardens I know is in Middleburg, Virginia, in the United States, where two vast borders sweep towards the foothills of the Blue Mountains. Huge clumps of peonies and iris were beautifully planted with a background of good shrubs, cleverly interspersed with evergreens. This kind of treatment can be used for even the smallest garden: planting to create a view, or frame an existing one, using shrubs in the herbaceous border to save work, placing evergreens to give winter life and summer contrast, and planting in clumps to create a simple restful effect.

Choosing the plants

In the garden you use the same technique as for flower arranging, grouping for contrast and allowing leaves to play a major part. When arranging a vase, the best way to avoid a spotty effect is to place together one or two flowers of the same colour. For example, an outline of twiggy flowering shrub such as forsythia, then some pieces of the green hellebore with delicate but solid heads, a centre focal point of two rounded heads of *Petasites japonicus*, or three or five yellow tulips with a few stems of straw-coloured hyacinth on either side. Exactly the same principles can be followed when you plan your border: in this case the forsythia and large-leaved petasites would be at the back, with the smaller plants in front providing different leaf forms and colour. Alternatively try putting three golden-leaved hosta together with three green-leaved ones, with dark-leaved bergenia or tellima next to the gold hosta, then maybe a russet leucothöe or two, and behind them a clump of grey artichoke and grey onopordum thistle together with a greyish-leaved eucalyptus. To contrast with the grey mass, you can have a pink or yellow-flowering rhododendron, then two clumps of euphorbia as another contrast in leaf form but with a colour to blend with the hosta in front of it. Try to group plants that set each other off and look well together even when not in flower. My favourite green hellebores, for example, look so well in the early spring against an evergreen hedge or under the bare twigs of *Cornus mas*. The lime green of *Alchemilla mollis* can be used to set off *Alstroemeria ligtu* hybrids both in vase and in border.

7

It is also fun to work out nice ideas for underplanting, but this is much more a matter of trial and error: I did try polyanthus under forsythia, but have never yet had the luck to find them all in flower at the same time. And only after twenty-odd years have I succeeded in getting my hardy cyclamen to flower well under a silver birch. However, this should not stop you from trying out ideas, for it is amazing how quickly the years fly by.

One big problem when deciding on which plants to grow is that, having spent so much on your house – usually more than one ever intended – there seems to be little left for the garden. So you may feel that you want to grow most things yourself and many from seed. Do bear in mind how long this will take, though, and invest in a few large shrubs and trees and some of the plants that will take longest to grow, such as peonies, roses, hellebores, alchemilla, onopordum, *Alstroemeria ligtu* hybrids, euphorbias, hostas, delphinium and a few plants for the rock garden. Hopefully, many of your gardener friends will have spare plants and will be happy to give you seedlings and cuttings, and I do advise you to accept these even if they are not exactly what you want, for they can always be replaced at a later date.

I tend to plant much too close together, pessimistically assuming that not everything is going to grow, but I suppose the ideal would be to plant each subject with enough space to grow to full maturity. If you are strong-minded and can do this, I suggest filling in during the early years with annuals, especially those like atriplex and moluccella, which are also lovely for picking and drying.

You will find that I have chosen only a few annuals that I find particularly useful for flower arranging. Unfortunately most of these are not easily bought as plants, so you will have to grow them yourself. But if you like to have a few annuals in the border giving colour through July and August, buy some young plants, such as antirrhinums, stocks, petunias and verbena. I find some of the brilliantly coloured geraniums very useful if used as annuals. Plant these in clumps of five plants to make a good splash of colour where some of the early flowers, like perennial poppies, have left a gap. All of these annual plants may be bought easily from your local garden centre or nursery.

If I could choose only ten plants to grow for flower arranging, the ones I would choose, and would hate to live without, are:

> *Alchemilla mollis*
> Artichoke (*Cynara scolymus*)
> *Arum italicum* 'Pictum'
> Bergenias
> Euphorbias
> Hedera
> Hellebore
> Hosta
> *Phytolacca americana*
> Sedum

All of these may be used in arrangements for many months in the year.

Choosing trees, shrubs and climbers

Your choice of trees and shrubs, to quite a large extent, depends upon the type of soil in your garden. There are so many excellent trees and shrubs that I think it is a great waste of effort to struggle with things that are unsuited to your conditions. However, gardening is such a challenge anyway that it is sometimes fun to get something growing even when you have been warned against it! Remember to choose for the shape, texture and colour of leaves as well as flowers. Foliage with good winter colour, leaves that reflect the glow of autumn, yellow-greens in early spring to give that feeling of sunlight – all these points are important. Winter-flowering shrubs are something I feel everyone should try to grow, particularly if you are a flower arranger, as these precious pieces picked in the depths of winter give more sheer delight than a wealth of bloom in midsummer.

The importance of a good lawn

I think the best way to achieve a good lawn is by sowing grass seed, but I know that this is not always practicable. We really had no choice, for instance: a sea of clay, rough ground with nettles and indeed every conceivable weed, two small children with nowhere to play outside – we decided very quickly that our first priority was to turf a lawn. The result has never been very good. However, we put geese on another area of rough grass for a year, and with constant fertilizing and cutting it has improved out of all recognition and is undoubtedly our best piece of lawn today. In my view, frequent cutting can make a good lawn even from poor grass. In my garden I soon found that even if I worked in it for every minute I could spare during the week, it was only when my husband cut the grass at the weekend that the garden began to look good.

Patio gardens

The paved area with its decorative pots must surely have started life in towns where space is limited and nearly everyone craves for something green and something which lives and needs tending. But the pattern is changing and the patio garden has come to the country, too. As we have so little sun in Britain we all want to make the most of the smallest ray, hence the sunroom and the patio are both welcome additions to many homes. And because of lack of help in the garden it seems to me that pot gardening for the summer is becoming more and more popular and patios are proliferating.

Patio gardens come in two categories. One is a copy of the old Spanish, or perhaps Italian, courtyard garden where pots are massed together, rather like plants in a garden. And in these Mediterranean countries I am always fascinated to see what they grow in the pots, such unexpected things turn up, like aucuba – what I call the spotted laurel – which appears to be a great favourite, as is bergenia. These seem to me strange pot plants but they thrive and give a lovely feeling of coolness in a blistering hot Spanish sun, and the shade of the courtyards must be like heaven to those who live with that burning heat every day.

The other type of patio garden has the elegant Grecian-type pot showing off one plant of good shape or even a bonsai, or perhaps just two well-planted pots of mixed summer flowers strategically placed so that they enhance the patio area. (Incidentally, there is now available a marvellous variety of standard fuchsias which make superb pot plants.)

I find that masses of pots of many varieties of plants can tend to look messy and confusing, though I have a friend in California who must have ninety plants on her terrace which look very effective. Personally, the thought of the daily watering would quickly persuade me to have only a few.

There are certain basic principles about making a sitting-out area, and I would say immediately that you should make it twice as large as you intended. From my own observation people never seem to leave enough room for the number of chairs that they actually use. You will also need a table and space to move around it comfortably so make a really large terrace, if you can, with room enough, too, for pots and tubs.

There are various ways of dealing with pots and tubs. A friend of mind has a rotation system which is very successful. As he has practically no garden, he capitalizes on a terrace on which he has only two large tubs showing at a time, although in fact he has eight pots or tubs in all. In winter two are planted with a small winter-flowering *Viburnum tinus* called 'Evelyn Price'. This evergreen has clusters of pinky-white flowers, and blooms almost continuously all winter long. Meanwhile he has planted two tubs of mixed bulbs for spring and they are placed on view when they break into flower. For high summer he has tubs of the most beautiful lilies I have ever seen including *Lilium regale* and with its wonderful gold stamens, *L. auratum*, the sun lily of Japan. (Lilies do grow very well indeed with the protection of a pot.) And as lilies are his speciality he also puts out many different lilies in pots which make a lovely show.

Lastly, the tubs are replaced by two large hydrangea plants and these bloom from August to October. But, don't forget that to make this system work you do need an area near the house to keep the out-of-season pots, or if not near the house, well out of sight and near a tap or access to water. Tubs and pots need plenty of water especially in the summer months. If you are able to submerge the pots under soil level they do not dry out nearly so quickly.

Swimming pools

The ease with which we can now heat our swimming pools has meant that there are many more pools in Britain than ever before. It also means another garden area which can be pretty bleak-looking with lots of uninteresting concrete which calls for groups of pots, or tubs. I think if you have any choice of where to place a pool then I would suggest keeping it away from the house a little because though it may look pretty in summer it appears very forlorn for about seven months of the year. Since it is not a good idea to have deciduous trees or shrubs near the pool, planting is restricted to evergreens and the colour must be provided by pots, urns or tubs. Should you be making the pool a feature of the garden then very careful planning and planting is needed and kidney-shaped pools or any shape other than the dreary rectangle must be the first thought. If you have lots of space, then a wide paved area round the pool gives you plenty of sitting space and room for pots and tubs for colour in summer. And in late autumn you can change the pots and plant them suitably to last the winter, as mentioned above.

Tubs and hanging baskets

From pots at ground level to hanging baskets: these are becoming very popular. Anything raised above eye level is effective and petunias are one of the best subjects for a hanging basket as they flower all summer and show off so much better in a basket than they do in a border in the garden.

I think the mixed basket is probably the most popular. The trailing varieties of lobelia are ideal and it is worth remembering how important blue is in a mixed planting. The lobelia 'Blue Cascade' is a lovely Cambridge blue and I can thoroughly recommend it. Another good trailer is the ivy-leaved geranium and for a wide range of colour there are the petunias.

I well remember seeing in Florida two magnificent wrought-iron urns filled entirely with white petunias and nothing else. They looked superb. I tried it here but with no great success. Maybe my setting was not so elegant, though single colour pots of plants do look extremely good, or perhaps there was not quite enough space to show them off to advantage. This is something that is definitely worth another try.

When planting hanging baskets it pays to use the very best soil and layer it well with sphagnum moss. For pots and tubs good loam is necessary as most plants have to survive with a small quantity of soil. I never feed mine enough during the summer and then really regret it. I am determined to do better next year.

Plants for tubs and hanging baskets

One of the plants which has improved so dramatically over these last few years is the begonia. The small *semperflorens* with their excellent and wide colour range are superb in pots, tubs and hanging baskets. They are also excellent for use as a bedding plant as well, for they flower right into October, or at least until the first frost. I have never been a lover of tuberous-rooted begonias though they are magnificent as a handsome planting in parks or large areas where they have plenty of space to show off to their best advantage. But these little *semperflorens* are another matter altogether, and a great delight. 'Venus Rose' is one of my favourites. It stays a good shade of pink all summer as does 'Rosanova', and 'Dancia Scarlet' has the added attraction of dark bronze foliage which is a lovely plus.

There are many mixed packets of begonia seed on the market and these, given a bed to themselves, provide great pleasure and constant colour from the first flowering to the first frost, with little or no special care, apart from watering. If you like the more unusual then it might be worth trying 'Coco Ducolour'. It does need careful planting and placing to show it off to the best advantage, but the white flowers edged with red and the well-shaped plants with their bronze foliage really appeal to me.

For the pots and tubs there are so many plants and even fruit trees that can be grown in them that the choice is very wide – starting in the early spring with camellias and going on to mixed bulbs and forget-me-nots. And I still enjoy forget-me-nots planted with the early double tulips, especially with 'Murillo' or 'Peach Blossom', old-fashioned perhaps but nevertheless very pretty.

I know many people plant daffodils in pots but to me they never look happy. Daffodils, I think, really look their best growing naturally in grass. There are many of the hybrid white, pink and very special colours which have to be specially cared for and these I grow in clumps together in the border, but I do not enjoy them in tubs. This, of course, is my personal opinion, and many may not agree with me. Ideal plants are hyacinths and short double tulips, and the little pink double daisy *Bellis perennis* is most attractive either on its own or with forget-me-nots and short tulips.

For summer, roses can be grown in a tub and do very well and it is useful to have them in tubs if you have a small area with nowhere else to put them. Then again, petunias, geraniums, lobelia, tobacco plants, begonias are all excellent subjects for a patio garden. Lilies in summer followed by pots of hydrangeas all give good colour range and a different look which makes the area interesting all the year round.

Another plant not usually considered as a pot plant but very effective, is sedum and 'Autumn Joy' gives a mass of colour for many weeks from September until the frost. And the butterflies love it.

I was very interested on a recent visit to China to find that nearly everything that was grown and tended was edible – understandable with such a vast population to feed, but every now and again one saw a few little pots clustered

11

outside a dwelling and on many occasions they turned out to be decorative kale plants and very pretty they looked. So maybe that is another idea for the winter patio.

Window boxes are used more in town than in the country though I have seen old stables which have been converted into gardenless country houses where window boxes look very attractive. Good strong wooden boxes are still the best if you can get them but if possible use a liner, or rather two liners, so that you can ring the changes with say, miniature conifers and euonymus interspersed with *Solanum capsicastrum* (Winter Cherry) to add colour in winter. The second box can be filled with bulbs and eventually in summer with geraniums perhaps, and petunias, lobelia and a wide choice of plants. Extravagant, but beautiful, are hydrangeas forced early and planted out in late May to stay until the frost – but beware! they do need a lot of water.

Apart from tubs and pots, old sinks can be useful in a patio garden or even newer ones, treated with sand and cement to give a rough surface, look very well lining a terrace and of course give constant interest all the year. A dwarf conifer or two provide an excellent outline shape and colour, and one of the best is *Juniperus communis compressa*; any Alpine specialist could give you more varieties.

Some well-shaped rocks placed strategically so that they do not take up too much room, will do much to set off the plants. Basically rock and shallow-rooted plants are suitable: in spring, perhaps, aubretias and yellow alyssum, rock garden dianthus and later campanulas with alpine phlox for marvellous colour. Try to choose plants with compact habit like succulents or sempervivums so that the sinks do not get overgrown and untidy. Miniature fuchsias look good and even berried plants for autumn like *Cotoneaster congesta*, which has little white flowers followed by red berries once it is well established. There is no end to the interest of a miniature sink garden.

Finally, to complete this section on patio gardens, window boxes, tubs, troughs and ornamental pots a few more words on the most important thing of all which I may not have stressed significantly and that is good planting and high quality soil. A really good loam is so important and if this is difficult to get it is well worthwhile to buy a bag or bags of John Innes or a similar compost recommended for window boxes or tubs. Good drainage is essential, so break up bricks or coarse rubble and place this in the bottom of the tub or box, then with a little sphagnum moss and good loam fill the pot. Do not overfill as it is difficult to water and if the soil is too high then the water runs off the top and never gets really down to the roots. I find that 'planting' an empty 8 cm (3 in) flower pot into the tub is a very easy way of making sure that the water really does get down to the roots. A little liquid fertilizer every few weeks during the flowering season is important and then you have really done all you can to see that these planted pots and tubs grow well and give the maximum of colour and pleasure throughout the season.

Wild flowers and how to use them

The prospect of wild flowers growing in grass is a thrilling one, but I must sound a note of warning! If you have a large garden and an out of the way place where grass and wild flowers may grow in happy confusion, that is fine. But should your garden be small I would strongly recommend you to move with caution – after the first few weeks of delight the long grass will start to look a mess and very unattractive. It will also be difficult to get it back into shape as a lawn again. I believe Lady Bird Johnson was responsible for having thousands

12

of seeds scattered on the road verges of Washington during her husband's presidency, and I think that was a lovely thing to do.

If you are thinking of gathering wild flowers from the countryside it is important to have a clear view about conservation. Nowadays with the ever-increasing amount of building it is essential that we watch over our precious native plants. This is especially necessary in rural areas where the rarer species such as orchis, fritillaria, lily of the valley and other delightful flowers are at risk. The sorts of wild flowers you can safely pick are what I call 'wayside flowers' – wild flowers that grow along the sides of roads and which will be cut down anyway by the council when the verges are 'tidied'. You will be surprised how many wild flowers you will find – I have used dog daisies, which spring up in hundreds whenever any waste land is disturbed, sorrel and docks, hemlock, cow parsnip, parsley and carrot (better know in the USA as Queen Anne's lace), willow herb and grasses of all kinds. They all flourish abundantly and picking them will not worry the conservationists.

Perhaps the best way of describing a wild flower is to say it is a flower which propagates itself in those place where it can survive and thrive. I suppose every flower is a native of some part of the world – orchids in Malaysia, for example, and acrolinium in Australia. I remember seeing sheets of the pink and white daisy-like flowers lining the roads north of Perth in Western Australia. It is extremely popular with arrangers who specialise in dried flowers as it dries particularly well. I believe that brides in Jamaica love having Queen Anne's lace in their wedding bouquets, whereas here where it grows in such abundance we would scarcely think of using it. Possibly because it would not last long before wilting.

This brings me to one of the problems in using wild flowers for arrangements. Growing, as they generally do, in poor soil wild flowers often have long tap roots to enable them to survive. If these roots are severed the flowers will wilt very quickly. So if you are intending to gather wayside flowers I suggest you should keep a strong plastic bag handy in the car. As you cut, say, cow parsley or bluebells place them head-first in the bag. Everyone puts them stalks-first into bags and this is how problems start. If you keep the heads out of the air the flowers suffer much less from lack of moisture. As quickly as you can after picking them, place the stems in a bucket of really warm water. This will give them the best chance of lasting reasonably well. I find that of the many wild flowers I like to use, bluebells and cow parsley, or cow parsnip, are the favourites. They last better if not on very long stems. Bluebells, like wall-flowers, should be cut on stems no longer than four or five inches (12–15 cm), then mass them in a box or basket. In this way they last very well and the scent is out of this world; they appear to like being packed closely together for they always seem to last better this way.

Cowslips massed are also lovely, but primroses look particularly well on a bed of moss. As their stems are naturally short, they enjoy the moisture they get from the damp moss. A spring garden arrangement made in a shallow dish is an excellent way to use them. Place some wire mesh in the dish and cover it with the moss. Then insert a few stems of hazel catkins to give height and tuck into the moss bunches of primroses, snowdrops and perhaps a few early daffodils and crocuses. This will give you the loveliest spring garden and wild flower arrangement. During the War we were evacuated to Berkshire and next door was a wood full of wild daffodils – they looked absolutely enchanting. Now, of course, they are far too precious to pick.

Wild roses. Try to pick them with a lot of buds as they will all open in water and last so much longer like this. They can be arranged in a basket and they also look well in a glass vase.

Opposite.
The author's
front door.

I find that the berries of the mountain ash tree, rose hips and hawthorn berries all look very effective in a copper or brass bowl. Black privet mixed with dark red snapdragons and some white flowers, such as roses or dahlias, also makes a striking arrangement.

Much wild material makes a splendid background for garden flowers so I often look for spikes of red dock, teasles, and bullrushes, while in the USA bittersweet and milkweed pods are invaluable allies. Old Man's Beard, the wild clematis, is enormously effective in arrangements and can be preserved easily. You should treat it in the same way as beech leaves by placing the ends of the stems in a solution of one part glycerine to two parts of water. Leave them for several days until they change colour and go brown.

Finally, the most important point of all about getting wild flowers for arrangements – you must be sure to condition them as well as possible. I have mentioned that they should be placed in a polythene bag when first cut, then the re-cut ends put into very hot water. This is the same treatment as for garden flowers which do not stand well when cut. The boiling water technique may be used for a mixed collection of wild and garden flowers – hydrangeas, roses, dahlias, clematis, wild roses, cow parsley, willow herb and other wild flowers – treating them all the same. Place the end of the stems into an inch of boiling water, count up to thirty, and then stand them in cold water for several hours so that they may have a really long drink. (I have only mentioned, as examples, a few of the garden flowers that benefit from this treatment. My *Complete Flower Arranging* gives in full the appropriate conditioning for flowers and leaves of the more than 400 plants described in it.)

Vases and containers

Today the word 'container' is used more widely than 'flower vase', maybe because we are using receptacles from around the house which started life for a very different purpose. Copper kettles and jugs make ideal flower vases, as do pewter mugs, teapots, tea urns, wooden boxes and tea caddies. Silver wine-coolers, entrée dishes, candlesticks are all ideal and so much more interesting than a traditional cut-glass flower vase.

Search round the house to see what you can find, and if you go to buy a vase try and get one in neutral colours, say in white-grey or dusky pink, so that you can use it with a wide variety of colourings. Although bright colours may be lovely for a special occasion, they can be very restricting for everyday use. If you become an arranger then you will automatically become a vase collector. You will find copper containers very useful for berries, bronze-coloured chrysanthemums and dahlias in the autumn. Glass or silver for roses, cow parsley and gypsophila; these light, delicate flowers show at their best in glass, and are fragile and cool-looking on a summer's day. Blue and red glass are both most effective, blue filled with delphiniums, red with brilliant, vibrant red colours. A wooden box or bowl looks lovely with bright orange and yellow marigolds and it is also excellent for showing off the subtle tones and hues of dried materials. Try to make the container part of the arrangement so that it blends with the flowers and does not stick out like a sore thumb. If you have nice porcelain, then picking up the colourings of the pattern of the china can also be very rewarding. A vegetable dish from your dinner service makes an ideal dinner table centre-piece, similarly the soup tureen or a sauce-boat can look superb. They all blend so well together when the table is set with the same china.

As you will see from the illustrations in this book, I use a wide range of containers and have collected them over the years. I have a great love for

alabaster and spent hours searching for it and for bronze containers. Unhappily both are almost impossible to come by nowadays. However, there is a wide variety of baskets of all shapes and sizes, and these can be very inexpensive. Baskets are nice to use at any time of year; in spring with a mass of daffodils, in summer with mixed garden flowers, annuals of all kinds, and as you will see in the illustration overleaf from page 54, a basket filled with wild daisies has a charm of its own. Alternatively you can make much more lavish arrangements using a basket filled with both pot plants and cut flowers mixed together. If the baskets don't come with a liner you can always find a cheap plastic or china bowl to fit inside them. But it is important to make sure it is big enough to hold sufficient water for the flowers.

If you live in a town or do not have the opportunity to pick flowers or to gather other arranging materials, containers and vases assume a special importance. (If you have a garden with lots of materials the container is not so important because even an oven dish can be disguised by having the flowers and foliage cover the front so that it is quite invisible.) My advice is to buy one really nice container that will hold plenty of water and which you will find easy to arrange. Should you have to buy all your flowers then I suggest you should get a vase that will look pretty with just a bunch of freesias, baby carnations, or a few stems of single chrysanthemums. They are all easily obtainable and long-lasting.

Never allow your enthusiasm for nice containers to encourage you to have too many arrangements at one time! In the winter one large arrangement of dried flowers or of pretty mixed green foliage is a good stand-by. Apart from that I would have one small arrangement on a side-table or coffee-table. Something sweet-smelling, possibly, is all that is necessary unless you are entertaining friends. A vase of flowers as you come into the house always gives a welcome and this is one of the most effective places for having flowers when they are in short supply. Finally, vases and containers of flowers need daily attention; you will need to add fresh water to them and you should inspect the arrangements, cutting out any dead or dying flowers. They should be cut rather than pulled out as you may completely upset the entire arrangement.

Opposite.
Summer colours in the author's garden.

CALENDAR OF MATERIALS

In order that the lists should not be inordinately long, I have arranged the plants under the months in which they are in flower. In the case of foliage, which may be used a number of times throughout the year, I have listed the subject under the months in which I find it exceptionally useful.

JANUARY

Alnus (Alder)
Aralia
Aucuba japonica
Camellia
Cedrus atlantica 'Glauca'

Choisya ternata
Elaeagnus pungens
Eucalyptus
Euonymus
Garrya elliptica

Hedera (Ivy)
Jasminum (Jasmine)
Magnolia grandiflora
Mahonia
Viburnum

FEBRUARY

Alnus (Alder)
Aucuba japonica
Arum italicum
Bergenia
Camellia
Cedrus atlantica 'Glauca'
Chimonanthus
    (Winter Sweet)
Choisya ternata
Crocus

Elaeagnus pungens
Eranthis (Winter Aconite)
Eucalyptus
Euonymus
Galanghus (Snowdrop)
Garrya elliptica
Hedera (Ivy)
Helleborus – corsicus,
    foetidus, orientalis
    hybrids

Jasminum (Jasmine)
Magnolia grandiflora
Mahonia
Narcissus
Petasites
Prunus
Pulmonaria
Salix (Willow)
Viburnum

MARCH

Alnus (Alder)
Aucuba japonica
Arum italicum
Bergenia
Camellia
Carpinus betulus
    (Hornbeam)
Cedrus atlantica 'Glauca'
Chimonanthus
    (Winter Sweet)
Chionodoxa
Choisya ternata
Corylus
Crocus
Cyclamen coum

Daphne mezereum
Elaeagnus pungens
Eranthis (Winter Aconite)
Erica carnea
Eucalyptus
Euonymus
Forsythia
Galanthus (Snowdrop)
Hamamelis mollis
    (Witch Hazel)
Hedera (Ivy)
Helleborus – corsicus,
    foetidus, orientalis
    hybrids

Jasminum (Jasmine)
Leucojum (Snowflake)
Magnolia grandiflora
Mahonia
Narcissus
Petasites
Primula
Prunus
Pulsatilla
Ribes
Rhododendron
Salix (Willow)
Viburnum
Zantedeschia

APRIL

Acer (Maple)
Allium
Arum italicum
Bergenia
Camellia
Chimonanthus
  (Winter Sweet)
Cornus
Corylopsis
Cynara (Artichoke)
Daphne

Elaeagnus pungens
Erythronium
Forsythia
Fritillaria
Hedera (Ivy)
Helleborus – corsicus,
  foetidus, orientalis
  hybrids
Hyacinth
Magnolia grandiflora
Narcissus

Polygonatum
  (Solomon's Seal)
Prunus
Ranunculus
Rhododendron
Ribes
Salix (Willow)
Trollius
Tulip
Viburnum

MAY

Allium
Azalea
Camellia
Clematis
Convallaria majalis
  (Lily of the Valley)
Cornus kousa
Cynara (Artichoke)
Daphne
Dicentra

Dictamnus
Digitalis
Euphorbia
Hedera (Ivy)
Helleborus corsicus
Hemerocallis (Day Lily)
Hyacinth
Ligustrum
Lilac
Lonicera

Lupinus (Lupin)
Paeonia (Peony)
Prunus
Rheum
Rhododendron
Senecio
Tellima
Tiarella
Tulip
Wistaria

JUNE

Alstroemeria
Angelica
Astrantia
Betula (Birch)
Campanula
Clematis
Cynara (Artichoke)
Delphinium
Dictamnus
Digitalis
Epimedium
Eryngium
Euphorbia

Geranium
Heuchera
Hosta
Iris
Lathyrus (Sweet Pea)
Ligustrum
Lilac
Lonicera
Lupinus (Lupin)
Macleaya
Nepeta
Onopordum
Paeonia (Peony)

Papaver (Poppy)
Penstemon
Polygonum
Prunella
Rosa (Rose)
Senecio
Smilacina
Thalictrum
Tiarella
Verbascum
Vinca
Yucca

JULY

Acanthus
Achillea
Aconitum
Alchemilla
Anaphalis
Angelica
Artemisia
Ballota
Betula (Birch)
Campanula
Crocosmia
Cynara (Artichoke)
Dahlia
Delphinium
Dianthus
Eryngium

Filipendula
Gentiana (Gentian)
Geranium
Gladiolus
Heuchera
Hosta
Kniphofia (Red-hot Poker)
Lathyrus (Sweet Pea)
Lavatera
Lavendula (Lavender)
Ligustrum
Lily
Macleaya
Nepeta
Onopordum
Paeonia (Peony)

Papaver (Poppy)
Penstemon
Philadelphus
Phlox
Phytolacca
Polygonum
Rosa (Rose)
Salvia
Scabiosa (Scabious)
Sedum
Sisyrinchium
Stachys lanata
Thalictrum
Verbascum
Yucca

AUGUST

Acanthus
Achillea
Agapanthus
Alchemilla
Amaranthus
Anaphalis
Angelica
Antirrhinum
Artemisia
Atriplex
Ballota
Buddleia
Campanula
Cobaea scandens
Cortaderia (Pampas Grass)
Crocosmia

Cynara (Artichoke)
Dahlia
Delphinium
Dianthus
Eryngium
Filipendula
Gentiana (Gentian)
Geranium
Gladiolus
Hosta
Hydrangea
Lavatera
Ligustrum
Lily
Macleaya

Moluccella
Nepeta
Nicotiana
Philadelphus
Phlox
Phytolacca
Rosa (Rose)
Rudbeckia
Scabiosa (Scabious)
Sedum
Sisyrinchium
Stachys lanata
Veratrum
Yucca
Zinnia

SEPTEMBER

Acanthus
Agapanthus
Alchemilla
Amaranthus
Anemone
Artemisia
Calluna (Ling)
Carpinus betulus
   (Hornbeam)

Cobaea scandens
Cortaderia (Pampas Grass)
Cotinus
Dahlia
Gentiana (Gentian)
Geranium
Gladiolus
Hydrangea

Kniphofia (Red-hot Poker)
Lily
Nerine
Nicotiana
Phytolacca
Rosa (Rose)
Sedum
Zinnia

OCTOBER

Agapanthus
Ampelopsis (Virginia
   Creeper)
Arbutus
Artemisia
Berberis
Celastrus (Bittersweet)
Cimicifuga
Cobaea scandens
Colchicum
Cortaderia (Pampas Grass)

Cotoneaster
Cyclamen neapolitanum
Dahlia
Epimedium
Fagus (Beech)
Forsythia
Gentiana (Gentian)
Gladiolus
Hydrangea
Nerine

Osmunda
Pernettya
Phytolacca
Pyracantha
Rodgersia
Rosa (Rose)
Scrophularia
Sedum
Symphoricarpus (Snowberry)
Vitis

NOVEMBER

Berberis
Cedrus atlantica 'Glauca'
Chrysanthemum

Cotoneaster
Elaeagnus
Euonymus

Hedera (Ivy)
Pachysandra
Viburnum

DECEMBER

Alnus (Alder)
Aralia
Bergenia
Cedrus atlantica 'Glauca'
Cotoneaster

Elaeagnus
Euonymus
Garrya elliptica
Hedera (Ivy)
Helleborus niger

Magnolia grandiflora
Mahonia
Pachysandra
Viburnum

19

Principles of Arranging and Conditioning

In this book I have concentrated on plants from your garden that can be used for flower arranging all the year round, and this results in a rather special approach to the actual design of the arrangements. With each changing season the arrangements will change too, in shape, texture and type: you will make flowing, massed or mixed arrangements in midsummer when there is plenty of material available, and more simple, economical groups in the winter and early spring.

Naturally, in January you will have to search your garden for bits and pieces, but if it has been a mild winter, it is amazing what you can find to pick, and it is generally possible to make a good all-green arrangement based on one unusual piece, such as a branch of *Garrya elliptica* with catkins, or of contorted willow or hazel, with some leaves of bergenia and the variegated euonymus – a real stand-by. Camellia foliage is a very special asset in midwinter, and this is also when aucuba comes into its own.

Very early in the year forsythia stems can be brought into the house for forcing, and so can branches of flowering currant. Catkined branches of hazel also force well, and provide excellent outline shape for any arrangement. The earliest flowering trees and shrubs – *Viburnum fragrans*, *Hamamelis mollis* and Winter Sweet, and that wonderful tree that blooms so well off and on all winter, *Prunus subhirtella* 'Autumnalis' – make good outline material and often bring scent into the house too. They can also be used to provide the tall stems for a moss garden, which is an arrangement in a shallow dish where layers of wire netting are covered with fresh moss (it is always a good idea to collect the moss well before Christmas, when it is plentiful, and keep it in a polythene bag). After positioning the flowering branch, you can place into the moss small bunches of snowdrops, aconites, crocus and so on. I often make the first moss garden of the year in a saucer, and use a larger container as the flowers and other material become more abundant.

There are very few tall flowers in the garden at this time of year, so if you want an arrangement for some special occasion, then it means buying a few flowers, at any rate until the early daffodils appear.

By the time early summer arrives you should have plenty to pick for your arrangements. Sometimes the fewer the flowers available, the better the arrangements turn out to be. It can be very confusing to have such a wealth of material that you don't know where to start, and generally speaking mass arrangements are more difficult to do well. It is only possible to do a vase of all one type of flower when there is a profusion, as with daffodils, roses, sweet peas or dahlias. Except in those cases, you will nearly always have to tackle a vase using many different and unrelated flowers and foliage. One word of advice: try to make every flower show as an individual subject. If you always remember this simple principle, you will never be guilty of overcrowding.

A 'mixed green' group is without doubt one of the most effective and attractive types of arrangement at any time of year. It can be created from a very few leaves or using a great mass of foliage in different colours – yellows and greys as well as all the greens – and perhaps with green flowers or seed heads added. These arrangements vary in shape and texture more than any other kind of group.

Through the winter I find that I use more and more dried arrangements, but I think it is best of all if you can use part dried and part fresh material. A few fresh chrysanthemums help a dried group, and later some stems of green hellebore are a wonderful addition. The fresh flower stems can be put into a small separate container within the larger vase of drieds, but often I simply put water in with the dried flowers. It does no harm, and only involves cutting a small piece off the ends of the stems if they become wet and soggy, but dipping the ends in varnish or polyurethane makes an excellent seal. It also means that you have to rearrange the dried flowers again when the fresh ones have died, and this ensures that you won't keep the same old collection gathering dust in a corner all winter.

One permanent dried group is effective as decoration in the house, but do remember to move it round to different positions so that you don't tire of seeing it always in the same place. An excellent group can be made from a mixture of some glycerined materials and some feathery dried seed heads, with the help of dried yarrow or hydrangea heads for added colour, and to give a good solid central point.

Principles and methods

Even after all these years the arrangements that give me the greatest pleasure are the ones that I pick into my hand as I wander round my garden, often with a particular container in mind. This way I find that I don't pick things that are much too tall and then have to discard them or waste a good deal. The only exception comes when taking, for instance, low branches from a flowering tree (those planted in grass often get in the way of the grass cutter) in which case you should always take the branch back to the trunk, and later cut off the lengths you require. Apart from this, picking for a certain vase means that you will cut all material to the correct lengths and no time will be lost before you can condition it – and it is important to do this quickly to make everything last as long as possible.

Personal choice comes into the method you choose to hold the stems in the container – a pin-holder, an Oasis-type block or wire netting. I still use a lot of chicken wire, but this may be because neither pin-holders nor Oasis existed when I first started – it's all so long ago! I think you should use whichever method you find easiest. Pin-holders are excellent for a few daffodils, but quite useless for mass arrangements, where wire is better. It is essential that a pin-holder should be really firm, and you can fix it with either some very sticky fixative, or with plasticine: roll a piece of plasticine in your hands until you have a strip, make this into a circle to fit the base of the pin-holder, and then press the pin-holder with its plasticine base firmly into place in the container. Make sure that all the surfaces are quite dry or the plasticine will not stick properly.

I personally feel that chicken wire, or a combination of Oasis and wire, is essential for a table centre arrangement. It is necessary to have a build-up of wire netting to come to the top of the container, so that stems placed in the centre of the vase do not fall over, and those threaded through the wire horizontally are held with their stem ends in the water and yet flow gracefully

21

over the lip of the container. As you will be sitting and looking at the arrangement, it is very important in this case that the flowers flow well over the edges of the vase, as otherwise you will be able to see all the mechanics.

For the upright urn-type of vase and arrangement, the tallest stem is the most important, for if this should slip, it will not only disarrange the whole vase, but is almost impossible to correct. So be sure to fix the main stem very firmly by whichever method you have chosen. This stem can be placed either to the right or left of the centre – I find that if it is off centre it will make the arrangement less stiffly symmetrical, with a result that will be more pleasing to the eye than if the whole is dead centre. Wherever you place it, the tallest stem must be absolutely vertical. The next stage is to fill in a roughly fan-shaped background, for which I suggest using lighter material. The pieces on either side should be slightly lower than the central stem. The guide on proportions is that the overall height of the arrangement should be one and a half to twice the height of the container, and the overall width should be about the same as the height. These are only rough figures, but I think that they are helpful.

Having achieved the outline shape with foliage or delicate flower sprays, then you add the central or focal point, made with an uneven number of flowers. Whenever possible I like to use flat-headed flowers or ones with many petals, such as open roses, dahlias or chrysanthemums, as these give a clear and distinctive central point where the eye focuses first. Two or three stems of these flowers should be placed so that their heads come well over the rim of the vase. Then place the next two well back, recessed so that they intensify the colour effect. It is interesting that the colour you place in the centre like this will dominate the vase, so if you have only three pink flowers and you want the vase to look really pink, then you must try to place these right in the middle.

Remember to place all stems in your arrangements so that they lead towards the middle of the vase. Look at each stem as you pick it, and try to choose pieces that will curve naturally either to the left or right. Then position them so that they fall gracefully from the edge of the container. Such subjects as ivy, Old Man's Beard, *Alchemilla mollis* and Solomon's Seal are good examples of stems that have a natural curve.

Try not to cut stems too short: by holding them against the vase, you can get a pretty good idea of how long you want them to be before you actually cut them. Once placed in position, it is best not to take them in and out too often, as this does prevent them living so long, for they hate constant handling.

Lastly, make sure that all the stems are well under the water-line, especially those you have placed to flow out on either side; and it is always important to see that the vase is filled to the very top with water.

When making a simple arrangement, such as the one shown overleaf from page 87 in the shallow greeny-blue oblong container, I used a pin-holder, and cut the stems to different lengths so that they would all flow from the central point. I have grown to love these simple vases – they have a peaceful effect and are so pleasant to have in the house.

Green arrangements take a little longer to pick and condition, for they have to be more carefully thought out, and nicely contrasting shapes and colours of material chosen. Use some tall slender spiky leaf or branch for the outline of the vase – the different shapes of leaves are as important as the colours. In green arrangements I always like to use some kind of variegated foliage, for I feel this brings to the arrangement the same light touch that the growing plant provides in the garden. A different kind of colour contrast can be achieved by the use of grey material – leaves of artichoke, senecio or artemisia for instance. As with other arrangements the centre should be created by using a round leaf or rounded green head, such as allium, green zinnia or *Euphorbia polychroma* in spring. I think it is well worth taking the extra trouble involved in making green arrangements, for you can create something quite different almost every week as material from the garden changes, the finished effect is most attractive, and these groups last particularly well.

Different again are arrangements of flowers and unrelated foliage, and here colour plays an important part. It is fascinating to create vases with particular colour themes, either shades of one colour or providing contrasts. I love the simple effect of two-colour arrangements, and have suggested many in this book: green and white, green and blue, black and white, pink and grey and so on. A lovely colour contrast can be achieved by using dark grapes, reddish berberis and some red beetroot leaves with white roses, similar to the arrangement shown opposite page 47. Autumn is a marvellous time of year for creating vases of flowers and foliage that blend together: for instance, turning autumn leaves with apricot-coloured dahlias and roses and a stem of late lupin. Many other combinations are given under the various plant entries.

Conditioning

Although I have mentioned the best method of conditioning under each plant description, I would like to add a brief summary of this very important aspect of flower arranging.

When I started doing flowers, we were told to hammer all hardy and woody stems and cut all soft ones, and then give everything a long drink of warm water. Though this is still good advice today, we have learnt a great deal more about the movement of sap, and air bubbles that can prevent the cut stems from drinking freely, and so we now realize the value of burning or boiling the stem ends to help the flowers to last much longer.

The method I would recommend is to place the ends of stems, as soon as possible after cutting, into a jug containing 2.5 cm (1 in) of really boiling water, count to twenty and then fill the jug up with cold water and leave the stems to drink for several hours, and preferably overnight. If the stems are tender, they should be allowed less time in the boiling water, if they are woody they can be allowed to stand in it for several minutes and no harm is done.

Poppies should be re-boiled if you have to cut the stems a second time; I try to cut and boil them at different lengths to avoid this. They are about the only flowers that do need to be re-boiled – most flowers only need to be treated once.

If you have a gas flame, you can burn the ends of the stems in that equally well. The Dutch and Japanese method of cutting the ends of the stems under water has the same effect of releasing the air bubble, and this practice can also be used successfully.

Small and Miniature Flower Arrangements

How small is a small flower arrangement? It's hard to define the size at all accurately. One might say, at random, 30 cm (a foot) overall and then stretch it to 60 cm (two feet) and it would still be small when compared with the kind of 3 m (ten foot) group one would use in a church or for a banquet or ball. It is largely a matter of comparison – we could assume that small flower arrangements are those that fit into the average home. Then we get stuck again, as the size of container will depend on the size of room and furniture which, of course, differ widely.

For example, when I got married just after the war, there were quite a few shortages and though I had collected various bits and pieces there were many things which were not available for a long time afterwards. However, because I love flowers and delighted in making arrangements, mostly with hedgerow material and gifts from friends with overgrown gardens, I usually had one large arrangement in the sitting room, far larger than warranted by tradition, but it filled what would otherwise have been an empty space. So I learned very quickly that a flower arrangement could be as large as you like (even if the room was not very big) provided, as in our case, it was taking the place of the piece of furniture which we did not possess.

I have acquired more pieces of furniture since then, but the large arrangement stays as it always did, but maybe for a different reason. To quote an American who came here a few years ago on our Open Garden Day: looking at this particular group, she turned to her daughter and said, 'How come that in my large house I cannot have a large arrangement when they can have it in this iddy-biddy-cottage?' And the daughter replied, 'No reason, Ma, but that perhaps you just couldn't arrange it.'

So use your discretion when you place your flowers. Should you have many lovely pieces of china, figurines, photographs, and so on, be careful not to overcrowd – you may just have to keep the arrangement that little bit smaller. The size of an arrangement is dependent on the surroundings and it is up to the individual to make his or her own decision.

Containers for small arrangements

Containers can be found around the house and used for small arrangements. They don't have to be vases. They could be, perhaps, a pretty cup and saucer, a coffee cup, a small milk jug or even an old silver teapot or sauce-boat filled with spring flowers.

Glass is pretty especially when filled with gypsophila (Baby's Breath), sweet peas or white petunias. Custard glasses and brandy snifters are useful for this. And silver – a silver salt cellar could be a size between small and miniature, and silver sugar bowls or *sucriers* filled with a mixed summer bunch are ideal. Mugs and small jugs are, of course, useful and candlesticks with metal candle cups placed in the top are lovely for a summer evening party, or for Christmas with cascading red ribbons tied to a posy at the place of each guest. There are very many objects around the house that one has never thought to use.

Next we come to the vases which are on the market today and are available in department stores or florist shops, including many types of Italian ceramic white vases. So if you cannot find anything suitable at home it might be an idea to treat yourself to one really nice container, an easily arranged vase which will not require too much material. It would be money well spent.

Boxes, old tea caddies, biscuit boxes, anything which has a lid are particularly good for small arrangements because the lid gives background and so limits the number of flowers which you have to use. They are the most economical of flower containers as you have to fill only one side.

Baskets of all kinds and small baskets of pretty shape are most useful all year round: to hold berries in autumn, dried small flowers in winter and, as shown for example overleaf from p. 54, fresh summer flowers.

Small ornamental vases, such as the shell-shaped, fluted vases so popular with flower arrangers for years, look lovely filled with just one type of flower and equally good with a handful of mixed flowers in summer.

Copper looks lovely filled with pink, or with apricot and red flowers. A copper pot filled with marigolds or a brass measure arranged with nasturtiums can be beautiful. The choice of container is important and so is the placement – copper and brass on oak and pine, ceramic and crystal on walnut, and so on. The attractiveness of your arrangements will be greatly enhanced if you remember to consider details of this sort.

The suitability of flowers to container is of major importance, not only do the flowers have to be in proportion but they must harmonize with the container. I find that daffodils are best in copper, wood or in baskets. Tulips look lovely in ornate, colourful ceramic containers, white flowers in a white vase, or making a complete contrast, in bottle-green or black. The world of flower arranging is inexhaustible, and after doing flowers for so many years I am continually surprised by finding myself unintentionally combining flowers, foliage and colours in completely new ways. It is nothing to do with me but something to do with the infinite variety of Nature.

Making a small arrangement

Small arrangements are suitable for everyone in some room or other. They are ideal placed on a coffee table, or on the side of a mantelpiece, on a small dining table as well as in the bedroom or the guest room.

For a low table, boxes are perfect containers, filled with bluebells (which must be cut on short stems or they will not last), or with wallflowers packed in tightly, also on short stems. It is the only method I can recommend for wallflowers, whose scent is, of course, superb. Later on, try filling the box with honeysuckle and a few short-stemmed and highly-scented sweet peas.

As I sit now on a dull winter's day just after the snow has gone, I am enjoying the perfume from a winter box consisting of a small spray of *Viburnum fragrans*, and the very first snowdrops, a few stems of erica, and winter jasmine which was brought into the house frozen and brown-looking and which opened out into lovely yellow sprays almost overnight. Always try to add a sprig of something sweet-scented in these little boxes.

If you have a garden to pick from and a good variety of these small containers

25

around the house you will always find the odd coloured or green leaf and a few flowers at almost any time of year, enough to make an attractive arrangement – in a margarine carton if necessary – and these little treasures are, for me, always the most pleasing. Incidentally, one of the most charming and welcome presents you can give someone in hospital is a small arrangement in a margarine container – preferably one with flowers printed on it. You simply fill the container with damp Oasis and at practically any time of the year you can find small flowers, and snippets of larger flowers, which will make a delightful arrangement. Somehow, when one is unwell and in bed, an arrangement of this size seems particularly acceptable and appropriate!

But not everyone is so fortunate as to have a wide choice of flowering oddments and then the vase you use becomes very important. A small white cupid vase is just right for holding any small bunch of bought flowers, say, snowdrops, or primroses, violets, lily of the valley, baby cyclamen, gentians, or freesia – any of these will give great pleasure. So if you live in a flat or have only a small garden to pick from, then it is important to choose a really pretty container which will make the most of a bunch from the shops.

To make an early spring garden for your table you will need a saucer, as deep as possible, or an ashtray or any small shallow bowl. Put several layers of crushed wire netting tied securely into the bowl and add a layer of moss. Then gather, in small bunches, as many different types of flowers as you can find – a few stems of blue polyanthus, yellow jasmine, snowdrops, crocus, sprays of flowering shrubs like viburnum and even stems of catkins. A little arrangement like this will certainly add life and colour to any room in the last days of winter.

Wine glasses are ideal containers for delicate flowers especially champagne and sherry glasses and brandy snifters. If you are arranging, say, dianthus (pinks) in summer, lily of the valley, cow parsley or Queen Anne's lace, it is best to make a pretty little bunch in your hand and then tie it either with a piece of cotton thread or an elastic band to keep the stems in place. This way the stems can be seen clearly through the glass without the basic mechanics showing. Alternatively, you can place two layers of wire netting cut to fit over the top of the glass, held in place with clear narrow Sellotape (Scotch tape), so that the glass is still clear and the stems can be seen unspoiled by Oasis or wire.

I have made an arrangement with glasses and bottles for which I admit I got the idea from an American book. It consisted of a series of glass vases and some miniature whisky and gin bottles, as served on aeroplanes. These I placed on a large round mirror in the centre of the dining table and filled each little container with a few stems of different flowers – pansies, a nerine, polyanthus, gentian, little cyclamen, a few pieces of nicotiana and the last stems of late-flowering alchemilla. It really was very effective indeed and could be done at any time of the year, not only in late autumn as I have described. Some small flower lights, or night lights, placed in custard or stemless sherry glasses would give a pretty effect, placed alternately with the small flower vases.

A cake-stand or comport in china or glass makes another effective flower container for a small dining table. Put in a quarter brick of well-soaked Oasis and cover this with a layer of wire and tie in firmly. Decorate with small bunches of green grapes and, ideally, gardenias or if you can't get them try five white camellias or white roses.

Small baskets filled with summer flowers all make very pretty little arrangements. If you have an attractive basket you will easily find a liner to hold the water, like a small Pyrex ovenware dish. Then fill the baskets with nasturtiums, small marigolds, forget-me-nots, primroses, rosebuds, and in the autumn with berries and Old Man's Beard. You will find the results enchanting.

Or in the spring dig up a few roots of primroses, or snowdrop bulbs from the garden (*not* from the wild) and plant them in a little basket. This is the right thing to do because it not only makes a charming arrangement for the house, but it splits up your snowdrops and encourages them to increase themselves.

The small picture-frame vase is very popular for a guest room and, for some strange reason, these vases seem to preserve the flowers extraordinarily well. It amazes me how the flowers in these vases last twice as well as in any other vase I know. They are ideal for camellias, as you have to pick only a short stem, and they last wonderfully. These vases are now available, not only at Constance Spry shops, but at many others as well.

Miniature arrangements

Miniature arrangements differ from 'small' by the very fact that a true miniature should not exceed 10 cm (4 in) in height, depth and width, so they are impractical for the average home.

My first miniature flower arrangements were started many years ago when my father brought me back a pair of darling little vases only suitable for a doll's house and this was how they were used. I little thought then that many years later I would be invited to talk at a local W.I. meeting on miniature flower arrangements, at which all the little vases, shells and tiny boxes came into their own.

At the show where I was first asked to judge the miniatures, I could not believe the popularity of (and the vast number of entries for) this class. Up till then it had seemed to me only for the few. But how wrong I was, though I well remember someone saying on that occasion that this was just a passing fancy and would soon wear off. That was a number of years ago! Without doubt it must be one of the most popular classes in our shows today, both for those who enjoy arranging them and for the general public who come to admire.

I like miniatures for a different reason. Personally I find them hard to do and suspect I do not have enough patience for them! Also I have nowhere in my house to display miniatures to advantage. But they are a marvellous exercise and there are many people who do them beautifully. For me, their real appeal is that they are very often works of art, done by a group of nimble-fingered and most creative people.

Miniatures are an unusual class at a show as they attract not only flower arrangers but other artistic and talented people. And it is a class wide open to everybody. It does not require a large garden to pick from or a lot of expensive flowers, and it brings out a creative spirit in many people who never realized that they possessed this sort of talent.

While a true miniature is 10 cm (4 in) overall, some shows have a class for 16 cm (6 in) and it is amazing how clumsy these look in comparison. When one is judging at a show, the perfect miniature always stands out. For a true miniature you are always scaling down – each flower part or leaf represents a larger flower, and when a miniature is enlarged by photography each of these must be in proportion. For instance, a small blade of grass represents an iris leaf, a small leaf of variegated ivy a hosta, a tiny floret of philadelphus represents a dahlia. Part of a flower or a stamen or a segment of a flower can represent a larger flower.

You will find your skill and ingenuity exercised in finding suitable containers. The range is very wide and can cover such everyday things as salt cellars, thimbles or sea-shells as well as exotica found in bazaars in different parts of the world.

Oasis is a great help in keeping the flowers in place but you may find difficulty, as I do, in getting these tiny stems into Oasis. Making a hole first with a wire or pin will help. Sometimes it may be easier to twist up fine fuse wire and impale the stems on them. Small tweezers are often a good substitute for clumsy fingers. Finally, try looking at the arrangement through the lens of a camera and nearly all the faults will be quickly spotted. Contrast of shape and texture is just as important in these miniature groups as in a large arrangement.

DRIED FLOWERS: PRESERVING AND ARRANGING

Dried flower arrangements have become increasingly popular as the price of fresh flowers in winter continues to go up and the ever-rising cost of oil makes heated greenhouses more and more expensive to run.

For myself, dried or any kind of preserved flowers can never replace the value or delight one gets from fresh flowers, especially in winter. I think I still prefer to preserve background material in glycerine and use this with fresh flowers or foliage until one can pick a bunch of spring flowers. But the occasional pot plant can sometimes take their place and last Christmas was made easy for me because of a superb white azalea which has been sheer delight.

There are many aspects of dried flowers and foliage and different ways of using them. You can make colourful posies which will last all winter, remaining pretty and cheerful, or for background material you can use the more sombre and neutral colourings which are ideal when mixed with a few salmon or apricot chrysanthemums, or some variegated leaves. In this way you can make a large arrangement when flowers are scarce and expensive.

Many flowers of attractive colouring can be grown from seed for drying and more lovely grasses become available every year.

Drying by hanging or air drying

The following method is used for all seed heads and some flower spikes such as delphiniums, which dry very well this way.

Wait until the flower head is open right up the stem and then cut it. All the leaves should be removed from the stems as soon as they are picked. This is important for two reasons. It is a good idea to assist dehydration as much as possible because leaves left on the stem retain the moisture in the stem and so prolong the drying period. And secondly, it is much easier to remove the leaves from the stem before they become dry and brittle. There is a risk, when removing them after drying, of breaking the stem. Place in deep water overnight.

It is important to have ready a dry, airy place for quick drying, as stems don't take long to mildew. Hang the seed heads in bunches tied together with string or elastic bands and make the bunches small to avoid overcrowding. In fact, I really prefer to tie each stem individually, as this gives a perfect specimen. If they are bunched too closely together one head can get caught in another and as you pull these apart when they are dry they tend to get damaged. Heads of yellow achillea damage very easily, and if the heads are all tied tightly together the stem of one flower presses into the flower head of another leaving a nasty hole when it finally dries, and this ruins the finished specimen. I usually stand

Opposite. Mixed primroses. These are wonderful value if transferred into the garden. The blue ones stay blue but die out more quickly.

Overleaf left. Variegated ivy, heather, *Arum italicum* 'Pictum' leaves, chincherinchee, *Petasites japonicus* 'Giganteus', *Iris reticulata, Tellima grandiflora, Helleborus nigra* and *foetidus*, golden polyanthus and *Mahonia bealii* make a pretty spring arrangement.

them in a flower vase so that the heads remain apart while drying.

Remember that it is by drying quickly that you will get the best results. If drying in a shed or garage, watch the seed heads carefully because if they dehydrate very rapidly they shrivel and tend to slip out of the strings holding them together. Place bundles well apart so they get as much air as possible circulating round them.

Light materials like grasses take about a week or so to dry, and heavier stems of, say, seed heads of hollyhocks, sedum, cardoons and lupins, take about three weeks. When dry these can be cut down and stored in boxes in a dry place. Always keep a lid on the box to exclude light, as they fade very quickly.

The more precious seed and flower heads, like statice and acrolinium, I tie in small bunches and dry them over the boiler in the kitchen. They dry very quickly like this and are not in the way too long!

Drying in water

I find the only way to dry hydrangea heads well is, strangely enough, with their feet in water and their heads in a warm atmosphere. Cut the heads when the colour starts to change from pink to red, and blue to a greeny colour. Remove all the leaves and stand the stems in about 5 cm (2 in) of water and place the jar on or near a boiler or in an airing cupboard. The warmer they are the quicker they dry and the heads will stay a better colour.

I dry a few stems of the charming green bell-like spikes of moluccella or 'Bells of Ireland', by first standing them in shallow water on a pin-holder so that they take on charming natural curves. Then I transfer them to a jam jar, still in a little water, until they are completely dry. They are strange as sometimes they stay green and sometimes turn a parchment colour. I always place a few stems into a solution of glycerine as this gives a glossy texture and keeps them from dropping. Seed heads of hosta also dry well like this and you can watch the green closed seed heads gradually opening out and turning back to reveal all their seeds.

Preserving in glycerine

Preservation by glycerine is long-lasting and the stems keep their natural shape and form, just deepening in colour as they absorb the glycerine.

Leaves and branches are the best subjects for this method. Mix one part of glycerine and two parts of hot water and pour this into a narrow jar or jug so that the solution goes as far up the stem as possible. Hammer woody stems well, about 8 cm (3 in) up the stem and be sure to soak thoroughly in water any branch which is freshly picked, as they can flag. After an overnight drink, put the stems in the glycerine solution, leave them for about ten days or until the stems have changed colour. Green leaves turn brown and you can gradually see the mixture creeping up the stem and changing colour.

Thick leaves benefit from a coating of the mixture: dip a little piece of cotton wool in the glycerine solution and coat the leaves. This prevents them from curling and can be repeated as often as you like.

Hard, leathery leaves of mahonia and laurel take twice as long as branches of beech, so watch carefully and as soon as the glycerine has almost reached the top of the branches, remove them from the container and hang upside down for a couple of days.

Study each branch carefully before putting it into glycerine as it is most wasteful to use branches which you know will be far too tall for your purpose. So first prune carefully, removing any poor branches or insect-eaten leaves.

I like to preserve my beech leaves early in the season before the leaves get damaged by insects. Beech leaves are the most popular with flower arrangers but I have had a lot of fun experimenting with such things as Old Man's Beard or wild clematis, and *Moluccella laevis*, but these stems should be left in the solution only five days. Then hang them upside down and let the solution run down into the head. Laurel and *Magnolia grandiflora* are both lovely natural evergreens and it may seem foolish to preserve them, but they do go the most irresistible bronze colour and last like this forever.

I have also found that by submerging a whole spray of ivy in berry form, they last very well, as does *Bergenia crassifolia*. And by removing all the leaves from a stem of hornbeam keys, and by defoliating a branch of lime-flower buds before they burst into flower, you can get branching stems of delicate tracery which make an ideal background for any dried or winter flower arrangement.

I tried putting some flower sprays of *Eryngium giganteum* 'Miss Willmott's Ghost', the thistle-like plant, in the solution with great success. The flowers stayed wide open and had a lovely shiny look and feel. Grasses, too, take glycerine well and as with all things placed in the glycerine solution, they are no longer brittle and never shed.

Pressing

Ferns press well and should you have enough Royal Fern (*Osmunda regalis*) to spare, it is a really successful way to keep it and the leaves will last all winter. As the stems are rather long they are liable to break in the middle but with the support of a thin cane or dial stick placed behind the main rib and caught with a wire in about three places, they stand well and quite firmly.

Smaller ferns will stand on their own and make a nice touch of green added to a small bowl or basket of mixed dried flowers such as statice, helichrysum and yellow yarrow.

Bracken can be pressed and used in small pieces painted and glittered for Christmas. It is advisable to soak the bracken overnight in a solution of starch and water, dry off on blotting paper next day before pressing. This helps to stiffen it before painting.

Beech sprays that have turned a lovely autumnal colour press well and add a flat spray of good colour as a background for other dried and preserved flower or seed heads.

Preserving in silica gel

This method is used very much more in the United States than in Britain because American houses and apartments are kept at a constant heat and at a very much higher temperature. And it is for this reason that the beautiful displays they arrange of these treated flowers look as good after a few months as they did when first arranged. Sadly, in my old cottage it is very hard to keep the rooms sufficiently warm and damp-free to prevent flowers preserved in this way from fading and losing all their lovely colour. The boxes in which you preserve them must be kept at 15.6° (60°F) at least while the drying is taking place. If you can manage this then it is well worth a try as the results are really beautiful.

First of all take a large box with a lid and in the bottom put a layer of silica gel powder which you can get from a garden centre. You have to put a wire in each flower head, though it need only be a short one as you can add a longer wire later on. Take, for example, a fully open rose, zinnia, dahlia (not too many petals) or marigold and place on a layer of silica gel bending the stem so that the

Overleaf right. An informal spring display of narcissi, pink and blue hyacinths, polyanthus, forsythia, pink cherry blossom and viburnum foliage arranged in a pewter jug. Jugs are always suitable for less formal arrangements.

Opposite. Hellebores – here 'Ballard's Black' and a seedling hybrid. Epimedium leaves – *grandiflorum* 'Rose Queen' – burnish in winter and are much better used when mature than in the summer. Dried purple sedum, stems of fan-tail willow.

31

flower head is looking at you. Then sift on more powder until the whole of each flower is submerged. Sometimes it is easier to place the flower head face down but you must be sure the powder gets right under the petals.

Place the lid on the box and put it in a warm place, such as a linen cupboard or boiler house. As I have already mentioned the boxes must be kept at a constant heat of at least 15.6° (60°F) while the drying is going on. This will take at least thirty-six hours.

Stems of delphiniums, larkspur and American dogwood dry extremely well, but you need a very large box and a great deal of powder for these stems. Ideal for this method are flowers for small arrangements and pictures – little pieces of forget-me-not, helleborus, snowdrops, primroses, violets, crocus and the like which all preserve beautifully.

Preserving in silica gel is a marvellous way to make a truly lovely everlasting bouquet or arrangement.

To sum up, there are two different approaches to preserved materials. One is to dry for colour, especially flowers like statice and helichrysum whose colour range today is much wider than it used to be. With acrolinium, achillea (yarrow), hydrangeas, delphiniums, larkspur, grasses and the like, you can make a colourful arrangement that will last all winter.

The second use is as background material – beech branches, seed heads, and the leaves of plants such as mahonia and laurel make a good background for the fresh flowers available. For me, the combination of fresh and dried is the answer to winter arrangements.

A footnote: many people ask about putting dried stems in water. It is all right to do this as the stems come to no harm and when using them a second time you just cut off the soggy end and start again.

Acanthus

This hardy perennial grows well in full sun or shade, making it a worthwhile plant for any fair-sized garden, with handsome foliage and tall flower spikes, purplish with distinct white under-petals.

Cultivation   Plant in a sunny or semi-shaded spot, from October to March. Any good garden soil is suitable. Cut the flower stems down to ground level after flowering.

Conditioning and preserving   Flower stems should be picked when the florets are open right up the stem: if picked with unopened buds, the stems tend to flop over and rarely recover. The stem ends should be dipped in boiling water followed by a long drink in deep cold water for several hours. Try as I may, I cannot get young leaves to hold up in water; better results can sometimes be achieved with mature leaves, if the stem ends are dipped in boiling water and then submerged completely in cold water, or, better still, a weak solution of starch.

The flower spikes dry well for winter use. I have found the most successful way is to allow them to dry off in the vase in which they are arranged. If this is not possible, they can be hung upside down to dry in a warm room.

Arranging   I love to use the long flower stems, but as these are generally around 1 m (3–4 ft) in height, they are only suitable for large arrangements, for cutting the stems short would destroy the beautiful proportions. They make an excellent background for a large group of mixed flowers in midsummer. The arrangement in the English delftware drug jar opposite page 79 is a very good example of how the rounded heads of agapanthus and hydrangea are enhanced by the pointed structural value of the acanthus spikes. Sadly, the beautifully decorative leaves do not last well in water.

Acanthus mollis, A. spinosus, height around 1 m (3–4 ft), planting distance 60–90 cm (2–3 ft).

Acer

Maples are worth every inch of space for their lovely coloured foliage, not only in autumn but in spring. Of the large trees, *A. platanoides*, the Norway Maple, is one of the delights of early spring, with the dark branches smothered in lime-green flowers. Its variety 'Drummondii' is a most striking variegated foliage tree, with green leaves that are margined with cream, and are a good colour all summer. *A. pseudoplatanus* 'Nizetii' has foliage ranging in colour from almost white to pale gold, suffused with pink, and is excellent for the small garden. *A. rubrum* 'Schlesingeri', the Canadian Red Maple, has wonderful autumn colour. *A. pennsylvanicum* is notable for its beautiful white striated bark and good autumn colour. *A. ginnala* is one of the best for brilliant autumn colour, and has delicate deeply cut leaves. *A. griseum* has bark which peels off to show a cinnamon colour beneath, and has particularly good red and scarlet leaves in autumn. *A. negundo* 'Aureum' has bright golden yellow leaves, while *A. pseudoplatanus* 'Brilliantissimum' (one of the best for flower arranging) has young foliage of a soft apricot colour in spring.

Cultivation   Acers prefer moist soil, in sun or partial shade; *A. rubrum* does best on an acid soil. Plant from October to March. If possible plant acers where they will be protected from cold winds and where the early morning sun will not reach the foliage when it is covered by a spring frost. Acers grown especially for autumn colour need shelter if possible from strong winds, as these will ruin the effect in a day or two. No pruning is usually necessary.

Acer ginnala, height 4.5–6 m (15–20 ft), spread 3 m (10 ft); A. griseum, height 4.5 m (15 ft), spread 2–3 m (8–10 ft); A. negundo 'Aureum', height 6–8 m (20–25 ft), spread 4–6 m (12–20 ft); A. pennsylvanicum, height 5–6 m (18–20 ft), spread 3–4 m (10–12 ft); A. platanoides, A. platanoides 'Drummondii', height 9–11 m (30–35 ft), spread 4–6 m (12–20 ft); A. pseudoplatanus 'Brilliantissimum', A. pseudoplatanus 'Nizetti', height 11 m (35 ft), spread 4.5 m (15 ft);

33

A. rubrum
'Schlesingeri', height 6–8
m (20–25 ft), spread 2–3
m (8–10 ft).

Conditioning and preserving   Conditioning is most important, for the acers do not last well in water without special care. The stems of *A. platanoides* should be pounded with a hammer and then given a long drink in warm water. The young foliage of *A. pseudoplatanus* 'Brilliantissimum' needs the same treatment, but I find that the early growth of smaller acers lasts better if, after hammering, the leaves are submerged completely under water for a whole night, or longer. The autumn-coloured leaves are always unreliable, though I think it helps a little to submerge the whole stems in a starch solution (made to the strength for table linen on the instructions) instead of just water.

Arranging   The flower heads of *A. platanoides* are a joy to arrange in early spring, their brilliant lime green a foil for late daffodils and yellow tulips, or equally lovely in a vase of 'mixed greens'. Next, the new buds and young foliage of *A. pseudoplatanus* 'Brilliantissimum' make this a wonderful tree to pick from, and to look at in the garden, as the leaves usually stay slightly variegated even after the early coral colour has died down to a light green. Stems go beautifully with apricot-coloured tulips, or contrast well with almost-black tulips and white cherry blossom in a black container.

Achillea   Yarrow

Achillea filipendulina
'Gold Plate', height 1.2
m (4 ft), spread 60 cm (2
ft).

The gold-coloured flat heads and the stiff stems with attractive fern-like leaves make a splendid long-lasting show in the perennial border and provide excellent material for the flower arranger. Achillea 'Moonshine' is perhaps my favourite. The pale creamy-yellow heads are so much more useful for mixing with a greater number of colours, and it dries beautifully. Bressingham Nurseries have a fascinating range of new colours coming out, with a range from apricot to reds, that will be worth looking out for.

Cultivation   Plant from October to March in any good well-drained garden soil. Achilleas like full sun. Cut the stems down to ground level in the general autumn clearing up.

Conditioning and preserving   The flowers last well with no special treatment. Though the stalks can be hung upside down to dry, I prefer to stand them in a jug in a little warm water, making sure the heads are not touching. They dry quickly like this and keep their shape. Covering the heads with borax gives a little better colour, but you may think, as I do, that it is hardly worth the extra trouble.

Arranging   Though I use these heads freshly cut, for me achillea is invaluable when dried and used in winter as it keeps such a good colour. It is effective with yellow mixed flowers in summer and looks well in the centre of a mixed foliage arrangement. The flat heads should always be placed so that they face you as they make a marvellous focal point in any display. They last superbly – a joy in summer when so many flowers shed their petals. They can be used on short stems of 5 cm (2 in), or full length up to 1.2 m (4 ft).

Aconitum lycoctonum   Monkshood

Height 1.3 m (4½ ft),
planting distance 1 m (3
ft).

The more common varieties of monkshood have blue-mauve flower spikes resembling those of a delphinium, but the one I would like to recommend here is *A. lycoctonum*, very delicate in form with yellowish to lime-green flowers. To be fair, I feel that this is a plant for the larger garden, as it really takes up quite a lot of space and flowers for a comparatively short time – and also really needs staking. However, as this is a book about flowers that I would like to have in the garden and for arranging, I am anxious to include it here.

Cultivation   This is a hardy perennial, easily raised from seed. It will grow in any good garden soil in sun or partial shade. Cut the old stems down to ground level in the autumn.

Conditioning and preserving   Give a long drink in deep warm water. The seed heads dry well if hung upside down in a warm place.

Arranging   It is lovely to mix with a group of yellow and white flowers, and I find that one or two stems really add so much to a small mixed summer flower arrangement. The seed heads are pretty whether used when green or allowed to dry completely, turning brown.

Acrolinium

A wild flower which grows in droves of pink and white in Western Australia and is grown in Britain as an annual. Its daisy-like, starry blooms are mainly used as dried flowers.

Height 22 cm (9 in), planting distance 20 cm (8 in).

Cultivation   Sow direct in open ground in April or under glass in March to be pricked out in May. They are grown mainly for drying, and as they are not decorative in the garden, they are best planted in a cutting area. In wet weather they look miserable as they are by nature sunlovers, and only open well in the warmth of the sun.

Conditioning and drying   Cut when flowers are mature and fully open, and tie in small bunches. Try not to overcrowd them as the flowers get damaged easily. When really dry, store in a box in a dry place to avoid loss of colour.

Arranging   These pretty little pink and white flowers are at their best added to other small dried flowers and used for little arrangements which will keep their colour well and be a lasting bright spot all winter. Some stems of dried grey artemisia and a few grasses add greatly to the light effect for these small groups.

Adam's Needle see *Yucca filamentosa*

Agapanthus

The Headbourne varieties are the best hybrids of this popular perennial plant. Carrying round heads of clustered florets on stout, smooth stems that grow 60–90 cm (2–3 ft) high, they are most welcome for the flower arranger as they give a blue flower head at a time when there are few other tall blue flowers. I have always felt that agapanthus was not hardy, but today there seem to be several hardy strains. Whether grown against a wall, or in the herbaceous or shrub border, they provide a lovely patch of blue and a nice change of form, with their decorative strap-like basal leaves.

Headbourne hybrids, height 60–90 cm (2–3 ft), planting distance 60 cm (2 ft).

Cultivation   Plant in April or May in any good garden soil, but preferably against a south- or west-facing wall. It is a worthwhile precaution to protect the plants against winter frosts by covering them in October or November with a 15 cm (6 in) layer of peat, straw or bracken.

Conditioning and preserving   The flower heads last very well with no special treatment but, rather like azaleas, it is important to remove each floret as it dies, or the whole head begins to look dead long before it is really over. The

35

buds continue to open in water, so you can keep the flower stems in a vase for a few weeks.

For preserving, leave the flower heads on the stems until the seed is well formed, then cut and hang the stems upside down to dry off thoroughly. They can then be used whole, or taken apart and used individually in smaller vases.

Arranging I think one of the best examples of the use of agapanthus can be seen in the arrangement with acanthus in the English delftware jar opposite page 79, though they will mix well in any large arrangement, using the stems short or full length. They add that vital touch of blue so important in mixed flower groups, or make an excellent focal point for a foliage arrangement in late July through to September, the combination of blue colour and rounded shape making an excellent foil against mixed leaves.

Alchemilla mollis

Height 30–45 cm (12–18 in), planting distance 40 cm (15 in).

Alchemilla, a perennial, is a 'must' for every garden, with its lime-green or sulphury-yellow feathery sprays of flower, which I use continuously from June to August. The flower stems branch from compact umbels of cup-like leaves which, because of their silky hairs, retain rain drops to glitter like quicksilver after showers.

Cultivation Plant from October to March in any good well-drained soil, in sun or partial shade. Twiggy sticks may be needed to support the plants if they are growing strongly. Cut almost to ground level in the autumn. A moisture-lover, it does not do well in hot and dry areas.

Conditioning and drying It really needs no special treatment, but it is best to remove a few of the leaves, as these tend to die long before the flower, and then give the stems a long drink in deep water. Remove all foliage.

The flower dries well, though loses some colour. Drying is best done by allowing stems to dry off in the vase in which they are arranged.

Arranging Because of the delicate form and wonderful blending colour of the flowers, I am tempted to use alchemilla in almost all my arrangements. It lasts so well, and adds such a soft touch that I look forward to it flowering, and it is a joy to find a piece that has blossomed in late autumn. The colour mixes well with pinks, reds, blues, yellows and any all-green arrangement.

Alder see Alnus

Allium

Allium caeruleum (A. azureum), height 60 cm (2 ft), planting distance 15 cm (6 in); A. giganteum, height 1.2 m (4 ft), planting distance 30 cm (12 in); A. ostrowskianum, height 30 cm (12 in), planting distance 7.5–10

Onion, leek and garlic all belong to this family, and the species grown for their flowers are also faintly onion-scented, which may be off-putting for some people, but they are good as cut flowers despite this.

My favourite is *A. siculum* from Sicily, its large dark-red bell-like flowers with the outer petals striped in blue-green, borne on curving 90 cm (3 ft) stems. The loose umbels of up to thirty flowers, appearing in May and June, are very unusual and striking. The shorter *A. caeruleum* has rounded heads of deep-blue flowers in June and July. Others I would recommend are *A. giganteum*, a real giant with huge heads of purple flowers on 1.2 m (4 ft) stems; *A. rosenbachianum*, one of the best for arranging with large heads of purple-lilac flowers; *A. ostrowskianum*, with short stems of bright pink flowers, excellent for the rock garden; and *A. roseum* 'Grandiflorum', a little taller with small rounded purple flowers, which dry so well and retain their colour all winter.

Cultivation   Plant from September to November – the earlier the better – in any good well-drained soil, in sun in an open bed, or among herbaceous plants. Mulch and give some soluble feed for the first year or two until the bulbs are established. Remove flower heads as they fade.

Conditioning and drying   I find a teaspoonful of bleach put into water in a vase stops the onion-like smell. The seed heads should be hung upside down in a dry atmosphere; take care that the heads do not touch each other.

Arranging   These rounded heads are useful for putting into summer mixed groups, and are marvellous to use when dried. They dry best if left in very shallow water in a warm place, or if hung upside down.

cm (3–4 in); A. rosenbachianum, height 60 cm (2 ft), planting distance 15–30 cm (6–12 in); A. roseum 'Grandiflorum', height 30 cm (12 in), planting distance 10–15 cm (4–6 in); A. siculum, height 60 cm–1.2 m (2–4 ft), planting distance 30 cm (12 in).

Alnus

Hardy deciduous trees, water-loving and usually found growing near streams or rivers, alders are beautiful all the year round. As soon as they lose their leaves, catkins start developing, and with some of the previous year's cones still on the branches, they remain attractive until May or June. *A. incana* 'Aurea' is one of the most attractive, with pink-tinged catkins in January.

Cultivation   Plant in any good soil, but not shallow chalky soils; excellent in cold wet places, the alder is exceptionally hardy. Plant October to March. No pruning is usually required.

Conditioning   Hammer the ends of the stems well, and put in warm water for several hours.

Arranging   Branches of fresh young catkins, with small clusters of black cones, provide one of the best outline shapes and can be used for weeks, as the catkins continue to develop in water. It makes an excellent background for a vase of spring flowers in moss, or for daffodils, and is a mainstay in many oriental-type arrangements. I often keep the best branches to use in dried groups in the winter.

Alnus incana 'Aurea', height 18–21 m, spread 6 m.

Alstroemeria

The ligtu hybrids are the only alstroemerias that I personally would consider growing. Once established, these perennials will give a profusion of multi-headed flowers, with a colour range of cream, apricot, orange and shades of pink. Blooming in June for several weeks, they add excellent colour in the border, and are rewarding as a cut flower since they last so well in water.

Cultivation   Always buy pot-grown plants, and plant very carefully without damaging the roots. March or April are the best months to plant. Choose a sheltered spot, preferably against a south or west-facing wall; any good garden soil is suitable. In all but the mildest areas protect in winter with a 15 cm (6 in) layer of bracken, peat or straw. Pick sparingly for the first year or two. Some support with pea sticks may be necessary. Cut the stems down to the ground after flowering.

Conditioning and preserving   A long drink in deep water immediately after picking is really all that is necessary.

The seed heads are attractive if allowed to form on the plant and then picked and hung upside down to dry. They can then be used full length for larger dried arrangements, or separate florets cut off for smaller arrangements.

Arranging   I think these flowers look very well in a vase on their own,

Alstroemeria ligtu hybrids, height 1 m (3 ft), planting distance 30–40 cm (12–15 in).

perhaps with a little green foliage, but not enough to distract from their delicate colours; the greenish feathery heads of *Alchemilla mollis* make a good foil. Otherwise they can be used in groups of apricots or pinks. One or two stems tucked into the centre of an arrangement give added colour for the focal point, and as they can be cut short or left with long stems, they can be used in this way for almost any size of arrangement.

Amaranthus

Amaranthus caudatus viridis, *height around 1 m (3–4 ft), planting distance 45 cm (18 in).*

This is the green form of Love-lies-Bleeding, which I find so much more attractive than the red. It is worth looking after for if the plant thrives the trusses may be twice as long as normal, and it is a most striking annual to have in the garden. It will seed easily and enjoys a medium or rich soil.

Cultivation Sow very thinly in their flowering situation in April in any reasonably fertile soil, and thin the seedlings as they become large enough to handle. Do the thinning in several stages until the plants are at the final distance.

Conditioning and preserving Remove all the leaves immediately after picking, for this plant does not take up enough moisture for both leaves and flowers. Place the stems in really hot water and leave them for several hours before arranging. If you are drying the stems, it is best to place them in shallow water in a warm room and allow to dry. Avoid drying the stems with the elegant, drooping trusses hanging upside down or otherwise they will dry erect!

Arranging The long, trailing tails of green chenille-like trusses make a splendid centre for a summer arrangement, and are equally effective in winter decorations when they have been dried.

Ampelopsis see Vitis

Anaphalis

Anaphalis margaritacea, *height 30–45 cm (12–18 in), planting distance 30–40 cm (12–15 in);* A. nubigena, *height 20–30 cm (8–12 in), planting distance 30 cm (12 in)*

Useful perennials with pleasant silvery foliage, providing a restful area in the border, particularly the dwarf *A. nubigena*.

Cultivation Plant from October to April in any good well-drained garden soil, in sun or shade. Good plants for dry conditions. *A. margaritacea* may need some support with twiggy sticks. Cut the stems down to the ground after flowering.

Conditioning and preserving The flower heads only last well in water if the stems are cut rather short. Condition by removing most of the foliage, then dip the stem ends into a little boiling water followed by a long drink.

For drying, bunch the flower heads on stems of about 13 cm (5 in), picking before the flowers have started to fluff, though they must be well open on the plant.

Arranging I find I use these flower heads mostly as dried material, in dried pictures, small arrangements and swags. However, they are nice for the centre of a green arrangement if used with short stems. I cut them about 5–7.5 cm (2 or 3 in) long, and tuck them into the middle of a group as a focal point.

Petasites japonicus 'Giganteus', iris, flowering currant, *Cornus mas*, snowflake, Christmas rose, *Helleborus foetidus*, *Prunus subhirtella* 'Autumnalis', pussy willow, snowdrops, scilla, daisy.

Hazel catkins, fan-tail willow, flowering cherry, 'Palace Purple' heuchera and ivy berries team up with the likes of snowflakes, helleborus 'Ballard's Black', widow iris, scillas, *Cornus mas* and polyanthus to form this elegant arrangement.

Valeriana phu, ligularia, *Euphorbia wulfenii*, *Arum italicum* 'Pictum', *Helleborus corsicus* and *foetidus*. I love various tones and shades of green, there is such an enormous variety and I never get tired of it.

'Connecticut Yankee' lily with *Arum italicum* 'Pictum', the leaves of which are useful for covering oasis and wire.

Anemone hybrida

Japanese anemones are particularly useful because they flower in early autumn. 'September Charm' and 'White Giant', both growing to around 1 m (3 or 4 ft), produce clear pink or white single flowers that last well when cut.

(A. japonica, A. elegans), height 60–90 cm (2–3 ft), planting distance 30–45 cm (12–18 in).

Cultivation Plant from October to March in any well-drained good garden soil, preferably in partial shade, although these anemones will grow in sun. They like a moist soil and often take several years to flower well. Cut the stems down to the ground after flowering.

Conditioning and preserving The flowers last well without any special treatment.

Individual flower heads can be dried excellently using silica gel.

Arranging Enchanting on their own, these anemones can also be used effectively with green to make a green and white arrangement, or the pink-flowered varieties with grey leaves to produce a charming pink and grey vase.

Angelica archangelica

This perennial is only suitable for a large garden, as it takes up lots of room and seeds so freely that it can become a real menace, though I love the big seed heads and fading pale green leaves. It will grow up to 1.8 m (6 ft) high, and needs staking in rough weather, so you can see it has limited value. The rounded seed heads can span a foot, but are usually about 23 cm (9 in) across. In spite of all its disadvantages, angelica is excellent for filling in space in a new garden.

Height 2–3 m (6–10 ft), spread 1 m (3 ft).

Cultivation Angelica is often grown as a biennial, but will live for several years if the flowers are removed. If plants are obtainable these may be planted in March in ordinary soil, preferably in a moist situation in sun or partial shade. Or seed may be sown in March or April in a prepared seed bed in the open. Transplant the seedlings 30 cm (12 in) apart when large enough, and move to their final quarters in March of the following year.

Conditioning and preserving All the stems, whether of flower or foliage, need the boiling water treatment: put the ends of the stems into 2.5 cm (1 in) of boiling water while you count up to ten, and then leave in deep cold water for as long as possible. Fill hollow stems with water and plug with Oasis.

To dry, leave the flower heads on the plant until the seed has formed, then cut and hang upside down.

Arranging As the heads are so big, they are only useful for large arrangements, such as church groups, when they make a good focal point in a mixed green vase. However, the umbels of flowers can be pulled apart and used in small arrangements.

Antirrhinum   Snapdragon or Lion's Mouth

These annuals are quite easily obtained from nurseries as young plants. The Double varieties and 'Penstemon Flowered' are much more difficult to come by so I recommend growing them from seed. They have a good colour range with a long flowering period, and 'Penstemon Flowered' has an attractive open tubular flower.

'Butterfly', height 60 cm (2 ft), planting distance 30–40 cm (12–18 in); 'Penstemon Flowered', height and planting distance 30 cm (12 in).

Cultivation Try to obtain sturdy, rich green plants, well hardened off, to plant in March or April in any ordinary garden soil, in full sun. Work in compost or manure before planting, and feed several times with a soluble

39

fertilizer during the growing period. When the plants are about 10 cm (4 in) high, pinch out the growing point to make them bushy. Remove dead flowers regularly. Water well in dry spells.

Conditioning   They seem to last better if they are placed in warm water. You should carefully remove each floret as it dies and this will keep the flowers looking very fresh.

Arranging   Antirrhinums add great charm to a mixed group of summer flowers and look very effective when used by themselves in similar-coloured arrangements. I like to put apricot with flame colours, and white antirrhinums in a white vase can look marvellously dramatic.

Aralia (Dizygotheca)

Aralia elata, A. elata 'Aureo-variegata', height and spread 6–9 m (20–30 ft).

This is a handsome shrub, it flourishes in the United States and does well in the warmth of Britain's town gardens. It has ivy-like flowers and large palmate-type leaves, which in *A. elata* 'Aureo-variegata' are blotched with yellow.

Cultivation   Plant October to March in any good soil. This aralia is very hardy but gives of its best in warm sheltered gardens. No pruning is normally required.

Conditioning and preserving   The leaves last better if the stem ends are put into boiling water and then allowed a long drink. It might be worth experimenting with preservation of the green-leaved form in a solution of glycerine and water, though I have not actually done this myself. The seed heads glycerine well in their berried stage.

Arranging   I use the well-shaped, dark-green leaves of aralia in winter, when I find it a good useful evergreen. The flower heads add interest and are effective in a cream and green group. The larger leaves of *A. elata* 'Aureo-variegata' can only be used on special occasions, when they play a great part at the base of a large summer green arrangement.

Arbutus unedo   Strawberry Tree

Height 4.5–6 m (15–20 ft), spread 3–4.5 m (10–15 ft).

Half-hardy evergreen, with white flowers and delightful strawberry-like fruits, which I have enjoyed using in arrangements in America. With a little care it can be grown successfully in the south of England, and makes a very decorative quick-growing tree.

Cultivation   Plant in October for preference, or March to May, in loamy soil. The situation should be sunny and sheltered from cold winds. This species is tolerant of lime. Give protection with straw, bracken or plastic sheeting until the plant is well established. It will then withstand quite strong winds and low temperatures. No pruning is usually needed beyond cutting back straggly shoots in spring to keep the tree shapely.

Conditioning   The fruit branches must be well hammered and the leaves must be removed, as the fruits do not last well if the leaves are allowed to take up the moisture. Though the 'strawberries' hang on the stems for a long time, I know of no way to preserve them.

Arranging   The fruits are the only part of the tree I find useful for arranging. The clusters add interest to any vase, looking particularly well with mixed fruits and red roses, arranged in a dark alabaster vase.

Artemisia

Grey foliage plants, which look well in the border and are useful for picking all through the summer months. *A. absinthium* is a small shrub. The only artemisia grown for its flowers is *A. lactiflora*, which has elegant cream plumes of flower.
Cultivation   Plant from October to April in any good well-drained garden soil, in full sun for preference. *A. lactiflora* may be grown in partial shade, and the stems should be cut down to the ground after flowering. *A. absinthium* should be pruned in April each year, cutting the stems to about 15–20 cm (6–8 in) above ground.
Conditioning and preserving   The plumes last longer if the stem ends are dipped into boiling water and then left in deep water for an hour or two. The plumes of 'Lambrook Silver' dry well in an arrangement in water, or if picked once the stem is in a mature state, and hung upside down to dry.
Arranging   The flower plumes are a great standby for background in any arrangement from July onwards, using the stems at almost any length.

Artemisia absinthium 'Lambrook Silver', height and spread 1 m (3 ft); A. lactiflora, height 1–1.5 m (3–5 ft), planting distance 45 cm (18 in).

Arum italicum 'Pictum'

This is one of the greatest treasures in any garden. The small spade-shaped spotted leaves come straight out of the ground in December or early January, resisting the stormy weather by closing up and unfurling as the sun shines. They grow on short stems of about 7.5–10 cm (3–4 in), but the leaves get much larger as the months go by, and in May the stems are often 15–18 cm (6 or 7 in) long and the big leaves up to 30 cm (12 in) or more in length, though their size does depend on the soil conditions. Producing seed heads of thick clusters of iridescent red berries in the autumn, they are very decorative in the garden – but the birds also enjoy them, and the stems become pulpy and soft if they are put in a vase.
Cultivation   Plant from September to December in any good garden soil, fairly moist, if possible in full sun.
Conditioning   It is best to submerge the leaves completely overnight, or in a weak solution of starch.
Arranging   The small leaves are such a good shape that they fit into any arrangement of foliage or of small spring flowers.

Height 45 cm (18 in), planting distance 30 cm (12 in).

Arum Lily see *Zantedeschia aethiopica*

Astrantia major

A shade-loving perennial that seeds freely, its wiry stems holding delicate flower heads, each a cluster of greenish-white or pinky florets within a collar of white bracts. A must in Sunningdale with its beautiful variegated foliage.
Cultivation   Plant from October to March in any good garden soil, in partial shade for preference, and in a damp corner if possible. Give the support of twiggy sticks as the flower stems require it. Cut the stems down to ground level in the autumn.
Conditioning and preserving   The flowers last well in water with no special treatment.
   I always think astrantia flowers should dry well, but in fact they don't. However, they can be preserved in a glycerine and water solution, turning a

Height 60 cm (2 ft), planting distance 40 cm (15 in).

41

creamy-buff and keeping a perfect shape, making them ideal for use in swags and garlands of dried flowers as well as in small dried arrangements.

Arranging These strange little flowers of nondescript appearance mix well in any small summer group. Though they grow on stems up to 30 cm (12 in) in height, I generally use them on shorter stems and tuck them well into the centre of a collection of small flowers.

Atriplex

Atriplex hortensis alba, A. hortensis 'Rubra' height around 1.3 m (4–4½ ft), planting distance 60 cm (2 ft).

Atriplex 'Rubra' produces tall stems with purple leaves and seeds. An annual, it grows easily from seed and once you have it, it is with you always – as a friend of mine once said, it seeds all the way to the bonfire! *A. alba*, the green form, has green leaves and spinach-like seed heads.

Cultivation Sow thinly in any good soil in a sunny spot in March or April. Gradually thin the seedlings until the plants are at their final distance. Water well in dry spells.

Conditioning and preserving The seed heads dry very well and as soon as the seeds are set it is best to remove every leaf and hang the stems upside down in a warm place to dry.

Arranging The seed heads are extremely useful as part of the background in arrangements. They are equally effective when used with purple tones or with contrasting colours. The green stems mix well in a green group or with blending colours.

Aucuba japonica   Spotted Laurel

Height 2–4 m (6–12 ft), spread 1.5–2 m (5–7 ft).

This is a plant I have come to love. A hardy evergreen, it lightens a dull patch, will grow almost anywhere and is rewarding for picking.

Cultivation Aucubas thrive in any reasonable soil. They may be grown in sun or semi-shade, or in tubs or other containers. Plant in October or March and April. They put up with the atmosphere in town gardens, and of course in the country as well as at the seaside. If grown in a container, feed with a soluble fertilizer according to the maker's instructions throughout the summer. No pruning is normally needed, but if the shrub becomes ungainly, old stems may be cut hard back.

Auricula see Primula

Autumn Crocus see Colchicum

Azalea

Deciduous varieties: 'Bouquet de Flore', 'W.S. Churchill', 'Coccinea Speciosa', 'Fire Glow',

(Though properly speaking these should appear with *Rhododendron*, I have put them in a separate section for the sake of clarity.)

These are shrubs that are well worth the extra effort required to give them the lime-free soil they need. I have had great success with them in one specially prepared area of my garden, and find that it is a corner which gives me more pleasure than almost any other. I value both the flowers in May, giving a wealth of colour, and the lovely tinted autumn foliage. I have limited myself to a choice of one of each colour which I know and like: 'W.S. Churchill', mandarin-red with a brighter red blotch; 'Bouquet de Flore', one of the best salmon-pinks, double; 'Coccinea Speciosa', with semi-double orange-flame coloured flowers, one of my favourites. I think if I were limited, I would grow only the flame colourings ('Fire Glow' is another brilliant one), with 'Persil', white with a pale yellow blotch.

As with roses and dahlias, my advice is always to try to see azaleas in flower before making a choice. I did not do this with my evergreen varieties, and although the foliage is good, I regret having only scarlet and vermilion-flowered plants, when I do not really care for either. I would prefer to plant only white-flowered ones, such as 'Adonis' and 'Palestrina', pure white and creamy white. For those of you who want colour, then I think that 'Vuyk's Scarlet' speaks for itself, as do 'Orange Beauty' and the interesting 'Blue Danube', the nearest thing to a true blue flower. These Japanese azaleas seem to grow well from one side of the United States to the other.

Cultivation Azaleas must have lime-free soil. If the garden soil is alkaline, it is still possible to grow azaleas in specially prepared sites lined with plastic sheeting, or in raised beds. Choose a sheltered site, in full sun, or semi-shade.

Conditioning and preserving The ends of the stems must be well hammered, and whenever possible allowed an overnight drink in deep water. It is essential to remove all florets as they fade and fall, as they can give the arrangement the appearance of being dead long before it really is. The Japanese varieties take up a glycerine solution well, but I seldom feel one has enough to make this worth while.

Arranging If you ever have the chance to pick enough, then nothing could be more lovely than a copper pot filled with apricot and pinkish azalea blossom, or a silver wine cooler of the white-flowered varieties with some 'Mount Tacoma' double white tulips. However, I usually feel that only the smallest pieces can be spared from the shrub, to use, for instance, with the early apricot-coloured foliage of *Acer pseudoplatanus* 'Brilliantissimum' and one or two 'Apricot Beauty' tulips. In October small pieces of the autumn-coloured foliage mix well with dark red or orange dahlias.

'Persil'. Height and spread 1.5–2 m (5–6 ft).

Japanese or evergreen varieties: 'Adonis', 'Blue Danube', 'Orange Beauty', 'Palestrina', 'Vuyk's Scarlet'. Height 60–90 cm (2–3 ft), spread 1–1.5 m (3–5 ft).

Ballota pseudo-dictamnus

The arching shrubby growth of ballota produces graceful stems for flower arranging, though you have to remove nearly all the leaves as they completely cover the small clusters of grey-green flower bracts that circle the stems.

Cultivation Plant in spring – March, April – in any good garden soil, in full sun, but choose a well-drained spot that does not lie wet in winter. Prune in April, shortening the growths by about half their length.

Conditioning and preserving Place the ends of the stems into 2.5 cm (1 in) of boiling water for a count of twenty, then stand in deep cold water for an hour or two.

Ballota bracts will dry quite well and keep a good green colour if the leaves are removed and the stems, with well-opened flowers, are bunched and hung upside down.

Arranging As the flowers grow all down the stems, you really need to cut them as long as possible, or you will destroy the grace of the flowers. I find them most effective in an arrangement of mixed flowers, adding a touch of delicate green more unusual than foliage.

Height 45–60 cm (18–24 in), spread 60 cm (2 ft).

43

Beech see *Fagus sylvatica*

Begonia

Height 15 cm (6 in), planting distance 20 cm (8 in).

Begonia semperflorens are excellent little plants for putting in tubs, hanging baskets and window boxes. Grown from seed and planted out after the frosts have gone, they have a good range of pinks and reds and white flowers, with foliage which varies from green to bronze.

Cultivation Grown from seed, these begonias need some heat. After pricking out, they should be planted out in late May and will flower from June to September/October. As the season progresses and the stems get longer, the flowers are more useful for cutting.

Conditioning To condition, just dip the ends of the stems in boiling water and then give them an overnight drink in deep water. The flowers do shed but buds open well in water and they last a surprisingly long time.

Arranging Though these begonias are not considered a cut flower they last very well and the touch of pink in a small mixed vase is very effective. Some of the deep red foliage is lovely but it is only useful for small arrangements as the plants are small and the stems short. The flower heads do fall, so give them a good shake before using.

Bells of Ireland see *Moluccella laevis*

Berberis

Berberis 'Buccaneer', height 1.5–2 m (5–6 ft), spread 1–1.5 m (4–5 ft); B. thunbergii, B. thunbergii 'Atropurpurea' (deciduous), height 1–1.5 m (4–5 ft), spread 1.5–2 m (5–6 ft); B. darwinii, height and spread 2.5–3 m (8–10 ft); B. linearifolia 'Orange King', height 2.3 m (8–10 ft), spread around 1 m (3–4 ft); B. verruculosa (evergreen), height and spread 1–1.5 m (3–5 ft).

Varied shrubs of many different kinds, quite easily grown. The evergreen varieties thrive well in the shade, though for really good autumn colour, the deciduous kinds need full sun. The wide range of heights means that you can find berberis varieties for both the front and back of the border.

B. 'Buccaneer' has lovely coloured berries pearly pink turning bright red with the red autumn foliage. All the cultivars of *B. thunbergii* share its pale straw-coloured flowers suffused with red, and superb autumn leaf colour. *B. thunbergii* 'Atropurpurea' has beautiful bronzy-red foliage which is supposed to turn true red in autumn; it does not do this for me, but it is still a lovely shrub, and provides contrast in the border. *B. thunbergii* 'Aurea' has striking golden foliage, turning light green.

The evergreen varieties have good contrast qualities. *B. darwinii* is one of the best, with orange-yellow flowers, purple berries and holly-like leaves. *B. linearifolia* 'Orange King' has the reputation of being one of the most beautiful, deep orange flowers darkening to red in April, and purple berries with greyish bloom. *B. verruculosa* has arching sprays of grey-backed leaves, yellow flowers and purple fruit with a rich bloom.

Cultivation Deciduous berberis may be planted from October to March, but the evergreen species are best planted either in September or October, or in March or April. They are not particular about soil; they will even grow quite well on rather poor shallow soils, but they do not like wet or waterlogged ground. Pruning is generally confined to cutting back straggly shoots to keep the bush shapely. Prune deciduous species in January or February, evergreens after flowering, usually in May or June.

Conditioning Handle with extreme care as the thorns are vicious and can even be poisonous. It is best to remove all thorns for 5–7.5 cm (2–3 in) up the stem; then hammer the ends well and allow a long deep drink in warm water. Though I know of no way to preserve berberis, the berries do stay on their stems for a long time without treatment.

Arranging   Berberis is one of the great joys to use in arrangements of autumnal coloured fruits and foliage. If you pick small pieces of brilliant colour, you will find that the leaves curl, but the berries will hang on for weeks until they have shrivelled completely. Their arching growth makes them easy to arrange, as they hang gracefully from any vase, though I think they look their best with autumn groups in copper or brass. I use sprays of *B. verruculosa* for green arrangements in both winter and summer.

Bergenia

Without doubt, bergenia is one of my favourite perennials: the rounded or heart-shaped fleshy leaves, useful in both summer and winter, make them a 'must' for every garden. They grow well in shade or full sun and act as excellent ground cover. *B. crassifolia* has spoon-shaped leaves that turn a bronze colour in winter, and has masses of delicate pink flowers in spring which are particularly welcome because they provide solid contrast to the more spiky spring bulbs. *B. cordifolia* has heart-shaped leaves that often turn beautiful autumnal colours as they die off. The new hybrid 'Ballawley' has a leaf shape which is a cross between the two mentioned above, and turns a lovely deep bronze in winter.

Bergenia purpurascens 'Ballawley', height 30–40 cm (12–15 in), planting distance 60 cm (2 ft); B. cordifolia, height and planting distance 30 cm (12 in); B. crassifolia, height and planting distance 30 cm (12 in).

Cultivation   Plant from October to March in any ordinary soil, including limy soils, in sun or partial shade. Cut off faded flower stems. Lift and divide plants every few years if they become overcrowded.

Conditioning   The leaves benefit from a good soak for a few hours in cold water. They are often limp if picked during a hard frost, but will soon recover if submerged in tepid water – and this means of course that they can be used however cold the weather.

Arranging   There is hardly a week in the year when I don't use some of these leaves. They are superb to add weight to the base of a foliage group, clustered in threes they add under-shadow to the arrangement, and will give a restful zone to a slightly cluttered arrangement of mixed flowers. The autumn-coloured leaves are marvellous with reds, or shades of apricot, in autumn. The magenta-pink flowers of *B. cordifolia* go well with reds in spring.

Betula

There is nothing more graceful than a stately silver birch, though I wish so much that I had also grown *B. papyrifera*, which has smooth dazzling white bark, peeling in paper-like layers, and golden leaves in autumn. *B. costata* is another lovely birch, with bark that is a well-marked silver in summer and orange in winter. *B. pendula* 'Youngii' and *B. pendula* 'Obelisk', both weeping forms of our common silver birch, make good subjects for the small garden, delightful in spring with green catkins, with golden colouring in autumn and lovely bark.

Betula costata, height 5–6 m (18–20 ft), spread 3–4 m (10–12 ft); B. papyrifera, height 6–9 m (20–30 ft), spread 3–4.5 m (10–15 ft); B. pendula 'Obelisk', height 4.5–5 m (15–18 ft), spread around 1 m (3–4 ft); B. pendula 'Youngii', height 6–9 m (20–30 ft), spread 3–4 m (10–12 ft).

Cultivation   The birches will grow in any reasonable soil, even hungry shallow soils, but prefer a good rich loam. Plant in sun or shade from October to March; their roots travel a considerable distance near the surface, so plant as far away as possible from flower beds.

Conditioning   Like all woody stems, they should be hammered and then allowed a long deep drink.

Arranging   The bursting young catkins and leaves make the branches of silver birch one of the loveliest outlines for a vase of daffodils or moss bed of young spring flowers. The bare branches have such graceful lines that they look beautiful at Christmas painted with clear glue and sprinkled with glitter, used by themselves, with holly berries or with white chrysanthemums.

Birch see *Betula*

Bittersweet see *Celastrus orbiculatus*

Black Snake-root see *Cimicifuga*

Blue Cedar see *Cedrus atlantica*

Briza maxima see *Grasses*

Buddleia

Buddleia alternifolia, height 4–6 m (12–20 ft), spread 3–5 m (10–15 ft); B. davidii 'Black Knight', B. davidii 'Harlequin', height and spread 2–3 m (8–10 ft); B. fallowiana 'Alba', height 1.5–3 m (5–10 ft), spread 1.2–1.8 m (4–6 ft).

For a quick effect these are among the best shrubs and nowadays come in a wonderful colour range, from the common mauve to deepest purple, almost pink or lovely white. The flowers appear at the end of the stems in close spikes of up to 20 cm (8 in). Apart from their rapid growth, a more important reason for including a buddleia in the garden is that they attract butterflies. However, they are not ideal for the flower arranger, as they are difficult to keep in water for any length of time.

Cultivation   Plant from October to March in any reasonably good soil, in sun or semi-shade. Buddleias do not object to a limy soil. *B. fallowiana* is not reliably hardy and should be planted against a south- or west-facing wall. *B. davidii* and its varieties are pruned in February or March. Cut back all the previous year's growth to within about 7.5 cm (3 in) of the point where it left the old stem. Thin out the shoots of *B. alternifolia* in July after flowering; about half to two-thirds of the old stems may be removed. *B. fallowiana* needs little pruning.

Conditioning and preserving   I have never found the answer to keeping buddleia for more than two days in water, and I have tried everything. Even for that short time it is advisable to strip off all the foliage, put the stem ends into 2.5 cm (1 in) of boiling water for a minute, and then leave them in deep water for as long as possible.

The seedheads dry well and make a useful contribution as outline for a dried group. They can be picked off the plant when dry, but it is better to pick them before this stage, strip off the leaves and hang them upside down to dry.

Arranging   Though effective for a party arrangement, in my experience buddleia is unreliable for more than a day or two. I have used sprays of white buddleia mixed with hoheria, white gladiolus and white chrysanthemums for an August wedding, but I felt it was safe to do this as the flowers only had to

Opposite. Petasites, *Helleborus foetidus*, fan-tail willow and Christmas rose.

mahonia

protea

epimedium

galax

alder catkins

bergenia

Cornus mas

ivy

A good early spring arrangement. Galax, widely sold in the US, is now appearing here occasionally. I have tried to grow it, without success. I bought the protea to add highlight.

last overnight. The deep purple-flowered buddleia looks very good with deep red roses and black grapes.

Calla Lily see *Zantedeschia aethiopica*

Calluna see *Erica*

Camellia

The foliage is, for me anyway, almost as beautiful as the flowers; glossy, dark-green rounded leaves on bushes that grow to 2–4 m (6 or 12 ft) high, though in Cornwall and warmer climates they can become huge. They are much hardier than was once thought, though personally I have never had any success in growing them, due I am sure to bad positioning. They grow well in Washington and many areas of the United States, even where the winters are very severe. Mrs Sydney Thompson in Bethesda, Washington, grew some of the best camellias I have ever seen, so I think I must try again. The whites are my favourites – perhaps because I carried white camellias as my wedding bouquet – especially 'Mathotiana Alba'. Other good ones are 'Elegans', anemone form salmon-rose; 'Mercury', light red; 'Donation' semi-double clear pink; and 'J.C. Williams', pale blush pink.

Camellia japonica 'Mathotiana Alba', 'Elegans', 'Mercury'. C. x williamsii 'Donation', 'J.C. Williams'. Height and spread 2–4 m (6–12 ft).

Cultivation Camellias must have lime-free soil. Plenty of peat or well-decayed leaf-mould should be worked into the ground at planting time. They are best planted in a north- or west-facing position because, as they flower early in the spring, the flowers may be damaged by frost if the early morning sun can reach them. When grown against a wall, see that they do not go short of water or bud dropping may result. Camellias should be planted in September or October, or March and April. C. 'J.C. Williams' and C. 'Donation' need protection of light woodlands or a west-facing wall. No pruning is normally required, but straggly shoots may be cut back in April.

Conditioning and preserving There is little I can suggest to prevent the flowers from dropping just as they start to fade, but I think it does help the leaves to last longer if the ends of the stems are burnt and then given a good long drink. Short pieces of foliage take up a glycerine solution well, and are attractive in dried arrangements.

Arranging Like me, you may find it difficult to bring yourself to pick these lovely flowers on long stems, though if ever you get the chance, they look well in a silver cake basket and make a spectacular table arrangement. The heads have a habit of falling off, so that it seems wasteful to pick them with long stems, though after the flower is over, I use the remaining stems of foliage and find they last for weeks.

I use camellia foliage after Christmas in mixed green arrangements, for it adds a certain quality that is hard to describe. Years ago we used to put waxed artificial flowers on fresh camellia branches for our contract work in London restaurants, and they not only lasted well but deceived many people, I am sure. Gradually, however, the real buds opened, and were invariably a different colour from the wax flowers, so that really destroyed the illusion!

Opposite. Elderberry, autumn crocus, hypericum, atriplex, white delphinium, 'Iceberg' rose, grapes, snapdragon, St John's Wort, blackberries, poke weed or *Phytolacca americana*, photographed in end of October.

47

Campanula

Campanula carpatica, *height 13–25 cm (5–10 in), planting distance 30–40 cm (12–15 in); C. glomerata, height up to 45 cm (18 in), planting distance 45–60 cm (18–24 in); C. lactiflora, height 1–1.5 m (3–5 ft), planting distance 45 cm (18 in); C. latifolia, height 1–1.5 m (4–5 ft), planting distance 45 cm (18 in); C. persicifolia, height 60–90 cm (2–3 ft), planting distance 30–45 cm (12–18 in); C. portenschlagiana, height 15 cm, planting distance 45–60 cm.*

One of the best-lasting summer perennials, a great asset for the flower arranger because the flowers continue to open in water from bud stage, and though paler and not so large as the first blooms, they do not drop their petals, which is a real joy after the lupin and delphinium period. *C. carpatica* is suitable for the rock garden, has lovely open flowers in clear white or blue. *C. portenschlagiana* makes a good edging plant and produces a mass of long-lasting purple bell flowers, but is not good as a cut flower. *C. persicifolia* is the best for cutting and is now a popular plant in the cut flower trade. My grandmother grew these and had a wonderful collection of seedlings, with cup and saucer form, in white and blue. I wish I had valued them then as I do today! *C. glomerata* has many forms, but the varieties that bloom in May and June are the most useful, as they bring that early touch of colour to the garden, and are excellent solid heads to pick, though they do not last as well as some other campanulas when cut. One of my favourites is *C. latifolia*, especially the white form 'Alba' and blue-flowered 'Gloaming' – but again these do not last well when cut. *C. lactiflora* 'Loddon Anna', pale pink, and 'Prichard's Variety', violet-blue, are well worth having in any garden. They last well in the border and when cut.

Cultivation   Plant from October to March in any normal garden soil, in sun or partial shade. The taller varieties may need the support of twiggy sticks. Remove flower spikes when the flowers have faded, and cut down the old stems of the tall campanulas in the autumn.

Conditioning   *C. latifolia, C. glomerata* and *C. lactiflora* all need to have their stem ends burnt, by placing them in about 2.5 cm (1 in) of boiling water, counting twenty, filling the can up to the top with cold water and leaving the stems to drink for several hours. As a child, I remember the ritual of hammering the stems and then standing them in a bucket of water in the cellar for two days: they seemed to last for ever afterwards. The only treatment needed to make *C. persicifolia* last well is a long drink of cold water for a few hours.

Arranging   *C. persicifolia* must be my first choice in this family as the variety that lasts best when cut. The white forms mix well with greens and in a vase of all white summer flowers. The blue-flowered forms are splendid in mixed arrangements. I love to use *C. latifolia* in a semi-oriental arrangement because it has such a beautiful form and stands out so well in a simple white shallow dish, maybe just three stems on a pin-holder and a few hosta leaves at the base. 'Loddon Anna', or any of the tall and stately heads of the *C. lactiflora* species, make a marvellous background for a large group for a summer wedding.

Carnation see Dianthus

Carpinus betulus   Hornbeam

Height around 6 m (20 ft), spread 3–4.5 m (10–15 ft).

A beautiful tree that few people plant, yet it is lovely in the spring, and the leaves turn russet gold in the autumn. It grows to the height of a beech or oak, so it needs planty of space. The green catkins in spring are followed by pretty keys in the autumn which often hang on to the branches long after the leaves have fallen.

Cultivation   The hornbeam will grow in any good garden soil, in sun or semi-shade. Plant from October to March. No pruning is required.

Conditioning and preserving   Stems of hornbeam keys should be hammered well and soaked before use. Remove all the leaves to reveal the keys, and they will then last surprisingly well in water.

If the keys are put into a solution of glycerine and water, they will acquire a slightly glossy appearance and last virtually for ever. They can be dried by hanging the keyed stems upside down after the leaves have been removed, but I am not really happy about this method as they tend to dry too straight. It might be better to leave them in a vase with just a little water, so that they dry off in their natural shapes.

Arranging Spring branches with catkins make a delicate outline for any early arrangement, but I think that the green autumn keys are superb. They mix well with green zinnias, moluccella and lime-green tobacco flowers, and make the outline for any foliage arrangement.

Cedrus atlantica 'Glauca' Blue Cedar

This is a tree for only the largest garden though I did have a friend who loved it so much, and felt that the colour was just what she needed for a certain part of the garden, that she decided to grow one, knowing full well that it would eventually swamp the whole area. I have never been back to find out if she ever had the courage to cut it down. This wonderful member of the pine family grows into a huge tree, adding an unusual touch of blue-green to the garden, with lovely foliage for flower arranging.

Height 12–15 m (40–50 ft), spread 4.5–5 m (15–18 ft).

Cultivation Plant in October or November, or in April. Stake the tree firmly and tie one leading shoot to it. It is necessary to keep the leader to one shoot until the tree can no longer be reached as it has a tendency to produce more than one leading shoot. Give a general fertilizer each spring until the tree is growing strongly. Some lower branches may have to be cut away.

Conditioning The ends of the stems should be well hammered and then allowed a long drink of warm water overnight, but try not to leave them in very deep water, as they lose colour when they get very wet; in fact, it is better to remove the lower pine needles so that you have a clear stem below the water level in the vase. If left undisturbed the needles do not drop too badly, and I have managed to keep stems in the house for up to 6 weeks.

Arranging Sprays of Blue Cedar are most useful for a winter arrangement, and with some lichen-covered branches and a few grey leaves of *Begonia rex* make a long-lasting winter group. The branches also provide an excellent colour contrast in a vase of 'Christmas greens'.

Celastrus orbiculatus Bittersweet

This very vigorous deciduous climber is a member of the family that includes the American Bittersweet (*C. scandens*). It is chiefly desirable for its brilliant scarlet seeds, contrasting marvellously with the yellow interiors of the seed capsules. These are showy and very long-lasting.

Height up to 9 m (30 ft).

Cultivation Plant from October to March in any good garden soil. It does not like a very alkaline soil, nor one that lies wet in winter. It is happiest on a south- or west-facing wall, or rambling over an old tree. Where it has plenty of room to spread, no pruning is required, but on walls or pergolas it may have to be kept in bounds by trimming it back in February. Thin out some of the oldest shoots, and cut back long growths to half their length – more severely if necessary.

Preserving Like the American Bittersweet, berried branches dry well if they are simply hung upside down.

49

Arranging   Sprays of the yellow bracts and red seeds are invaluable for using with autumn-tinted foliage and with dried flower groups.

Chimonanthus praecox   Winter Sweet

(C. fragrans), height and spread 2.5–3 m (8– 10 ft).

A hardy deciduous shrub with most sweetly scented winter flowers. They are nondescript, rather like small spiders on a branch, but one small sprig of these pale yellow flowers, deepening to red in the centre, will quickly scent a whole room. My shrub took seven years to bloom, but it was worth every minute of that long wait.

Cultivation   This shrub will grow in any soil, but is happiest in a sheltered position against a south- or west-facing wall. Plant from October to March. It may be grown as a free-standing bush in full sun, and will need little or no pruning. Any overcrowding stems may be cut out in March or April. Grown against a wall, the shoots that have flowered need to be pruned back in early spring to leave only about 7.5 cm (3 in) of stem.

Conditioning   The stems benefit from being put into warm water for a long drink after the ends have been hammered.

Arranging   I do not think the flowers show up well for flower arranging, but they make their presence felt by their fragrance. Tuck a small piece into a spring arrangement, and even if you cannot see it, you will know it is in the vase as soon as you come into the room.

Chionodoxa gigantea   Glory of the Snow

Height 20 cm (8 in), planting distance 10 cm (4 in).

Little star-shaped flowers which I find invaluable for that touch of blue that is so important for a mixed arrangement in early spring, or for a moss garden. My grandmother had what she called her 'blue bed' – a flower bed of about 3 m by 1.2 m (10 ft by 4 ft) against the end of the house, entirely filled with a mixture of chionodoxa and scilla, and a solid mass of blue when in flower. I have no idea how long it took to reach this size, but it was quite superb, and people came from miles around just to see it as soon as the snow had gone.

Cultivation   Plant in September to November – the earlier the better – in full sun in ordinary but well-drained garden soil. No further attention is needed, but if, after some years, the clumps of bulbs become congested, they should be lifted, divided, and replanted.

Arranging   Chionodoxa looks splendid in groups in a moss garden.

Choisya ternata   Mexican Orange Blossom

Height 1.5–2.5 m (5–8 ft), spread around 2 m (6–8 ft).

This wonderful shrub with glossy evergreen leaves produces clusters of scented white star-like flowers in May, and spasmodically throughout the rest of the year. It forms a rounded bush of aromatic foliage. There is a new golden-foliaged variety, 'Sun Dance'.

Cultivation   Choisyas prefer light well-drained soil and a sheltered position in full sun, although they will tolerate a certain amount of shade. In cold districts they need the protection of a south- or west-facing wall. Even in milder districts young growths may be damaged by frosts. Pruning consists merely of removing straggly shoots, or shortening them by a few inches, and of course cutting back to healthy wood any shoots that have been damaged by frosts.

Pruning is best done after flowering in spring, but removal of dead foliage may be done in March or April.

Conditioning and preserving   Hammer the stem ends well, or put them into 2.5 cm (1 in) of boiling water, in either case followed by a long drink before arranging.

Arranging   The foliage is particularly attractive in green arrangements, and can be used to give life to a dried group, especially after Christmas when they tend to look rather dull.

Chrysanthemum

From this large family of perennial flowers that are perhaps more widely grown than almost any other I have chosen only two varieties. The summer-flowering *C. maximum* 'Esther Read' which has a lovely double white flower, excellent for cutting and showy in the garden, deserves a place in every border. I cannot bear to see these lovely pure white flowers dyed every conceivable colour and sold all through the summer, but they are obviously very popular. 'Esther Read' grows to about 60 cm (2 ft), but there are many taller varieties of the Shasta Daisy.

Chrysanthemum Korean varieties, height 60 cm (2 ft), planting distance 45 cm (18 in); C. maximum 'Esther Read', height 60 cm (2 ft), planting distance 30–45 cm.

My second choice is the autumn-flowering Korean chrysanthemums, not really hardy perhaps, though with a good top-dressing of leaf-mould my plants have withstood many winters. There is a wide range of colours, but my favourites are the single apricots and 'Wedding Day', a beautiful white with a green centre.

Cultivation   Plant 'Esther Read' from October to April in any good garden soil, in full sun or partial shade. Cut down the old stems to the ground in the autumn.

Plant Korean chrysanthemums in April or May in any good garden soil, in sun or partial shade. Feed with a soluble fertilizer as directed by the makers, during the summer. Cut the old stems to the ground after flowering, and protect the plants with a 15 cm (6 in) layer of peat, straw or bracken.

Conditioning   Bruise or hammer the ends of the stems and leave in a bucket of cold water up to their necks for three hours or more.

Arranging   'Esther Read' chrysanthemums give good flower heads for arranging as they last well in water with no petal dropping, and I have known them keep for two weeks if picked fresh. They make a good show on their own with no unrelated foliage, but they can be used with other white flowers. They make a marvellous focal point in any vase as they have outstandingly clear faces. Korean chrysanthemums also look lovely on their own – perhaps massed in a basket – or used for a central point in any vase of mixed flowers, or autumn-coloured foliage.

Cimicifuga racemosa   Black Snake-root

Tall spikes of fluffy white flowers on coal-black stems, appearing in July and August, when there is little tall perennial material to cut and arrange. *C. racemosa purpurea* has the same flower form but its foliage is a wonderful maroon colour, as its name implies. The golden form is also useful.

Height around 1.7 m (5–6 ft), planting distance 60 cm.

Cultivation   Plant from October to April in any good garden soil, preferably in light shade in a site that is fairly moist. Support the flower stems with twiggy sticks if necessary, and cut the stems down to the ground after flowering.

Conditioning   I find that the flowers last a little better if the ends of the stems

51

are placed in boiling water for a few seconds before giving them a long drink of cold water.

Arranging   Stems of cimicifuga bring touches of delicacy to a vase of mixed flowers, and are graceful in a shallow dish arrangement on a pin-holder with their own leaves at the base.

Cineraria maritima see Senecio

Clematis

Clematis armandii, height 8–9 m (25–30 ft), spread 6–9 m (20–30 ft); C. macropetala, height 3–4 m (10–12 ft), spread around 2 m (6–8 ft); C. montana, C. montana 'Rubens', height 9–12 m (30–40 ft), spread 4.5–6 m (15–20 ft); C. orientalis, height 4.5–6 m (15–20 ft), spread 2–3 m (8–10 ft); C. tangutica, height and spread 4.5–6 m (15–20 ft). Clematis 'Duchess of Edinburgh', 'Hagley Hybrid', 'Madame le Coultre', 'Nelly Moser', 'W.E. Gladstone', height 2–4.5 m (8–15 ft), spread 1–2.5 m (4–8 ft).

For any wall or fence there is nothing more attractive than a climbing clematis. It is hard to make a choice from the many species and hybrids, so perhaps colour would be your best guide. *C. armandii* is well worth growing for the beautiful evergreen foliage, which provides a good wall cover all winter, and the trusses of ivory white flowers which appear in March and April. *C. macropetala*, has semi-double flowers, pendulous bells of mauve-blue, with lovely seed heads. *C. montana* is a rampant grower with good purple-tinged foliage and a wealth of single open white flowers (or pink in the case of *C. montana* 'Rubens'). *C. orientalis* 'Orange Peel' has delightful nodding heads of four thick petals resembling orange peel, which flower in September and October. *C. tangutica* flowers in August, and the pointed pendent little yellow lanterns are followed by good seed heads. Among the large-flowered hybrids, I would recommend 'Duchess of Edinburgh', with fragrant double white rosette-shaped flowers; 'Madame le Coultre', which has large blooms of single white flowers with yellow stamens; 'Hagley Hybrid', slower in growth but flowering over a long period; 'Nelly Moser', an old favourite and perhaps one of the most widely grown with its mauve-pink flowers, each sepal striped in deep carmine; and 'W.E. Gladstone', with enormous pale lilac blooms that can span 25 cm (10 in).

Cultivation   Clematis prefer an alkaline soil, but will grow reasonably well in any reasonable garden soil. They like to be in full sun, but they also like to have their roots in the shade, so it is wise to plant some dwarf shrubs at their base. When grown against a wall, they may need watering in dry spells. Plant from October to May. Pruning requirements vary with the different species and hybrids. Thin out shoots of *C. armandii* in February; *C. macropetala* and *C. montana* may be thinned out after flowering and new shoots trained in. Prune *C. orientalis* in spring if necessary, thinning out old shoots and shortening new ones if necessary; prune *C. tangutica* in March, cutting previous year's shoots to within 5–7 cm (2–3 in) of the base. The newly planted specimens of the foregoing may be cut back by about one-third of their length immediately after planting. The other clematis described, the hybrids, may be pruned hard back in February. Cut all shoots made in the previous year just above a joint, at about 30 cm (12 in) from the base. It is important to cut plants back to 15–23 cm (6–9 in) immediately after planting.

Conditioning and preserving   Conditioning is very important, as the flowers do not normally last well, though I do remember at a dinner given for the late Constance Spry in Sydney, Australia, the table was arranged with clematis, and when they started to fade two of us put a few in our glasses where a little champagne was left, and the blooms revived in seconds. So you could try using champagne if you think it worth it! Presumably this is the basis of the Japanese treatment for wistaria and clematis – they dip the ends of the stems in pure alcohol for a few hours. I put the ends of the stems into a little boiling water for a few moments, taking extra care that the steam does not reach the delicate flowers, and then if possible leave them overnight in water before arranging. I find they last very well in Oasis if one takes the precaution of giving them a long drink beforehand.

Arranging   One of the best ways of showing off these beautiful flowers is undoubtedly by floating them in a shallow bowl, and like this they last extremely well and make an attractive table decoration. I love to use one or two clematis as the centre of a group, for they have such a stunning flat face and they show up very distinctly, even from a distance. I have used 'Nelly Moser' like this in many arrangements, mainly because this variety flowers so frequently and well that I feel I can pick them freely. The smaller blooms of *C. montana* 'Rubens' look exquisite arranged alone in a plain or blue glass vase.

Cobaea

Better known as Cups and Saucers, Cathedral Bells or Dutchman's Pipe, this plant has lovely trumpets of green turning to pale mauve, and being a climber it is better trained on a fence or wall. If you can train the stems along a wire, you will get a wealth of bloom that may otherwise be difficult to see when the stems grow very high. In its native Mexico cobaea grows freely over fence and wall and it becomes a veritable menace in Australia.

Cobaea scandens, height 6 m, planting distance 60 cm.

Cultivation   This is a half-hardy perennial but is normally grown as an annual to form a quick screen over trellis, fences, or over a pergola. Sow the seeds in a heated greenhouse in March, prick off the seedlings and plant out when danger of frost is past. Place the seeds edgeways in the soil. This plant will grow in any reasonably fertile soil but appreciates some feeding in summer, and plenty of water in dry spells.

Conditioning and preserving   The trumpet flowers need little conditioning but should be given a drink of warm water in a narrow-necked container when picked. The seed heads do not dry well and I do not recommend your trying to preserve them.

Arranging   These delicate flowers arrange well with mixed greens or as the centre of any vase where their colour is enhancing to the arrangement. The seed heads are striking and look very attractive in a fruit and flower arrangement.

Colchicum   Autumn Crocus

Delightful autumn-flowering bulb that produces single and double crocus-like flowers in white and varying shades of purple. The flowers appear straight out of the ground before the leaves, making a lovely display. It is best to plant colchicum under azaleas or round specimen trees.

Colchicum autumnale, height 15 cm (6 in), planting distance 23 cm (9 in).

Cultivation   Plant in August or September in any reasonable soil, in full sun. Remove the dead leaves in June or July, and if desired, lift and transplant the bulbs.

Arranging   The large white colchicum is one of the flowers that is superb to arrange, looking best in a shallow silver bowl or entrée dish, arranged on a pin-holder which can be hidden by a piece of coral or moss; in this way they need no unrelated foliage. The purple ones need the help of some other flowers, and are prettiest mixed with gentian, nerines, the last pink roses and some *Erica* 'H.E. Beale'.

Comfrey see Symphytum

Convallaria majalis
Lily of the Valley

Height 20 cm (8 in), planting distance 10–15 cm (4–6 in).

Sweetly scented sprays of white bells, a most popular flower which has a strange habit of deciding for itself where it would like to grow. However carefully you plant it, it has a habit of spreading on to a nearby path, but try planting it there and in no way is it happy! However, it is well worth a spot in any garden; it likes shade and any soil, making it a good plant for the small town garden and excellent ground cover anywhere.

Cultivation Plant in September or October in any good garden soil, preferably in a moist and shaded site. If it is possible to redirect rain from the down pipe of a roof gutter into the bed, this will often encourage the plants to grow strongly.

Conditioning If picked straight from the garden, then an hour or two in deep warm water is all that is necessary. If bought out of season, then it is advisable to place the bunch, still wrapped, into deep warm water overnight, for it has usually been forced and will be very tender.

Arranging Because of their delicious scent, lilies of the valley are a joy to have in the house. They scarcely need arranging: just pick small bunches, surrounded by their own leaves, tie with string and pop into any pretty china bowl, sugar dish or sauce-boat.

Cornus
Dogwood

Cornus alba, C. alba 'Sibirica Variegata', C. alba 'Spaethii', height 2–3 m (8–10 ft), spread 2–3 m (6–10 ft); C. florida, height 3–4 m (10–12 ft), spread 6–8 m (20–25 ft); C. kousa, height and spread 2.5–3 m (8–10 ft); C. mas, height 2.5–4 m (8–12 ft), spread 2.5–3 m (8–10 ft); C. nuttallii, height 4.5–6 m (15–20 ft), spread 2.5–4 m (8–12 ft). All deciduous shrubs.

C. alba is a spreading Siberian shrub with brilliant red shoots in winter; *C. alba* 'Sibirica Variegata' has the added attraction of silver variegated foliage, and *C. alba* 'Spaethii' has golden variegated leaves. *C. sanguinea*, with red and black berries, grows wild and was used for making arrows in bygone days as the wood is extremely hard. But of all the cornus, *C. florida*, the American dogwood, is one of the most beautiful sights in the world. It is the state flower of Virginia, and is found growing wild in many areas there, the small yellowish flowers of *C. florida*, and the rosy-red bracts of the pink form, *C. florida* 'Rubra', producing sheets of pink during May in many places in the eastern areas of the United States. *C. nuttallii*, the Pacific dogwood, has buttons of white flowers surrounded by six creamy-white petal-like bracts; Frances Perry tells me that the bark of this tree made quinine substitute, and was greatly treasured in the American Civil War when real quinine was unobtainable because of the blockades. *C. kousa*, a tall, elegant Japanese shrub with white bracts growing along slender branches, may be one of the best varieties for Great Britain. *C. mas* is one that I have grown, and it is a sheer delight, with a mass of small clustered yellow flowers in February, well worth growing on account of its early flowers alone.

Cultivation Plant from October to March. They will succeed in partial shade, but the full colour of the stems is developed in a sunny situation. Any good garden soil is suitable, and they enjoy a moist situation. No pruning is usually necessary except that the species and varieties such as *C. alba*, which are grown for their highly coloured stems in winter, should be cut hard back almost to ground level in April.

Conditioning and preserving The stems should be pounded with a hammer, and then given at least twelve hours in water. This applies whether you are using flower stems or branches of foliage.

54

Narcissus cyclamineus 'February Gold', *Iris styllosa*, crocus, *Helleborus orientalis, foetidus* and 'Ballard's Black', pussy willow, *Cornus mas*, 'Ruby glow' heather, snowflake, alder catkins, winter jasmine and *Vibernum fragrans* – this is prettier than the more advanced hybrids and is very sweet smelling. Pick *Iris styllosa* in bud; it is the glory of a day only. An effective table arrangement in two china lambs.

Berberis, honesty, dock, white bearded iris, yellow iris, *Allium siculum*, goat-leaved honeysuckle, brown hazlenut leaves, purple cimicifuga, taken in June. No iris lasts very long, so it is important to pick them in bud.

Wild dog daisies, here with grasses, last so well; pick at different stages of opening. White single spray chrysanthemums would give the same effect.

Hosta, *Onopordum salteri*, *Siembodiana elegans*, ground elder, meadow rue, *Rosa rubrifolia*. Ground elder flowers are useful when there are no garden flowers around; pick them from the hedgerows and don't try to grow it!

I have seen a vase of preserved American dogwood that had been put into a flower-drying powder by Mrs Prewitt of Lexington, and I have never seen anything so beautiful in my life. I had to go and touch the flowers, and even then, on that chill November day, found it hard to believe my eyes.

Arranging   I use the tall red shoots of *C. alba* in green winter groups; although they lose some of their brilliant colour in the house, they are still distinctly red, and the shape of the bare stems as well as their colour will enhance any arrangement. If I can ever get any of the American dogwood, I love to use it in any form. When in flower it is superb in a vase by itself, as also are a few branches in autumn when the leaves have turned to a russet-red colour. The delicate bare branches of silver bark are a delight in winter, especially when used to make the outline for an oriental type of arrangement.

I pick small pieces of *C. mas* in January and force them out in a warm room; they open well and give a touch of colour to a few early spring bulbs.

Corylopsis

These delightful deciduous shrubs are not widely enough grown, to my way of thinking. *C. pauciflora* is a densely branched shrub with small hanging yellow catkin-like flowers, sweetly scented and flowering in early spring. *C. spicata* grows a little taller and has similar flowers, but with rounded, more glaucous leaves.

Corylopsis pauciflora, height 1–1.5 m (4–5 ft), spread 2–3 m (6–10 ft); C. spicata, height and spread 1–2 m (4–6 ft).

Cultivation   Plant October to March, if possible in lime-free soil, in sun or partial shade or, preferably, in thin woodland or against a south- or west-facing wall. As these shrubs flower early in the spring there is the danger of the blooms being damaged if early morning sun can reach them when they are covered with frost. If the soil is alkaline, work in plenty of moist peat – a 9 l (2 gallon) bucketful, to the square metre (square yard) at planting time. No pruning beyond the removal of old or weak shoots is usually necessary with this plant.

Conditioning   Hammer the ends of the stems well before giving them a long drink of water.

Arranging   A few stems of corylopsis with delicate little pale catkins look exceptionally pretty with a few daffodils or early species of tulips.

Corylus   Hazel

The deciduous hazel family is lovely in the wild form, with dancing yellow catkins on an early spring day. *C. avellana* 'Contorta', the Corkscrew Hazel, or Crazy Filbert as it is called in Australia, has great charm in winter and early spring, with attractively twisted branches and small catkin flowers. *C. maxima* 'Purpurea' has wonderful coloured foliage which rivals the copper beech for colour, and its catkins are a gorgeous pinky red.

Corylus avellana 'Contorta', height and spread 2.5–3 m (8–10 ft); C. maxima 'Purpurea', height and spread 5–6 m.

Cultivation   Plant in any good garden soil from October to March, in sun or partial shade – preferably in sun, but where they are protected from bitter north and east winds. Avoid wet or waterlogged sites. For the first few years encourage the plants to become bushy by cutting the new shoots back in spring by half their length. Then shorten shoots a little after flowering in March or April to maintain the production of flowering side shoots. If the bush becomes congested, thin out some of the old stems in late summer or autumn.

Conditioning   Hammer the woody stems well before giving a long drink.

Arranging   The contorted hazel is a 'must' for the flower arranger's garden: I use it continually, as a background for a line arrangement, or as outline for a green group. The catkins of the purple hazel are a delight, and so is the purple foliage – but it should not be cut until the leaves have matured on the branch a little, as it will then last very much longer in water.

Cotinus

Rhus

Cotinus coggygria 'Flame', 'Foliis Purpureis', height and spread 2.5–3 m (8–10 ft).

These deciduous smoke-bush trees are mainly grown for their coloured autumn foliage, but the common name comes from the smoke-like flower plumes which often remain on the bush until autumn. 'Flame' is reputed by Hillier to have brilliant orange-red foliage in autumn, whereas 'Foliis Purpureis' has, as its name implies, ruby red foliage and plumes of red flowers. If you are going to buy only one bush, it is always difficult to choose which to have, but I think my preference would be for the 'Foliis Purpureis' as it is more effective for a longer period. Sadly I lost mine quite suddenly, but have no idea why.

Cultivation   Plant from October to March in any reasonably fertile, well-drained garden soil, in full sun. Do not feed these shrubs if their glorious autumn colours are desired. Any pruning to keep the tree shapely is best done in March or April.

Conditioning   Put the ends of the stems into 2.5 cm (1 in) of boiling water, and then submerge the whole branch overnight. No foliage should be picked until it has been in full leaf for several weeks unless you change it as it droops.

Arranging   The leaves will not last well in water until they are mature. Then pieces of the red foliage look wonderful with the mixed reds of roses, gladioli, dahlias and autumn-coloured foliages and berries. The green-leaved varieties have more effective flower heads for the arranger.

Cotoneaster

Cotoneaster 'Cornubia', height and spread 4.5–6 m (15–20 ft); C. horizontalis, height 60 cm (2 ft), spread around 2 m (6–7 ft); C. wardii, height 1.5–2.5 m (5–8 ft), spread 1–2 m (3–7 ft); C. watereri, height and spread 3–4.5 m.

A large collection of ornamental evergreen or semi-evergreen shrubs, varying from prostrate forms to small trees. The majority are deciduous and all have good autumn colour. C. 'Cornubia', which grows into a small tree, has in addition to lovely autumnal colour, large clusters of red berries which often remain on their branches until after Christmas. The flat-growing C. horizontalis, the 'herringbone cotoneaster', grows well against a wall or fence or flat on the ground and has the rather curious tendency of attracting queen wasps – I have managed to kill many in the spring. C. wardii is a stiff, erect, medium-sized shrub with evergreen leaves, glossy on the top and white underneath, and sprays of bright orange-red berries. C. watereri is a fast-growing shrub, in form a little like C. 'Cornubia', with a wealth of berries which I find that the birds scatter.

Cultivation   Cotoneasters will grow in any soil. They like a sunny position, but will tolerate some shade. Plant from October to March. Little pruning is needed, but if the plants are growing too strongly they may be cut back in spring.

Conditioning   Hammer the ends of the stems well before putting into deep water overnight.

Arranging   Though I am sometimes tempted to pick one or two arching sprays of the delicate white flowers, I do so reluctantly, for it is the later sprays of berries that are my chief delight. They last so well that I find I can often keep them in a vase for several weeks. I use small pieces from November onwards, when they start to colour, and I find them a great help at Christmas if the holly is not berrying well. They are handsome used with mixed foliage groups, or with apricot-coloured dahlias, gladioli, late roses and other autumn flowers.

Cranesbill see *Geranium*

Crocosmia masonorum

A valuable late-flowering perennial with erect sword-like leaves from which slender flower stems of 60–90 cm (2–3 ft) arch out with their vivid orange clustered flowers. The foliage is as useful for the flower arranger as the flower. Once considered not to be hardy, it became very obscure, but is now widely grown with little trouble.

Height 75 cm (2½ ft), planting distance 30 cm (12 in).

Cultivation Plant in March or April in well-drained soil in a site sheltered from east and north winds. They need no support. Cut the withered stems and foliage down in March. In cold districts either lift and dry off the corms in October, keeping them free from frost, or cover them with a 15 cm (6 in) layer of peat, straw, bracken or half-decayed leaves.

Conditioning and preserving The flowers need little save a good long drink, as they last well in water.

The leaves can be preserved by putting the stem ends into a solution of glycerine, when they turn a lovely brown colour. They can also be pressed by putting the sprays between newspaper or blotting paper and placing them under a heavy book or carpet. Flower seed heads dry well on the plant and can be used for winter arrangements.

Arranging The leaves are superb and make a wonderful background to a later summer green group, which really needs good spikes as much as rounded flowers or leaves. The flower heads with their clear orange colour are good outline material for such heavier autumn flowers as dahlias and chrysanthemums.

Crocus

Nothing makes a warmer or more attractive show in the garden than these early flowering spring bulbs. The ordinary golden-yellow is one of my favourite colours, for it gives such a glow on a chilly but bright spring day. The crocus naturalizes well in grass and makes for good underplanting in the shrub border.

Crocus biflorus, C. chrysanthus, C. sieberi, C. tomasinianus, height 10 cm (4 in), planting distance 7.5–10 cm (3–4 in).

The species crocus are the best of all: if left undisturbed they increase well and are ideal for rock gardens and sinks. Among the most attractive are C. *biflorus*, the flowers white, feathered blue; *C. sieberi*, delicate blue with a golden throat; *C. tomasinianus*, a variety that increases and hybridizes well, producing a wide range of mauves, of which 'Whitwell Purple' is a good example; and many cultivars of C. *chrysanthus*, such as 'E.A. Bowles', canary yellow with bronze veining; 'Zwanenburg Bronze', an unusual bronze yellow; 'Golden Bunch', the earliest of all to flower; and 'Snow Bunting', white with a yellow throat.

Cultivation Plant in September, October or November, the earlier the better, in any good garden soil, even in grass. Plant the corms about 7.5 cm (3 in) deep. Remove the old foliage at the end of June. When the clumps become congested after a few years, lift them after the foliage has died down, separate the corms, and replant.

Arranging Perhaps the crocus is not one of the best flowers for the flower arranger, but I love to use them in a moss garden; and a bowl of white crocus grown in stones looks lovely in the house in January.

Cyclamen

Cyclamen coum, C. neapolitanum, C. repandum, *height 10 cm (4 in), planting distance 10–15 cm (4–6 in).*

Cyclamen are ideal for planting under silver birch, or in short grass, or in a rockery. *C. coum* produces flowers all winter, but is at its loveliest in spring, with deep red flowers. *C. repandum* has fragrant flowers in an attractive rose colour and well-marbled leaves. *C. neapolitanum* is perhaps the best known autumn-flowering cyclamen, and the white form is my favourite, producing small flowers on stems of not more than 7.5–10 cm (3–4 in).

Cultivation These hardy cyclamen thrive best in semi-shade, in any good soil that has been enriched with peat or leaf-mould. Dry corms are best planted in September or October, but better results are usually obtained if green pot-grown plants can be purchased and planted in March or April. The ideal spot for these cyclamen is in a lightly shaded woodland site with deep rich soil.

Arranging These tiny flowers need care in arranging as they can very easily be overshadowed. I use the flowers and leaves in really miniature arrangements, but I think it is almost best to arrange them on their own in a very small vase.

Cynara

Cynara scolymus (*globe artichoke*), C. cardunculus (*cardoon*), *height 1–1.5 m (4–5 ft), planting distance 60 cm (2 ft).*

Globe artichokes and cardoons are useful for flower arranging and worth a place in any garden, though they take up quite a lot of space. Both plants have good grey foliage and tall stems producing big globe heads which open into thistle-like flowers. If you do not want to eat the artichokes, they are nevertheless very attractive in all stages, good to cut and striking when dried.

Cultivation Plant in March or April in good soil enriched with compost or manure, in a well-drained, sunny site. Feed with a general fertilizer when new growth begins. Cut the stems and leaves down to 30 cm (12 in) above ground in late October, and earth them up as one would potatoes, but do not cover the stems. Lay bracken or straw in a layer of about 30 cm (12 in) thick up to, but not over, the stems. In periods of very severe frost cover the plants right over, but remove the covering when the weather turns mild again.

Each spring, in April, scrape the soil away and reduce the number of shoots on each plant to three. This will encourage the production of strong flower stems and large heads. Make a new planting with some of the offsets that are removed. After the plants have given three crops, destroy them. Young plants will have been coming along to take their place. Plants older than three years become less prolific.

Conditioning and preserving The flowers last very well in water with no additional help, but like all flowers they benefit from a really long drink before arrangement. The leaves do better if the ends of the stems are dipped into boiling water before they are given a long drink. Avoid submerging, for like most grey foliage the leaves have a covering of minute hairs, and if these get really wet for any length of time it tends to destroy the colour.

The flower heads dry well in full flower: leave them on the plant until they go a lovely brown colour, then pick them and hang upside down until thoroughly dry. They can be used like this, but are also attractive if the outside bracts are removed, leaving the centre of pale fawn-coloured fluff. It is advisable to spray the backs of the flowers with spray glue or cheap, sticky hair lacquer.

Arranging There are so many ways of using these plants: the leaves are excellent for foliage arrangements, as a background with greys, or with any summer flowers. It is best to cut the flower heads with short stems, as they are so heavy that they can topple over the whole arrangement quite easily. When in the green stage they make a good focal point, and later in the summer the purple thistle-like heads can be used in big groups, maybe cutting the stems to not more than 20 cm (8 in). I also use the dried heads, either purple or brown, as a central point in the same way, and therefore on very short stems.

Daffodil see Narcissus

Dahlia

The Pompon or Decorative types of dahlia are the best for flower arranging; the large-headed flowers are so difficult to arrange. There is an enormous range of colours available, so choose those shades which will blend best in your house. I particularly like the apricot shades for their warmth. 'Baseball' is a compact small white, 'Ponos' a clear pink, and for vivid red my choice would be 'Hawaii'. In the Decorative and Cactus classes 'Polar Beauty' is a good white, while 'Apricot Waverley Pearl' is one I find invaluable. 'Newby' and 'New Church' are both peach-coloured; 'Jescot Jim' is a good clear yellow, and 'Jescot Buttercup' a paler and more delicate colour; 'Delicious' and 'Jerry Hoek' are reliable pinks; 'Cherry Ripe', 'Hockley Maroon' and 'Doris Day' are good reds. 'Chorus Girl' is a lilac pink, which can be a useful blending colour. However small your garden may be you ought to grow some dahlias. For the last two years instead of lifting the tubers in the late autumn I have covered them with polythene and straw and have left them undisturbed in the ground. You may well lose some in a hard winter, but as I always used to lose some when I took them up I feel the risk is justified! Three new dahlias I would like to recommend are 'Angora', a Cactus-type with a lovely cream centre surrounded by a mass of heavily-cut petals as if it had been cut with pinking shears, a good new lilac, 'Lilac Time', and a superb gold, 'Gold Crown'. There is no better flower for cutting continuously for flower arranging. If you have sufficient room a cutting bed is ideal and a mixed collection bought inexpensively from a reliable nursery will give you excellent value for money, so long as you are not too fussed about the colours.

Pompons, Decorative and Cactus classes, height 30–150 cm (1–4½ ft), planting distance 45–60 cm (18–24 in).

Cultivation Plant late May or early June. The taller varieties will need staking. When the plants are about 30 cm (12 in) high nip out the growing point to encourage the production of side shoots. Mulch and water generously in dry spells and give foliar feeds two or three times after planting at fortnightly intervals. Lift the tubers in the autumn and store in a frost-free place.

Conditioning and preserving Dahlias like a little sugar in the water, but it is best to add an aspirin too as this helps to discourage algae from forming. Put the ends of the stems into a little boiling water and then give them a long drink. The small Pompons preserve well in any flower-drying powder but they must be kept in a dry atmosphere or they quickly lose colour.

Arranging Dahlias invariably flower well and one can pick them almost every day, so I like to have them in abundance in the house – large bowls of apricot and red and yellow and white, depending on the setting. I find the pink dahlias blend particularly well with nerines and mauve asters and add a splendid colour and glow to a red arrangement.

Daphne

Daphne cneorum
(Garland Flower), height
15 cm (6 in), spread 60–
90 cm (2–3 ft); D.
laureola, height 60–120
cm (2–4 ft), spread 1–2
m (3–6 ft); D.
mezereum, D.
mezereum 'Alba',
height 1–1.5 m (3–5 ft),
spread 60–120 cm (2–4
ft); D. odora 'Aureo-
marginata', height 1–1.5
m (3–5 ft), spread 1–2 m
(4–6 ft).

A family of moderate-sized shrubs, suitable for a small garden or even a rock garden, and sweetly scented. *D. cneorum*, evergreen, is best for the rock garden, with clusters of very fragrant deep pink flowers on prostrate branches in May. *D. laureola* is an evergreen and useful for a shady corner, as well as being good for arranging in winter. *D. mezereum*, with rose-mauve flowers, and *D. mezereum* 'Alba', deciduous, with white flowers, are very fragrant and often flower as early as January, a mass of colour before the leaves appear. The only snag is that this is a short-lived shrub, though easy to grow from seed. *D. odora* 'Aureo-marginata' has gorgeous lemony-scented flowers.

Cultivation   Daphnes are best planted in September or October, or in March or April. They thrive in any good garden soil and do not object to chalky soil. Plant in sun or partial shade, but make sure the site is well drained. No pruning is normally required beyond keeping the plants shapely by trimming back unwanted growths in March.

Conditioning · Put the ends of the stems into boiling water for one minute, and then let them have a long drink.

Arranging   Both *D. mezereum* and *D. odora* make their presence felt as soon as they are brought into the house, whatever you do with them. A piece of *D. mezereum* will add height, colour and fragrance to a moss garden. *D. odora* is pretty just on its own in any decorative small vase or piece of china.

Day Lily see Hemerocallis

Delphinium

Belladonna varieties,
'Blue Bees' and 'Peace',
height around 1 m (3–4
ft), planting distance 60
cm (2 ft); Pacific hybrids,
height around 2 m (6–7
ft), planting distance 60–
90 cm (2–3 ft).

Delphinium blue is so often talked about that it comes as quite a shock when you see lovely spikes of white delphiniums and some of the most subtle shades of pink and purple. The Pacific hybrids grow on tall stems, so they are good subjects for the back of the perennial border; though the smaller Belladonna types are becoming more and more popular as they need little staking, yet give the blue needed for garden and flower arranging.

Cultivation   Plant from October to March in any good garden soil enriched by digging in compost or manure. A sheltered but sunny site is desirable. Tall varieties need staking with four bamboo canes and string tied across from cane to cane to form a kind of network to support the flower spikes. The Belladonna varieties need only twiggy pea sticks to keep them upright.

After flowering, cut spikes to just above a strong leaf. New flowering shoots may appear to bloom in the late summer. In October or November cut the plants down to ground level.

Conditioning and preserving   The art of keeping delphiniums in water is mostly a question of being careful to pick them before all the flowers are open right up the stem, leaving some buds at the top. The buds will not open in water, but at this stage the lower flowers are not too far open and will last several days without dropping. I find that as they start to drop it is best to shake every bloom each morning, instead of leaving the petals to fall all the time and make such a mess. The tip of filling the hollow stem with water and plugging with Oasis or cotton wool can help, and I find that the old idea of adding a little starch to the water does seem to help prevent the petals dropping.

Delphiniums hold their colour well when dried if the stems are hung upside down: use the smaller stems or side shoots when the blooms are well open right up the stem. Single florets or small stems dry well in silica gel, or some similar drying powder, but when these are taken out of the powder and used in the house, they must always be kept in a very dry atmosphere. The green seed heads dry well if picked just as they have formed and hung upside down.

Arranging Delphiniums have a wide range of uses: nothing is prettier than a vase full of them on their own if you can spare enough. The white varieties are superb for any mixed white arrangement, and with philadelphus and white peonies, for instance, make the perfect wedding arrangement. A stem of purplish pink with pink roses emphasizes the pink, or with pale mauve picks out that colour. Blues and lime greens are another excellent colour scheme, and delphiniums make these arrangements easy. The small Belladonna varieties are so well worth growing, and they are marvellous to arrange; the stems are only about 90 cm (3 ft), and they can be used full length or on short stems, and strangely enough do not look out of proportion. So the large blooms of the Pacific hybrids need large containers, to show off the grace and elegance of these flowers. It is comforting to know that if they are too well grown and too big they are not so useful for the flower arranger.

Dianthus   Pinks

Pinks conjure up for me hot summer days from my childhood, and I always associate them with the scent of pinks edging the borders. It is a charming perennial – our vegetable beds were edged with 'Mrs Sinkins' and no pink in my opinion is more fragrant. The grey tussocks of foliage and wealth of small pink, red or white flowers make pinks ideal plants for the front of the border or for the rock garden.

Height up to 45 cm (18 in), planting distance 20–30 cm (8–12 in).

Cultivation Plant from October to March, or even later if the plants are pot grown. They prefer a sunny open site, well drained. They do not object to some lime in the soil. Some support with twiggy sticks is necessary for the taller pinks. Do not mulch pinks with organic material as this may cause the stems to rot. Feed after flowering with a good general fertilizer.

Conditioning and preserving No special conditioning is required, for they last well in water; but never leave them out of water before arranging, for if they once fade they will never recover. The small seed heads are useful for drying and using in miniatures or small winter dried arrangements.

Arranging As with so many sweet-scented flowers, pinks need little arranging, and can be picked into your hand in a bunch and popped into a small vase or pretty piece of decorative china: a little flower-painted cup is ideal. The stems are short and they can be used in any small summer arrangement, their tiny rounded faces making a good focal point in any small group.

Dicentra spectabilis

Often called 'Bleeding Heart', this perennial has great charm with decorative foliage and arching sprays of flowers that hang like small hearts when in bud, and appear very early, making it doubly useful as a cut flower as it is well ahead of many other herbaceous plants. It is low-growing and a welcome subject for the front of the border. If you take one of the flowers, turn it upside down and

Height 45–60 cm (18–24 in), planting distance 45 cm.

61

NEW FLOWER ARRANGING FROM YOUR GARDEN

pull back the petals, you will reveal what looks like a lady in her bath – a little trick that gave us a lot of fun when we were children. The white dicentra, which I have only just acquired, *Dicentra spectabilis alba*, is outstandingly beautiful. It has all the charm of its pink relation but is purest white.

Cultivation Plant from October to March in any good garden soil; work in compost or manure before planting. Dicentras thrive in full sun, but do not object to some shade. As they flower so early they do need protection from cold winds, and are best planted in a south-west or west-facing position, where the sun will not reach them too early on frosty mornings.

Conditioning and preserving Dip the ends of the stems into boiling water until you count ten – it needs very little time as the stems are fleshy and boiling water creeps up them very quickly – then allow an hour or so in deep cold water.

Small sprays can be preserved in silica gel, giving good arching shapes that can be used in little flower pictures, but they do not stand well enough without support in dried arrangements.

Arranging Stems with a natural curve are heaven-sent for the flower arranger, and dicentra is effective as outline material for any small arrangement, whether of a mixed group with tulips and other bulbs, or of a vase on its own.

Dictamnus albus

(D. fraxinella), height 60 cm, planting distance 45 cm.

This is known as the 'Burning Bush' and, if you hold a lighted match to the base of the flower stem on the evening of a hot day, it will ignite and burn off oil without harming the bush. I long to try this but have never dared. The flowers are rather similar to a lupin at first glance, but with long stamens in white and mauve-pink.

Cultivation Plant from October to March in a sunny, open well-drained site. Any reasonably good soil is suitable, preferably alkaline. Acid soils may be given a dressing of lime. Cut the plant to ground level in the autumn. No staking required.

Conditioning and preserving The flower spikes should be given a long warm drink.

The good seed heads dry well if cut and hung upside down.

Arranging The flower spikes are pretty, very unusual and last well in water, making them ideal for use in all-white or green and white arrangements. There is a purple form (*D. albus* 'Purpureus') which enhances any mixture of interesting material.

Digitalis   Foxglove

D. grandiflora (D. ambigua), height 60–90 cm (2–3 ft); D. parviflora, height 90 cm (3 ft), planting distance 45 cm (18 in); D. purpurea 'Sutton's Apricot', height up to 1.5 m (5 ft), planting distance 60 cm (2 ft).

The biennial foxglove, 'Sutton's Apricot', is superb, particularly in woodland as it thrives in partial shade. The tall spikes of apricot last well in water. Among the perennials, *D. grandiflora* has dark green foliage and pale yellow bells, while *D. parviflora* has flowers of mauve-pink and buff.

Cultivation Plant from October to March in any good garden soil, in sun or, preferably, light shade, in a moist spot if possible. They will flourish, however, in a dry shade if well watered.

Seeds may be sown in May in a prepared seed bed outdoors. Transplant the seedlings 15 cm (6 in) apart when large enough, and transfer to their permanent positions in autumn or spring.

62

'Gruss an Aachen' roses, which have two flowerings, arranged with summer-flowering jasmine and sweet peas, which last well. All are sweet smelling.

Hydrangea, tobacco, 'Iceberg' rose, gladioli, petunias, snapdragon, lime (with leaves removed to reveal the seeds). Petunias are not often used but last well. Replace a rose if you have to; a bud has little value as a focal point.

Yellow bearded iris, *Euphorbia robbiae*, *Hosta fortunei* 'Albo-picta', 'Mont Blanc' lily, sweet smelling and bought in. As each flower comes out, and they all do, lasting a couple of days, you may have to rearrange a little bit. Use all you can from the garden and supplement where necessary.

'Caroline Testout' rose. Specimen vases are coming back into popularity. They look very pretty in the right place with one beautiful flower and some greenery.

Cut away the main spike when the flowers fade to encourage side growths, and in autumn cut the plant down to ground level.

Conditioning and preserving   Put the ends of the stems into warm water and allow them to have a long drink. To dry, pick stems when the seed heads have formed, remove all the foliage and hang upside down until dry.

Arranging   *D. parviflora* has such unusual colouring that I find it goes well with many colour combinations, and it has a short stocky growth habit that is most useful. The taller foxgloves produce stems of up to 1.5 m (5 ft), making them ideal for the large wedding group or any church arrangement, and the soft colouring of the Sutton's variety enables one to use it with all kinds of yellow and apricot groups. Do be careful to pick with stems as long as possible, as these flowers lose their elegance if arranged on too-short stems.

Dizygotheca see *Aralia*

Dogwood see *Cornus*

Elaeagnus

The only members of this family that I would grow are *E. pungens* 'Maculata', a shrub with thick leathery leaves in two shades of superb green, heavily splashed with yellow-gold in winter; and *E. pungens* 'Variegata', with cream-yellow marginal variegation. Both plants bring a touch of sunlight in winter, and I cannot recommend these evergreens too highly.

Elaeagnus pungens 'Maculata', E. pungens 'Variegata', height and spread up to 3 m (10 ft).

Cultivation   Plant in September or October, or in April in any soil, even thin sandy or limy soils, in full sun or in partial shade. No pruning beyond trimming straggly shoots in April is normally required. Sometimes the variegated form produces green shoots which should be cut out at the base.

Conditioning and preserving   All varieties last well in water. The ends of the stems should be put in boiling water, or hammered well, and then given a long deep drink.

Elaeagnus takes up a glycerine solution very well. Hammer the stem ends well, and leave them standing in the solution in strong light for best results, for about four weeks, or until you can see the change in colour.

Arranging   The vivid colouring of these leaves provides excellent contrast in mixed green arrangements, and also makes good background material for the first daffodils.

Elymus arenaria see *Grasses*

Epimedium x rubrum

These perennials have become more popular in recent years, not only because of their interesting foliage for flower arrangers, but also as a ground cover plant. The leaves are wonderful to cut when they have matured on the plant. The flowers are adorable, coming before the leaves on wiry stems supporting delicate columbine-like sprays in white, pale or deeper pink. Sadly, they do not

Height 30–40 cm (12–15 in), planting distance 30 cm.

63

last well, though I have used them on special occasions; but it is the foliage that I use continuously through late summer and autumn, when the leaves turn wonderful bronzy colours.

Cultivation   Plant from October to March in partial shade in any reasonable soil. If there is danger of the plants drying out in summer, they will need watering in dry spells. No pruning is required.

Conditioning   It is essential at all times to dip the ends of the leaf stems into boiling water up to a count of twenty, and then let them have a long drink of cold deep water. The flowers need the same treatment. If you should decide to use the young spring foliage, try submerging it completely and leaving overnight in cold water.

Arranging   The autumn-coloured leaves look marvellous with sprays of berries, dark red dahlias, blackberries, and dark beetroot leaves; but they have many other uses because of their unusual form and striking colouring. The foliage is also superb in spring, and I often think that the creamy-apricot colour of the new leaf growth is as effective as the tiny sprays of flowers; however, it is not advisable to pick them, as at this stage of growth they cannot be made to last for more than a few hours in water.

Eranthis hyemalis Winter Aconite

Height 10 cm (4 in), planting distance 7.5 cm (3 in).

A hardy tuberous-rooted perennial, this small, buttercup-like flower surrounded by a ruff of green heralds the spring, and I must include it here for that reason. It is best propagated by division during the summer when a leaf is showing, for the dry bulbs are difficult to establish.

Cultivation   Plant in September to November in full sun or in partial shade. No further attention is needed.

Arranging   Winter aconites have very short stems, but they are ideal for a small moss garden, as they give it that invaluable touch of yellow.

Erica and Calluna

Erica carnea, height 15–30 cm (6–12 in), spread 45–60 cm (18–24 in); E. mediterranea, height 2–3 m (6–10 ft), spread around 1 m (3–4 ft); Calluna vulgaris 'H.E. Beale', height 23 cm (9 in), spread 60 cm (2 ft).

Small heathers with flowers ranging in colour from white through pinks to reds, the ericas make good ground cover, and it is possible to choose your varieties so that you have some in flower every month of the year. Several varieties have the added attraction of golden or russet foliage in the autumn.

   E. carnea 'Springwood Pink' and 'Springwood White' flower from December to March; 'Eileen Porter' has deep carmine red flowers from October to April; *E. mediterranea* 'Superba' with pink flowers from March to May, and 'W.T. Rackliff' perhaps the best white, flowering from March to April, and a little taller. Best of all for the flower arranger is the Ling, *Calluna vulgaris* 'H.E. Beale', with long spikes of deep double flowers in September and October.

Cultivation   Plant in October or November, March, April or May. *E. carnea* and its varieties grow on any soil, acid or alkaline, and *E. mediterranea* does not mind some lime in the soil. *Calluna vulgaris*, however, does not like lime, and plenty of peat should be worked into the soil for this species and its varieties. Plant in full sun. See that the plants never go short of water, especially in the first year or two after planting.

Conditioning and preserving   There is little I can suggest to make these flowers last well in water. The flower spikes of 'H.E. Beale' once arranged will dry off in water, only needing an occasional dusting! I have also been recommended to try sticking the stems into a potato, the moisture from which will keep the heather fresh and the colour good as it gradually dries off.

Arranging   I think in all fairness it must be said that heathers are not particularly good for flower arranging, but are worth growing for continuous colour in the garden. Nevertheless, I do like to use some small pieces in a spring vase, for even though they do not last well and shed their foliage, they do not look really dead.

Eryngium giganteum

A hardy biennial with grey-green foliage and flowers with a silvery collar of prickly spines surrounding a blue-grey head. They are most decorative both in the house and garden.

Height 1 m (3–4 ft), planting distance 60 cm (2 ft).

Cultivation   This biennial species dies after flowering, so seed should be sown each year in a pot or box of a proprietary seed sowing compost in March in a greenhouse or cold frame. The seedlings are pricked off singly into Jiffy pots or Jiffy 7's, and planted out from October to March. Or seeds may be sown in the open ground in April, and the seedlings transplanted in the autumn. Any good garden soil is suitable, and a sunny site is best.

Conditioning and preserving   The fresh flower heads need little conditioning, but benefit from a long deep drink of cold water.

If the stems of the open 'flowers' are put into a glycerine solution, they take on a slightly oily appearance and never shed their bracts, so I can thoroughly recommend this. You can dry them by hanging the heads upside down, but they do not stay open quite so well, so it really is worth the extra trouble of glycerining them as they are so beautiful and last for months.

Arranging   These thistle-like heads add a lovely centre to a green group, and are particularly striking in an arrangement of greys and pinks. In fact, I find that they enhance any arrangement, and I can never get enough of them.

Erythronium dens-canis

Erythronium, or Dog's Tooth Violet, is a corm worthy of a place in any garden, producing fragile little flowers in March and April. 'Kondo' may be one of the most popular varieties, but for me 'Pagoda' is best of all, the long stems carrying four or five large canary-gold flowers, the flat petals turned up at the tips, revealing conspicuous cinnamon antlers – a charming and graceful plant. 'Lilac Wonder' is probably the most widely grown, and I have seen a bank in North Wales covered with these flowers – a wonderful sight.

'Kondo', 'Lilac Wonder' and 'Pagoda', height and planting distance 15 cm (6 in).

Cultivation   Plant from September to November, preferably in a semi-shaded and fairly moist situation. Erythroniums prefer a rich, moisture-retentive soil.

Arranging   'Pagoda' is enchanting by itself arranged in a slim wine glass – a lovely way to see and enjoy this flower. Both pink and white forms enhance any vase of little spring flowers.

Eucalyptus

Gum trees are natives of Australia and Tasmania and most are not very hardy in Britain, so I have included only two species, both of which I feel are fairly reliable in milder parts. If you live in California, Florida or Australia, then, of course, your choice is unlimited. The eucalyptus makes a tall, elegant tree that

Eucalyptus gunnii, height 12 m (40 ft),

spread 4.5 m (15 ft); E.
parviflora, height and
spread 9 m (30 ft).

sheds its bark but not its leaves. *E. gunnii* has rounded leaves and very grey young foliage, but *E. parviflora* is hardier.

Cultivation   Eucalyptus like a well-drained, good garden soil and a sunny situation. Plant in June or July. See that they do not go short of water in the first two or three years after planting. No pruning is normally needed, but to provide plenty of foliage for cutting the trees may be 'stooled' – that is, the shoots are cut back to the base every year. Eucalyptus need to be given the support of strong stakes for the first three or four years after planting.

Conditioning and preserving   The ends of the stems should be hammered or put into boiling water, before being given a long drink.

Eucalyptus stems take up a glycerine solution very well and turn a lovely grey-brown colour, and make a wonderful background for lighter dried seed heads and grasses. Hammer the stems well and leave them in the solution for several weeks. Some people add a little brown dye to the mixture, and this strengthens the leaf colour. They are very expensive to buy in dried form, but I think they are probably worth it, since they last for weeks, or even years.

Arranging   The grey-silver leaves of eucalyptus last well in water, and there is nothing better for a winter vase, with stems of grey lichen-covered branches, and some leaves of *Begonia rex*. It can be used in large groups in January, when it comes into the flower markets from southern France.

Euonymus

Euonymus europaeus,
height 2–3 m (6–10 ft),
spread 1.5–3 m (5–10 ft);
E. fortunei 'Silver
Queen', height 2–3 m
(6–10 ft), spread 1–2 m
(4–6 ft); E. japonicus
'Aureo-pictus' and
'Ovatus Aureus', height
2–2.5 m (6–8 ft), spread
1.5 m (5 ft);
'Microphyllus
Variegatus', height 1 m
(3 ft), spread 60 cm–1 m
(2–3 ft).

A family of widely different shrubs, both evergreen and deciduous, though I think the slow-growing waxy-leaved evergreens are particularly useful for flower arrangers, as they are at their best in winter and early spring and many have silver or yellow variegated leaves.

E. europaeus, the spindle tree and a native of southern England, is a deciduous tree with fine coloured leaves in autumn and attractive pink capsules enclosing bright orange seeds. Among the best evergreens are: *E. fortunei* 'Silver Queen', with good green and white variegated leaves, a small spreading shrub that can also be induced to cover walls; *E. japonicus* 'Aureo-pictus', with shiny green and gold leaves that revert easily, but are still excellent for the flower arranger as they last so well in water; *E. japonicus* 'Microphyllus Variegatus', its very small leaves with a silver margin; and *E. japonicus* 'Ovatus Aureus' with leaves suffused and blotched yellow.

Cultivation   Euonymus will thrive in sun or partial shade in any good garden soil. Plant in September or October, March or April. Give the variegated forms some shelter – a wall, or other shrubs, against cold winds if possible. No pruning except to keep the shrubs shapely is usually needed, and any that has to be done may be done in February or March.

Conditioning   Hammer the stem ends well before soaking in warm water for several hours.

Arranging   Branches of the spindle tree, in the ornamental berrying stage, are an excellent foil to dried groups, and also go well with autumn arrangements in shades of pink and apricot. The variegated evergreen leaves add graceful lines and light touches to winter flower arrangements and mixed greens.

Euphorbia

Most hardy euphorbias make bushy plants that can be used in shrub or herbaceous borders and are rewarding for colour and length of their flowering period. As far as I am concerned, they are another 'must' both for house and garden. *E. veneta* (*E. wulfenii*) is the most handsome of all, with good foliage all the year round and, in Graham Thomas's words, 'evergreen bottlebrushes on long stems, composed of dark grey-green leaves, forming heads 15 cm (6 in) wide. These leafy shoots are biennial and in their second year bear a big head of greeny-yellow small flowers'. These cut superbly, but if left on the plant will last several months. Though the foliage of *Eucharacias* is similar, the flower heads are not so handsome, being darker green with a black eye. *E. polychroma* has stems of about 45 cm (18 in) and is a subject for the front of the border, a joy in early spring with massed heads of sulphur-yellow which are most effective. *E. griffithii* 'Fireglow' should be placed farther back, as it will grow up higher. It flowers a little later, in June, and the flower tips are brilliant burnt orange. *E. myrsinites* is more suitable for a rock garden or wall, flourishes on poor soil with lots of sun, and in those conditions produces good silver-green foliage which is attractive all the year, and heads of lime-yellow flowers in spring. *E. robbiae* is better in the odd corner and acts as a marvellous ground cover, with decorative dark-green tufted foliage, from which comes the yellowish-green flower spike.

If you live in a tropical area, then you will grow and love two other euphorbias: *E. fulgens*, which has arching sprays of tiny orange flowers clustered down the stems, and lasts very well indeed in water; and *E. pulcherrima*, the poinsettia that we know so well as a Christmas houseplant, which in its natural state grows to a bush around 1.5 m (5 or 6 ft) tall and produces an abundance of flowers with red or pink bracts that last for months.

Cultivation   Plant from September to April in good well-drained soil, preferably in a sunny site. *E. robbiae*, however, enjoys shade, but may need watering in dry spells. Trim flowering stems in autumn to keep the plants shapely.

Conditioning   All euphorbias ooze a white sticky juice, which is exceedingly poisonous and for some a nasty skin irritant. It is therefore very important to wash this off hands and secateurs, and to get the stems into water as soon as possible. I dip the ends into boiling water, counting up to twenty, and then allow at least twelve hours in deep cool water. The more water they take up at this stage, the longer they will last. The ends of the stems can be singed in a gas flame with equally good results, but they must still be given a really long drink.

Arranging   The distinctive lime-green colour of euphorbia flowers looks well in any arrangement or in the centre of an all-green group. I use the foliage of *E. veneta* during the winter, and the flower heads from May to July: they fade as they mature, but are a vivid yellow-green in early spring. *E. robbiae* has a long flowering period and the particular asset of being useful in autumn, when the flower heads turn orange and are good with dahlias, gladioli and other bright autumn flowers.

Euphorbia characias, *height around 1 m (3–4 ft), planting distance 90 cm (3 ft)*; E. griffithii 'Fireglow', *height 75 cm (2½ ft), planting distance 60 cm (2 ft)*; E. myrsinites, *height 15 cm (6 in), planting distance 30 cm (12 in)*; E. polychroma (E. epithymoides), *height 45 cm (18 in), planting distance 60 cm (2 ft)*; E. robbiae, *height 45 cm (18 in), planting distance 60 cm (2 ft)*; E. veneta (E. wulfenii), *height around 1 m (3–4 ft), planting distance 1.2 m (4 ft). Not hardy:* E. fulgens, *height 1.2 m (4 ft), spread 30–45 cm (12–18 in)*; E. pulcherrima, *height 1–1.5 m (4–5 ft), spread 30–60 cm (1–2 ft).*

Fagus sylvatica   Beech

Far too large for the average garden, do consider planting one of these huge deciduous trees for your children's children if you have the space and well-drained soil. *F. sylvatica purpurea* 'Atropunicea' is a fine form with extra-dark purple leaves. *F. sylvatica* 'Heterophylla Laciniata' is one of the fern-leaved beeches and a very lovely tree. *F. sylvatica* 'Tricolor' is a really beautiful tree,

Fagus sylvatica purpurea 'Atropunicea',

67

F. sylvatica
'Heterophylla Laciniata',
F. sylvatica *'Tricolor',*
height 4.5–5.5 m (15–18
ft), spread 4–4.5 m (12–
15 ft).

popular in the United States but not widely grown in Britain, though it deserves to be with its swinging cream, pink and maroon leaves.

Cultivation   The beeches thrive on all soils, alkaline or acid, provided they are not waterlogged, and they enjoy full sun. Plant from October to March. No pruning is required.

Conditioning and preserving   The mature stems should have their ends hammered and then left in deep water overnight. Young beech branches benefit from being totally submerged overnight, after the usual hammering treatment, of course.

To preserve beech, stand the stem ends in a solution of glycerine and water and leave until the foliage turns colour. It is best to use leaves that are not too old for this – in about July or August. Autumn-coloured leaves can be preserved by pressing the sprays under a carpet for several days.

Arranging   A stem of beech makes a fine background to any vase, especially in the autumn. I love to use copper beech with regale lilies, or as a background for dahlias, autumn berries and foliages.

Filipendula ulmaria 'Aurea'

Height 45 cm (18 in),
planting distance 30 cm
(12 in).

The only filipendula, a hardy perennial, I feel suitable for this book. In spring it is one of the most attractive foliage plants, with brilliant golden divided and veined leaves, both in basal clumps and right up the flower stem. As the plant flowers, the leaves lose some of their vivid colour, fading to a creamy yellow. The flowers are insignificant, and I usually cut them off to retain the beauty of the foliage a little longer. My plant grows on heavy soil, and I find that it spreads and seeds well.

Cultivation   Plant from October to March in partial shade in a moist spot if possible. The plant is not fussy about soil. Cut the stems down to the ground in autumn.

Conditioning   The small leaves should have their ends dipped into 2.5 cm (1 in) of boiling water for a few seconds and then totally submerged under cold water for several hours. In this way you give them every chance to drink. If you pick and condition some each day, you can replace any that have wilted; but if this is not possible, remove any wilted leaves from the vase and submerge them again, overnight if possible.

Arranging   The well-shaped golden leaves are useful in a green arrangement or at the base of a group of small yellow flowers. I find that the leaves last better as they mature on the plant, but even then they are a little hard to condition, so I use them only where I can look after them as I described above. I occasionally use the flowers to add a light touch to a small mixed vase.

Firethorn see *Pyracantha*

Flowering Currant see *Ribes*

Forsythia

F. x intermedia
'Lynwood', 'Primulina',

One of the joys of early spring, with golden-yellow bell-shaped flowers that wreath the brown branches, on deciduous shrubs that grow up to around 2.5 m (8 or 9 ft). Forsythias are easy to grow and most rewarding, especially as they seem to flourish on hard pruning – or maybe, in my case, hard picking.

'Lynwood' has the largest golden flowers, borne in profusion along the branches; 'Primulina' is one of my favourites as the flowers are an exquisite primrose yellow; 'Spectabilis' is still deservedly one of the most popular; and *F. suspensa* 'Fortunei' has arching branches and leaves of good autumn colour.

'Spectabilis', F. suspensa 'Fortunei', height and spread around 2.6 m.

Cultivation   Plant forsythias from October to March or April. They thrive in full sun, but tolerate partial shade and will grow in any normal garden soil in town or country or at the seaside. They should be pruned after flowering by shortening shoots that have borne flowers by about a third of their length. Remove completely any old and worn-out shoots.

Conditioning   To force, hammer the stems well, place in warm water, and keep in a warm room. Change the water daily and remember to keep it warm.

Arranging   This is a good subject for forcing, so stems can be taken into the house in early January to produce flowering branches about five weeks later. I use them at any length, depending on the arrangement: small pieces for a moss garden to give the essential height, or large sprays for mixing with daffodils. It is one shrub that will tolerate near-slaughter, so one need have no scruples about cutting it hard. I also use the autumn-tinted foliage.

Foxglove see Digitalis

Fritillaria

The large bulb of the Crown Imperial, *F. imperialis*, produces a circle of elegant bell-shaped flowers in orange or yellow surmounted by the 'crown', a tuft of leaves resembling a pineapple. It makes a tall and handsome plant for the back of the border particularly valuable because it flowers so early, and is well worth growing for use in large groups.

Fritillaria caucasica, height and planting distance 30 cm (12 in); F. imperialis, height 60–90 cm (2–3 ft), planting distance 30 cm (12 in); F. meleagris, height 30–45 cm (12–18 in), planting distance 15 cm (6 in).

In contrast, *F. meleagris* stands not more than 45 cm (18 in) high with nodding heads chequered in pale and deep purple. Another small fritillary is one of the best for flower arranging: *F. caucasica* comes from Turkey and produces quite enchanting deep maroon-coloured bells, yellowish inside and with a silvery bloom on the outside petals.

Cultivation   Plant from September to November in any well-drained fertile soil, in full sun, although *F. imperialis* will grow in partial shade. Cut stems down to the ground as they die.

Conditioning   No special treatment is required.

Arranging   The large stems of Crown Imperial look well arranged alone in a copper or wood container. They take on graceful curves in water, and are ideal for a large church group, or in an arrangement inspired by a Flemish flower painting, in which they frequently appear. The tiny fritillaries add a distinctive charm to a small vase of early species tulips, grape hyacinths, small widow iris (*Hermodactylus tuberosa*) and tellima leaves.

Galanthus   Snowdrop

I think everyone must know the snowdrop: no garden would be complete without them. They are the first brave flowers to weather the snow, so good for planting in woodland or beneath shrubs or along the base of a hedge where they remain undisturbed, and they increase all the time.

Height 15–20 cm (6–8 in), planting distance 7.5–10 cm (3–4 in).

Cultivation   Plant bulbs in October or as soon after as possible. They succeed in grass in the open, under trees or in light woodland, as well as in the rock

4444

garden or in the front of a border. If snowdrops have to be removed, or the clumps divided, do this immediately after flowering.

Arranging   A whole mass of snowdrops dug out of the garden and planted in a big bowl not only looks marvellous but lasts exceedingly well. However, I also like to use them in a moss garden in clumps, with crocus, scilla and some small pieces of pussy willow or blossom.

Garrya elliptica

Height 2.5–4.5 m (8–15 ft), spread 2–4 m (6–12 ft).

I first grew this evergreen shrub because I was told that it would flourish even on a north wall, though in fact I now know it needs some protection in colder districts during winter. I feel it is a 'must' for both the gardener and the flower arranger, with beautiful grey catkins, particularly long on the male plants, and attractively clustered grey-green foliage. It can make a beautiful specimen tree if pruned well and allowed an island site, but in colder areas does well as a wall shrub. Mine grew so rapidly that my husband always said he didn't know why I wanted more windows in our cottage when I covered them all with garrya.

Cultivation   Thriving in sun or shade *G. elliptica* should be planted in April with as little root disturbance as possible – buy container-grown plants. Any well-drained reasonable garden soil is suitable, and against a west- or south-facing wall is the best site for this shrub. Whenever possible plant in a sunny spot, although some partial shade is tolerated. No pruning is necessary beyond keeping the shrub in bounds.

Conditioning and preserving   The stems should be pounded with a hammer and then allowed a long drink of water. If the stems are placed in glycerine solution they take it up very well and you get dark brown stems with attractive catkins still firm on their branches.

Arranging   This is a shrub that I cannot praise too highly. I use the catkins from December to February, on any length of stem from large branches of 1.2 m (4 ft) to smaller pieces. It looks particularly fine in all green arrangements with *Aucuba japonica*, or with lichen-covered branches and bergenia leaves, or as a background for Christmas arrangements.

Gentiana

Gentiana acaulis, height 7.5 cm (3 in), planting distance 30 cm (12 in); G. asclepiadea (willow gentian), height 45–60 cm (18–24 in), planting distance 30–45 cm (12–18 in); G. sino-ornata, height 15 cm (6 in), planting distance 30 cm (12 in).

A hardy perennial, the willow gentian brings a lovely patch of blue to the garden in late July, and the flowers are so graceful in an arrangement. Growing on slender stems, the trumpet-shaped blue flowers are borne in the leaf axils down the stem. *G. sino-ornata* has vivid blue flowers on short stems, and if it grows well produces a sheet of blue in September. It loves the conditions in Scotland and I have never seen it growing better than there. *G. acaulis* has larger flowers of an even deeper blue and firm green leaves, flourishes on lime soils and flowers in the spring.

Cultivation   Plant *G. asclepiadea* and *G. acaulis* from September to March, in full sun, in reasonably fertile soil enriched with peat or garden compost. Plant *G. sino-ornata* in March or April in a sunny position; lime-free soil is essential. Work in peat or well-decayed leaf-mould at planting time.

Conditioning and preserving   The small gentians need little conditioning, but I do dip the stem ends of the tall gentian in a little boiling water and then allow a long drink.

   G. acaulis and *G. sino-ornata* flowers preserve well in silica gel. I find that the willow gentian dries well in water and keeps a good colour all winter if you

'Connecticut Yankee' lily. Add a little bleach – a teaspoon – to the water to keep it clear.

gentian sino-ornata

purple autumn crocus

delphinium

miniature
*Cyclamen
neapolitanum*

viola

'The Fairy'
floribunda rose

blue willow
gentian

*Kirengeshoma
palmata*

pansy

dianthus

Cimifuga cordifolia

'Day Dawn' potentilla

Gentians, cyclamen and roses ('the Fairy') in a mixed arrangement. Bunch the cyclamen with an elastic band because they tend to slip down into the water.

remove all the leaves and keep the stems in a vase of water in a warm place. They will also quite often dry off if they are simply left in the vase in which you have arranged them.

Arranging   The small gentians, *G. acaulis* and *G. sino-ornata*, add that important touch of blue to any small arrangement, and it is therefore desirable to have both as they flower at different times of year. A miniature white china vase filled with blue gentians looks really marvellous, but remember to place them in a good light as they tend to lose their colour in artificial light. I have only recently got my clump of willow gentian well enough established to be able to pick and enjoy these lovely arching sprays. Arranged with mauve asters, sprays of catmint and some pink roses, they add sharp colour and a graceful outline.

Opposite. 'Norah Leigh' phlox, green-headed sedum, 'Autumn Joy', golden foliage lasts very well.

Geranium   Cranesbill

All true geraniums are hardy, and are not to be confused with the indoor and summer bedding 'geraniums' which are pelargoniums. The cranesbills have a wide range of colours and heights, and though they are not good for cutting, I cannot pass *G. sanguineum* without recommending it. I have grown it for so many years and it has given me endless weeks of pleasure, with its large leafy clumps and brilliant magenta flowers, blooming for weeks and needing little attention. G. x 'Johnson's Blue' I think is the best blue geranium, and both these plants will adapt to the odd corner and give small good-coloured flowers to pick in high summer. 'Ballerina' and 'Wargrave Pink' are two welcome newcomers. They bloom well in shade and are a useful ground-cover plant.

Cultivation   Plant from October to March in sun or partial shade. Any reasonably fertile soil is suitable provided it does not lie wet in winter. Cut the flower stems to the ground after flowering, and cut the plant down to ground level in the autumn. The plants may need some support.

Conditioning   The flowers last longer if cut on short stems and given a long drink in warm water. The autumn-tinted leaves are tempting to pick and will survive well enough for 24 hours.

Arranging   If the magenta flowers of *G. sanguineum* are picked on short stems, they can be used to give a touch of brilliant colour to a small posy of mixed summer flowers. 'Johnson's Blue' short-stemmed blue-mauve flowers are a pretty addition to blue and mauve arrangements.

Geranium x 'Johnson's Blue', height 30 cm (12 in), planting distance 60 cm (2 ft); G. sanguineum, height 30 cm (12 in), planting distance 45 cm (18 in).

Gladiolus

Half-hardy corms, producing vigorous spikes of flowers in a wide variety of colours. This is one of the most useful flowers for arranging, and personally I grow them in a cutting area so that I can take as many as I need at any time. If you are limited for space, these are among the few flowers I think it is worth buying to arrange.

Though I find the large stemmed gladioli wonderfully useful for church flowers or large groups, there is something very attractive in the smaller varieties such as the Butterfly types, with their wavy petals and delicate stems of small flowers. They nearly all have a blotch in the centre of the flower. Three I would like to recommend are 'Dancing Doll', shell pink with carmine blotches on creamy yellow; 'Greenwich', soft yellow shaded lime green, becoming more yellow with age, and 'Tropical Sunset', a magnificent blood red with a purple-red centre. For clear colours in a small type of gladiolus the Primulinus varieties

Height 60 cm–1.2 m (2–4 ft), planting distance 10–15 cm (4–6 in).

71

are well worth buying. 'White City' is my favourite, starting cream and becoming pure white. 'Comic' has a lovely brownish-grey, smoky colour and 'Obelisk' is a clear fiery red.

Cultivation   Plant in full sun in any good garden soil enriched with manure or compost, from mid-March to late April. There are varieties that flower early, in mid-season, or late. By planting several batches of your favourite varieties at fortnightly intervals you can spread the supply of flowers over a long period. Plant the corms 10–15 cm (4–6 in) deep, and give support of canes in exposed gardens. Feed and water in summer. Gladioli need copious supplies of water. Lift the plants when the flowers are over in October, dry the corms, and store in a frost-free place.

Arranging   Gladioli are useful at all times for their stiff upright stems, which provide the outline that is so important, especially for large arrangements – in white for weddings; pink in vases of mixed pinks and blues perhaps; all shades of red in mixed and 'clashing' reds; 'Green Woodpecker' for green arrangements. They should never be cut short, but always used with at least 15 cm (6 in) of stem. Picked when in bud with just a touch of colour showing, and left in a cool place, they will remain at that stage for a long time, and will then come out in warm water overnight. I never take off the top buds, as I like the natural curving ends, though many people believe that it is only by removing the buds at the tip that you can ensure every floret will open fully. I am sure that they do this in any case; but it is very important to remove faded florets from the main stem.

Globe Flower see Trollius chinensis

Glory of the Snow see Chionodoxa gigantea

Grape Hyacinth see Hyacinthus

Grasses

Briza maxima, *height 45 cm (18 in), planting distance 20–30 cm (8–12 in)*; Cortaderia selloana (C. argentea), *height around 2 m (6–8 ft), planting distance 1–2 m (4–6 ft)*; Elymus arenaria, *height 1.2 m (4 ft), planting distance 30 cm (12 in)*; Lagurus ovatus, *height 30 cm (12 in), planting distance 15 cm (6 in)*.

Perennial grasses bring wonderful variations of colour and form to the shrub border with their clumps of feathery flowers and spiky foliage in many shades of green. In the same way they add variety and a light touch to summer arrangements and dried groups.

C. selloana, or pampas grass, is a majestic plant when in full flower, and can look well in grass or as a foreground to evergreen shrubs. E. arenaria, like silver wheat, has good grey foliage even before flowering, though it needs careful watching if it is not to take over the whole border.

Cultivation   Plant cortaderia and elymus from September to March. These grasses grow in any reasonable soil and prefer an open sunny site. Cut them down to ground level in October or November. B. maxima and L. ovatus, however, are annuals and may be sown in March or April in the open ground where they are to remain in their flowering position.

Conditioning and preserving   Give all grasses a long drink of water as soon as picked.

When they are in flower or in seed, the grasses will take up glycerine well. The nodding heads of B. maxima and L. ovatus are particularly well worth doing as they look rather shiny, don't shed and last for weeks. For glycerining, remember again to pick only when the flowers are really open.

Pampas and elymus dry well if left in 2.5 cm (1 in) of water in a warm room.

Arranging   The thin flowering stems in a glass goblet or wine glass look so effective placed either in front of a window or behind a light. I also love to use an arrangement of dried leaves and seed heads in the house in winter, and dried grasses really make the arrangement. Pick when the flowers are fully open.

Hamamelis Witch Hazel

H. mollis is one of the most attractive deciduous shrubs to grow and to arrange, with small yellow fragrant flowers rather like spiders blooming on bare branches from December to March, and good yellowish autumn foliage. 'Pallida', with dense primrose-coloured flowers, is a form I would love to grow too. The shrub from which we extract witch hazel lotion is *H. virginiana*, a native of America, where I have seen it growing on the Blue Mountains of Virginia. Unlike *H. mollis*, the flowers appear after the leaves, in September, but the shrub is well worth growing for its brilliant autumn leaf colour.

Cultivation   Plant from October to March in any well-drained ordinary garden soil provided it is not limy. *H. mollis* and its varieties enjoy full sun or partial shade, and shelter from bitter north or east winds. Give *H. virginiana* a more shaded, sheltered situation. No pruning other than cutting back straggly branches after flowering, to keep the tree shapely, is needed.

Conditioning   Hammer the stem ends well and then give a long drink of water.

Arranging   Winter-flowering shrubs are of course the most valuable of all material for the flower arranger, and pieces of *H. mollis* will enhance any early spring arrangement. It can be used on short stems or long, depending on what you can spare from your plant.

Hamamelis mollis, H. mollis 'Pallida', height and spread 2.5–4 m (8–12 ft); H. virginiana, height and spread 2.5–4 m (8–12 ft).

Hazel see Corylus

Hedera Ivy

Climbing evergreen plants that have retrieved some of their former popularity these last few years. It is interesting that most catalogues now say a well-built wall will not suffer if ivies are grown on it. I hope this is true, or my cottage could fall down round my ears at any moment! Self-clinging, with heart-shaped leaves, they make a wonderful contribution to a garden, and those with good variegation are also excellent for picking. *H. canariensis* 'Variegata' has shield-shaped olive green leaves with silver and white edging, pink tinted when young. *H. colchica* 'Dentata Variegata' has large leaves of soft green, with deep yellow variegation. *H. helix* 'Buttercup' has small bright gold leaves, while 'Gold Heart' (or 'Jubilee') is a fast-growing ivy of great distinction, the leaves dark green with a gold centre.

Cultivation   One useful tip: when taking a cutting, lay it along the ground and not, as so many people try to do, up the wall. Plant from September to March in any good garden soil and in any situation, sunny or in partial shade. The variegated ivies develop their best colour in full sun. No pruning is necessary, but the old leaves should be clipped over every spring, and of

Hedera canariensis 'Variegata', height and spread 6 m (20 ft); H. colchica 'Dentata Variegata', height and spread 6–9 m (20–30 ft); H. helix 'Buttercup', height and spread 2 m (6 ft); H. helix 'Gold Heart', height and spread 2.5 m.

73

course the plants must be cut back whenever they are escaping beyond their allotted space – especially if they are beginning to penetrate under tiles.

Conditioning and preserving   Put the ends of the stems into boiling water for a few moments, then leave in cold water overnight, and you will find that the sprays last marvellously well.

Stems of ivy and berries take up a solution of glycerine and water very well. They should be left in the solution for several weeks, when they will change colour from green to greeny-brown, and in that state will last for months.

Arranging   Ivies are wonderful for using in midwinter, arranged on their own in a wall vase, or placed where they can fall naturally. Sprays can be used in a green arrangement to provide the falling line that softens the whole effect.

Helichrysum

Height 90 cm (3 ft), planting distance 30 cm (1 ft).

Perhaps better known as Straw Flowers, these round daisy-heads are grown purely for drying, for use in winter. The daisy-like flower heads are surrounded by papery bracts and come in a good colour range – reds, pinks, orange, deep red, white, yellow and a lovely apricot colour. Dobies, I understand, have packets of self-coloured seed.

Helichrysum petulatum is a half-hardy annual with beautiful arching sprays of grey foliage, an excellent plant for tubs and hanging baskets. In a good sunny summer it will produce clusters of white daisy-like flowers which I have dried with great success. They mix very well in small dried arrangements.

Cultivation   Helichrysum seeds are best started in heat in March, pricked out and planted out as soon as the frosts are over. They are not very decorative, so grow them in a cutting area of the garden. For the variety *Helichrysum petulatum* try to keep the old plant and take cuttings in the spring for fresh young plants. Keep these in pots until the frosts are over and plant in tubs or baskets in late May. If you have no plant, sow seeds in March and follow the procedure mentioned above.

Conditioning and preserving   Straw Flowers should be picked from the plant as soon as the flower is rounded and shows colour and before the centre opens; this will enable the remaining buds to open on the plant. As soon as you pick a flower put a florist's wire up the stem into the flower head and stand in a flowerpot filled with sand to hold the stems firmly until they dry. These flowers develop quite quickly so be ready to pick the opening flowers every few days. As the wire which provides an artificial stem rusts, it is a good idea to cover it with green binding. To use the grey foliage of *Helichrysum petulatum* first place the ends of the stems in boiling water for a few seconds, and then allow a long drink in cold water, preferably overnight. Pick the little white flowers when well open but really white, as they tend to turn cream when fading. Tie in small bunches and hang up to dry in a warm place.

Arranging   As Straw Flowers are often used as the central point of dried flower arrangements, collect as many flowers as possible of the same tones for this colour area. If they are placed singly, they give a spotty effect. These rounded heads add good colour to any dried arrangement. Sprays of the charming grey foliage of *Helichrysum petulatum* can be added to mixed arrangements all summer and are effective with pinks and mauves.

Helleborus

Another necessity for both garden and flower arranger. *H. niger*, the Christmas Rose, has pure white wide-open nodding flowers held erect, with a cluster of bright yellow stamens in the centre of each bloom. *H. orientalis* hybrids (the Lenten roses), produce longer flower stems and a lovely range of colours from greenish-white or pink and purple tinged to an almost black plum colour, their nodding heads giving a wonderful show in spring. The green variety that most of us still think of as *H. corsicus* (but which at the moment is called *H. lividus ssp. corsicus*) has the most beautiful foliage, each leaf made up of three prickly edged grey-green leaflets, lasting well when cut. The flowers are open green clustered heads of a mass of flowers standing on stems of about 45 cm (18 in). Some of my plants must be at least 20 years old, and seem to have had little attention but a top dressing of well-rotted manure in spring. *H. foetidus* has green bell-shaped pendent flowers and well cut, deeply divided dark-green foliage. The new cross between *niger* and *corsicus*, giving us *nigicore*, is one of the most exceptional plants in my garden. Its form is like *corsicus* with heads held high in large clusters of creamy-white flowers. 'Ballard's Black' is one of the darkest of all.

Cultivation   Plant from October to March in any reasonably fertile soil, in partial shade. If a moist spot can be found that does not lie too wet in winter, so much the better. The only attention required, beyond mulching with compost or mushroom manure in April, is to cut down withered leaves or stems from time to time.

Conditioning and preserving   All hellebores last better if their stem ends are hammered or dipped into 2.5 cm (1 in) of boiling water for several minutes, and they are allowed to stand in deep water with a little pure alcohol for twelve hours or more. I find that by then pricking the stems in several places, from just under the head to the base of the stem, they last pretty well. The *orientalis* hybrids flag after a few days, and then it is important to submerge them in cold water overnight; this can be repeated several times. A lot of trouble perhaps, but well worth it from my point of view, when flowers at this time of year are scarce and precious.

The seed heads of *H. niger* and some *H. orientalis* hybrids dry well if they are picked after the seed heads have formed on the plants, the stems placed in a little water and left in a warm place.

The flowers of *H. lividus ssp. corsicus* dry well in silica gel, if you choose widely open florets.

Arranging   The Christmas Rose can be forced under a pane of glass to ensure that the flowers are really out by Christmas, for nothing makes a more beautiful Christmas Day table decoration than a bowl of variegated holly, yellow jasmine and *H. niger*. They are a real joy, too, arranged with *Iris unguicularis*, winter jasmine, sweet-scented sarcococca or *Chimonanthus fragrans*. The *H. orientalis* hybrids are difficult to condition to make them last any length of time, but they are beautiful arranged in a shallow bowl so that the stems are well under the water. I have a small ornamental Italian vase in the shape of a lamb which holds flowers in its back, and for some reason the *H. orientalis* hybrids last extremely well in it, maybe just because the stems are in deep water.

All the green-flowered hellebores are wonderful to arrange, the lovely heads lasting very well indeed, and I pick them from January to June, using small florets in an early spring moss garden, and the full-length stems for the next few months.

Helleborus foetidus, *height 60 cm (2 ft), planting distance 45–60 cm (18–24 in)*; H. lividus *sub-species* corsicus, *height and planting distance 60 cm (2 ft)*; H. niger, *height 30–45 cm (12–18 in), planting distance 45 cm (18 in)*; H. orientalis, *height 45–60 cm (18–24 in), planting distance 60 cm (2 ft)*.

Hemerocallis

Day Lily

Hybrids, height 60–90 in (2–3 ft), planting distance 45 cm (18 in).

This plant is to be recommended as much for its early spring foliage of brilliant green as for its flowers. Day lilies are widely grown in America, with flowers in really beautiful colourings, making the common orange-yellow dull by comparison. They need little attention but, grown with care, some of these new hybrids make a fine display. The flowers really do last for only one day, but the buds continue to come out, even in water.

Cultivation   Plant in any reasonably fertile soil from October to March, in sun or partial shade. Water well in very dry spells. Tidy the plants up in autumn, cutting them back to within 2.5–5 cm (1–2 in) of the ground.

Conditioning   The early spring foliage lasts better if the stem ends are dipped into boiling water and then given a long drink for several hours; as the summer goes on, this treatment is no longer necessary. The flower stems need no special treatment, though as always they benefit from a long drink of warm water before arranging.

Arranging   I use the early foliage a great deal as it is graceful and iris-like, providing a sharp touch of emerald green in a foliage arrangement or in a vase of spring flowers. Although I enjoy the flowers I cannot really recommend them for the focal point of an arrangement, since each flower lasts only for the day, and you may well find that you have to wait for a couple of days without your vital centre until the next flower comes out. However, the buff and brownish colouring of some day lilies is so lovely that it is worth using them somewhere, even if the effect is short-lived. The florets look effective floating in a shallow bowl.

Heuchera

Bressingham hybrids: 'Bridget Bloom', 'Greenfinch', 'Scintillation', height 45–60 cm (18–24 in), planting distance 30 cm (12 in).

The evergreen ivy-shaped marbled leaves of this hardy perennial make it a marvellous plant for ground cover and for flower arranging, with foliage that is copper in spring and bronze in winter. The delicate stems of small bell-shaped flowers range from pale-pink to scarlet in the Bressingham hybrids. 'Greenfinch' is outstanding with real green flower spikes. A new and very welcome addition to this family is H. 'Palace Purple' and, though the flowers are nothing special, the remarkable purple leaf colouring is really wonderful. If they are grown with grey foliage plants the contrast is most striking.

Cultivation   Plant between October and April preferably in light quick-draining soil, in sun or partial shade. The plants tend to lift themselves out of the soil, so they appreciate a mulch of compost, peat or mushroom manure.

Conditioning   The flower stems last well if allowed just a long drink in warm water. The leaves should be submerged overnight, or at least for a few hours.

Arranging   The delicate flower stems add a graceful touch to a vase of small summer flowers in pretty coral shades. I use the leaves all the year round: they make a restful placement at the base of miniature arrangements, some having excellent markings and lovely bronzy colours.

Honesty see Lunaria

Honeysuckle see Lonicera

Hornbeam see *Carpinus betulus*

Hosta

With the wide range of these wonderful leaf plants, it is really difficult to pick out the best, and I think you must be guided by the amount of space you can allow for hardy perennials. They produce large clumps of superb foliage, the size of leaf depending on the growing conditions: if in good damp soil and half-shade, the leaves are enormous and some get as big as 50 cm (20 in) in length, but the average size is about 30 cm (12 in). Having so many forms and colours of green, they are decorative in the garden from May to October, or until the first frosts, and they are also wonderful to use in arrangements, making the hosta a 'must' for everyone. *H. albo-marginata* has one of the smaller leaves – about 23 cm (9 in) – sage green edged with a white band. *H. x* 'Thomas Hogg' has a white edge on a large leaf, as does the rarer *H. crispula*. *H. fortunei* 'Albo-picta' is perhaps my favourite, especially in spring when the leaves unfurl and display their lovely bright butter-yellow leaves edged with pale green – a remarkable sight. The yellow colour gradually fades and by midsummer the whole leaf is green. *H. sieboldiana* 'Elegans' is the greyest of all. The leaves can grow to 20 cm (8 in) in width, on stems of at least 60–90 cm (2–3 ft), making them extremely useful for picking. The flowers are sturdier than most hostas and a paler lilac colour. The smallest hosta that I use for flower arranging is *H. undulata*, with slightly contorted leaves, rich green and striped with central bands of white which vary on every leaf, and good deep-purple flower spikes on stems 45 cm (18 in) high. I also have a hosta with large greyish leaves edged in gold which I think must be *H. fortunei* 'Aureomarginata'. It appears to be rather rare, but is well worth searching for. Some smaller species of hosta from Japan are collectors' plants, but have little value for arranging. The American hosta, *H.* 'Frances Williams', is super, grey with a lime-green edge. *H.* 'Gold Standard' starts green and turns gold; it is most unusual. A smaller form, *H.* 'Wogan's Gold', really is a good small-leaved hosta.

Cultivation Plant from October to March, in sun or, for the variegated forms, preferably in partial shade. Any reasonably fertile soil is suitable, but it is wise to dig in plenty of peat, compost or mushroom manure. Choose if possible a moist site, or arrange to water generously in dry spells if the soil tends to dry out. Tidy the plants up in autumn and give them a mulch in April.

Conditioning and preserving An added joy about this plant is that the leaves stand so well in water. When they are in their early stages of growth I dip the stem ends into 2.5 cm (1 in) of boiling water and then submerge the leaves completely under cold water overnight. Then I place them in a polythene bag for several days, which stiffens them. But by the end of May little treatment is necessary, other than a long deep drink for several hours, or if possible overnight. The flowers last well with no special care.

To preserve the seed heads it is best to leave them on the plant till well formed and starting to dry, but be sure to pick before they have opened. Place them in a jug with a little water in a warm place and you can watch with delight as the heads burst open to reveal the jet-black clustered seeds. Unexpectedly they stay like this all winter.

The leaves can be pressed in autumn in the usual way between blotting paper or newspaper. In Canada they are placed between sheets of greaseproof paper and pressed with a warm iron and then allowed to dry off completely for another 24 hours under a heavy weight. By this means they keep their colour

Hosta albo-marginata, *height and planting distance 45 cm (18 in);* H. crispula, *height and planting distance 60 cm (2 ft);* H. fortunei *'Albo-picta', height 45–60 cm (18–24 in), planting distance 45 cm (18 in);* H. sieboldiana, *height and planting distance 60 cm (2 ft);* H. x *'Thomas Hogg', height 60 cm (2 ft), planting distance 45 cm (18 in).*

extremely well, though sometimes, if they are a little limp, it is necessary to place a piece of florist's wire at their backs and tape it on. They can then be placed at the base of a dried flower arrangement, providing a good solid leaf of natural colour.

Arranging   There is scarcely a day all through the summer when I do not use a leaf of hosta. In early May, the leaves of *H. fortunei* 'Albo-picta' make the undershadow for a vase of near-blacks and lime greens using Delavayi peonies and dark auriculas. Hosta leaves are also excellent to use in any green group, as you can see from the illustrations. The tall and elegant flower stems, with their lilac pendulous bells, are good in any mixed flower group, especially with mauves and pinks.

Hyacinthus

Hyacinth

*Height and planting
distance 23 cm (9 in).*

With their fragrant spikes of pink, white or blue flowers, hyacinths are among the most rewarding flowers to grow, naturalizing well, particularly in light chalky soils.

Muscari

Grape Hyacinth

*Height 20–25 cm (8–10
in), planting distance 10
cm (4 in).*

Grape hyacinths make excellent underplanting for magnolias and late-flowering shrubs.

Cultivation   Hyacinths, forms of *H. orientalis*, are very expensive nowadays and many people only use them to grow in bowls and then plant them in the garden after flowering. They grow in full sun or light shade, in any reasonably good soil, and make a good edging to a rose bed or shrub border.

Grape hyacinths, muscari, grow in sun or partial shade in any good garden soil.

Plant hyacinths and muscari bulbs in October or as soon after as possible. Muscari naturalize so well by self-sown seed that they may become a nuisance in a rock garden, for example.

Arranging   Hyacinths are among the best bulbs for planting into bowls in the autumn so that you can have their sweetly scented flowers in the house in midwinter. I prefer not to mix the colours, but to use containers as large as I can afford, each filled with hyacinths of one colour. I love using them as cut flowers, and though it is possible to buy them in bunches these days, I find I can nearly always pick from my bowls, for once the main flowering is over, there are often a few stragglers left that can best be used in a vase of cut flowers. If you can get a really large number of stems, there is one arrangement that is quite superb, and that is an enormous vase just of hyacinths, either all in one colour, or in mixed colours, in which case it is important to group the flowers – say five each of pink, white, blue and mauve.

The little grape hyacinths are at their most effective in tiny spring arrangements or in a moss garden.

Hydrangea

*Hydrangea
arborescens, height and
spread 1–2 (4–6 ft); H.
macrophylla hortensis,*

The wonderful range of shades of pink, blue and white makes these shrub-like plants valuable for the garden and for cutting. They bloom for several months, and have the added attraction of drying well with heads that keep their colour and are so useful all winter. *H. hortensis* is the most commonly grown and gives wonderful colour effects. *H. arborescens* is one of my favourites as the flowers are more delicate in form, having rounded heads on slender stems. The

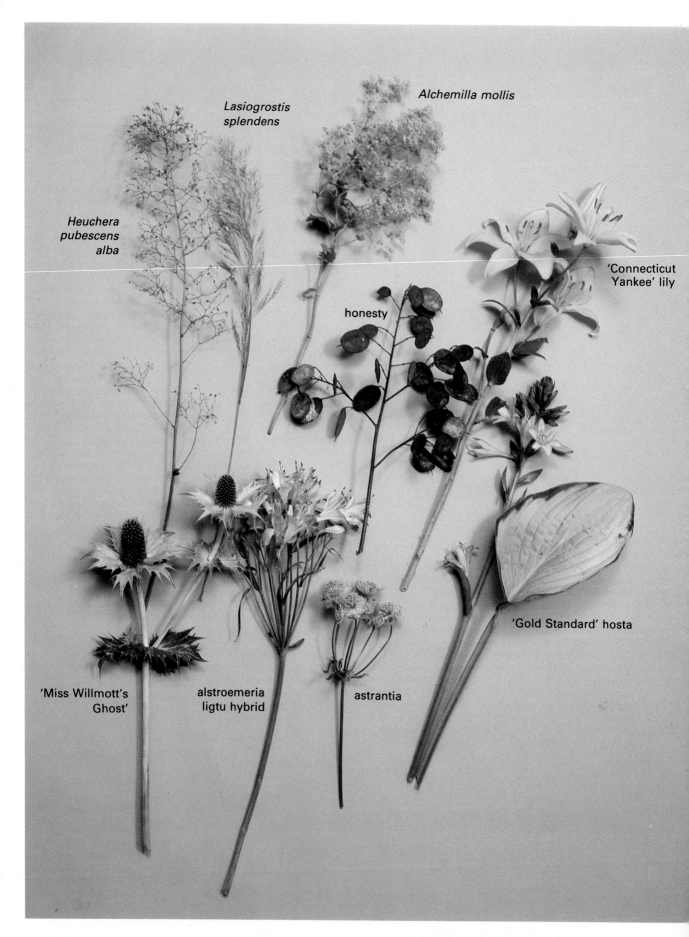

Lasiogrostis
splendens

Alchemilla mollis

Heuchera
pubescens
alba

'Connecticut
Yankee' lily

honesty

'Gold Standard' hosta

'Miss Willmott's
Ghost'

alstroemeria
ligtu hybrid

astrantia

This arrangement is made using an old work-box – be very careful to line well to prevent any water from damaging the wood. Not suitable for every-day use, but lovely for special occasions.
Other flowers not shown in the detailed photograph include sedum, purple delphinium and *Lilium regale*.

creamy-white colour soon fades to lime green, making it particularly useful in all stages of the flowering period. *H. paniculata* is heavenly if it grows well for you. It does well in the north of Scotland and in North America. Both *H. arborescens* and *H. paniculata* flower on new wood, so they need fairly hard, careful pruning each year. *H. sargentiana*, which grows tall and looks very decorative in the garden, is, I find, quite difficult to arrange. *H. quercifolia*, sometimes known as the Oak Leaf hydrangea, has superb autumnal tints in the foliage and lasts surprisingly well when cut.

Cultivation Plant from October to April in good garden soil which has had peat, manure or compost worked into it. They will thrive in full sun or light shade, and should be so sited that the early morning sun does not reach the tender new shoots on a frosty morning. Mulch annually with suitable material in April. Leave flower heads on the stems until March. Cut out weak shoots in March if the bush is congested, and on old plants of *H. macrophylla* cut out some shoots at ground level every year to encourage new growth.

Conditioning and preserving All heads last better if the ends of the stems are placed in 2.5 cm (1 in) of boiling water and then given a long drink up to their necks in water. Spraying the heads with one of the small mist sprays you can buy now is invaluable, and if the blooms are very young I find that keeping them in water overnight with the heads covered in wet paper helps them to stay much fresher. I find that they dry well with the ends of the stems in water and the heads in a warm, dry atmosphere – the kitchen or the linen cupboard, for example. The heads keep their colour better if they are dried quickly. For a satiny brown head, stand the stems of the flower heads in a solution of glycerine and water. They turn brown and make a most unusual arrangement.

Arranging Hydrangea heads need to be well matured on the plant before you cut them for an arrangement, having been out on the bush for over a week. The heads will then stand well and provide solid colour value in the centre of the vase. Use them in a massed arrangement with all the hydrangea colours mixed. You can also use the white heads for a green and white arrangement, the blues with blue and mauve, or with the spiky heads of pink and purple larkspur and delphiniums, pink roses, etc. As the heads turn green they will then contribute much to a foliage and green arrangement, the heads of *H. arborescens* being particularly attractive.

height and spread 1–2 m (4–6 ft); H. paniculata, height and spread 3–4.5 m (10–15 ft); H. quercifolia, height and spread 1–2 m (4–6 ft); H. sargentiana, height and spread 2.5–3 m (8–10 ft).

Opposite. Honesty, white delphinium, *Hydrangea arborescens*, hollyhocks, *Rosa rubrifolia*, artemisia, acanthus, agapanthus. The blue delft jar looks dramatic with this sort of arrangement. To make the hollyhocks last, burn the end for one minute in boiling water and then transfer to a deep bucket of cold water for as long as possible. Having done this, every single flower should open.

Iris

The flag or bearded iris blooms in May, growing out of clumps of decorative blade-shaped grey-green foliage, in itself decorative all year. The colour range of these flowers is fantastic, and often the upper and lower petals are of completely different shades, though I prefer the self-coloured types for arranging, such as 'White City' and 'Magic Hills', good grey-whites; 'Canary Bird' and 'Golden Planet', clear yellows; 'Prairie Sunset', a beautiful pinky-apricot blend of unusual colouring; 'Tuscan', a copper brown; and two unusual blues, 'Blue Admiral' and 'My Smoky'.

   I. pseudacorus 'Variegata' is worth a place in any garden, with handsome yellow and green striped foliage in the early spring. *I. pallida* 'Argenteo-variegata' has shorter white and green striped leaves. *I. foetidissima* has good dark-green shiny foliage, but I grow it for the seed pods, which burst in autumn displaying bright orange berries that stay in the pods nearly all winter if picked and kept indoors. The flowers of *I. sibirica* are in various shades of blue, and last well when cut.

   A very desirable plant for the base of a south-facing wall is *I. unguicularis* (*I.*

Bearded iris, height 60 cm–1.5 m (2–5 ft), planting distance 45 cm (18 in); Iris foetidissima, height and planting distance 45 cm (18 in); I. histrioides, height and planting distance 10 cm (4 in); I. pallida 'Argenteo-variegata', height 90 cm (3 ft), planting distance 45 cm (18 in); I. pseudacorus 'Variegata', height around 1 m (3–4 ft), planting distance 60–90 cm (2–3 ft); I. reticulata, height 15 cm (6 in), planting distance 10 cm (4 in); I. sibirica, height 60–90 cm (2–3 ft), planting distance 60 cm (2 ft); I. unguicularis (I. stylosa), height 30 cm (12 in), planting distance 45 cm (18 in).

stylosa) which flowers from November to March, producing masses of fragile, scented purple flowers on short stems. Finally, two very early irises especially suitable for the rock or sink garden: *I. histrioides*, pale china blue with short sturdy stems, but producing a sheet of blue once established; and *I. reticulata*, in all the purple and blue shades, which grow a little taller and last well when cut.

Cultivation Plant the bulbous irises *I. histrioides* and *I. reticulata* from September to the end of November in full sun in light quick-draining but fertile soil. They need no attention beyond removal of the dead foliage in June.

Plant bearded irises and *I. pallida* in June or July, or in September, in any reasonably fertile soil, in full sun. *I. pseudacorus* may be planted in March, April or in September and October. It will grow happily in up to 45 cm (18 in) of water, but when grown in a border will be much shorter. Plant *I. foetidissima* in a moist border for preference in October or November, *I. sibirica* in preferably moist conditions, in September, October or April. *I. unguicularis* may be planted in September or April, preferably in a border at the foot of a south-facing wall. All these irises thrive in an open situation in reasonably fertile garden soil.

Conditioning and preserving No special treatment is needed, though they should be given a long drink before arranging. Remember to remove each flower as it fades, for it will soon be replaced by a new one as the buds open in water.

To preserve the seed pods of *I. foetidissima*, I think it best to stand the stems in a little water and allow them to dry off in a warm room.

Arranging The most interesting arrangements are started off by the use of one unusual-coloured flower which catches my eye, and then I see what would blend or contrast with it. Some of the tall bearded irises have this effect, and I find them ideal in groups based on Dutch flower paintings. Their foliage, too, is useful in large arrangements all the year round. *I. unguicularis* flowers are a joy, appearing so early in the year, though they should be picked in bud so that one can have the delight of watching the delicate purple blooms unfurl. They do not last longer than two or three days, but can be replaced quite easily, and in an arrangement with Christmas Roses, winter jasmine, the first crocus and winter aconites, make a vase to cheer any winter's day.

Because of their short stems, *I. histrioides* may last better if arranged in a bed of moss, putting a layer of moss over wire netting, so that the early primroses and crocus, snowdrops and these iris all get added moisture, however short their stems.

The seed heads of *I. foetidissima* make a good central point in an autumn arrangement, the bright orange berries going well with pieces of autumn-coloured foliage. The leaves of *I. pseudacorus* 'Variegata', buttercup yellow in early spring, bring an effect of sunlight to any arrangement, and are helpful in a vase of mixed foliage.

Ivy see *Hedera*

Jasminum   Jasmine

Jasminum nudiflorum, height and spread around

Jasmine is one of the most popular climbers and is simple to grow. The little yellow flowers of *J. nudiflorum*, winter jasmine, cheer any winter day, grow easily and cover a wall quite quickly.

J. officinale is the sweetly scented summer white jasmine, of which 'Affine' is

80

the best form. Nothing gives more pleasure than the perfume of these blooms on a summer night, so I grow the plant under my windows.

Cultivation   Plant from September to April in any good garden soil. These two species like full sun but will be quite happy if planted on an east or north-facing wall. They need some support – *J. nudiflorum* loves to be trained round a 2 m (6 ft) high wigwam of bean poles or against a wall or fence. So does *J. officinale*, but left to ramble up through a tree, it will reach 9 m (30 ft).

Conditioning and preserving   Both types benefit from having the stem ends dipped in boiling water and left in cool water for an hour.

The winter jasmine can be preserved in any flower-drying powder.

Arranging   Little stalks of winter jasmine go beautifully with the first snow-drops and crocus, and can be used to give height to a moss garden. Arranged with variegated holly and Christmas Roses, it makes a perfect Christmas arrangement. Pieces of white summer jasmine will scent any room and do not need to be specially arranged.

3 m (9–10 ft); J. officinale 'Affine', height up to 9 m (30 ft), spread 2–3 m (6–10 ft).

Jonquil see Narcissus

Kniphofia   Red-hot Poker

Hardy perennials ranging from 1.8 m (6 ft) down to 45 cm (18 in), coming in so many different forms that the blooming period covers several months, from June to October. All have flame-like flowers on thick stiff stems. My favourites are the unusual creamy white 'Maid of Orleans'; the pure deep yellow 'Brimstone', which is late flowering; 'Earliest of All', the first of the flame-coloured forms and a good apricot-red; and 'Bee's Sunset' which I have heard described as a glowing orange. All these have gone a long way to improve the original form, *K. uvaria*, but the original plant still gives a wonderful display in the late summer/autumn.

Cultivation   Plant from October to March in full sun, in any reasonably fertile soil. Tie the leaves together wigwam fashion in October to protect the crown of the plant from frost. 'Maid of Orleans' is not so hardy as other varieties, and in really severe spells may need a 15 cm (6 in) covering of straw or bracken. Trim the old foliage away in the spring.

Conditioning   They last extremely well in water with no more care than a really long deep drink after picking. So far I have found no way of preserving them.

Arranging   There are few flowers that have tall orange or apricot-coloured spikes, and for this reason and because they last well when cut, I find red-hot pokers most helpful from June to October. They add the vital tall slim background material for so many apricot and orange arrangements, with full-blown apricot roses, late dahlias and turning autumn foliage. They can be used on stems of their full height of around 1 m (3 or 4 ft) or cut shorter, but to avoid losing the grace of the plant I would advise against cutting a stem of less than 15 cm (6 in) below the flower head. These shorter pieces can be used at any angle, at the sides of an arrangement as well as in the centre where greater height is needed.

'Brimstone', 'Bee's Sunset', 'Earliest of All', 'Jenny Bloom', 'Maid of Orleans', height around 1 m (3–3½ ft), planting distance 60 cm (2 ft).

Lagurus ovatus see Grasses

Lamb's Ears see Stachys lanata

Lathyrus odoratus
Sweet Pea

Height 30 cm–2.5 m (9 in–8 ft).

No house or garden should be without these sweetly scented delights. I grow the dwarf varieties up short sticks. Unwin's 'Jet Set' is a good, sweet-scented mixture and needs no support.

Cultivation Sow in a cold frame in October and plant out in March in a rich soil. Or plant in the open in late February or March. I grow mine up pea sticks.

Conditioning Sweet peas last well in Oasis – which always surprises me.

Arranging The only thing to do with sweet peas is to make a mass arrangement, blocking the colours – several stems of the same colour placed together – so you can bury your head in them and enjoy the fragrance.

Lavandula
Lavender

Lavandula spica, L. spica 'Hidcote', L. vera, height around 90 cm (3 ft).

Lavenders are valued for their fragrance, and for their long period of flowering. The tallest grow to about 90 cm (3 ft), are good for hedging in a small garden, and make an attractive edging round a large rose bed. *L. spica* 'Hidcote' is my favourite for compact growth, a wealth of deepest purple-blue flowers and grey foliage. There are now several improved forms of *L. spica* (old English lavender) with good grey foliage and long spikes of pale mauve flowers. *L. vera* (Dutch lavender) with broader silver leaves and tall soft-mauve flowers, is the one from which the oil is extracted.

Cultivation Plant from October to April in any good garden soil, in full sun. Lavenders will grow in semi-shade but tend to be soft and lanky. Pruning consists of trimming the new growths back in August or September. It is not wise to cut into old wood – far better to trim the young growths to keep the plants shapely.

Conditioning and preserving The flower spikes seem to last well with no special treatment. They even dry off in the vase of water.

To preserve for winter use for sachets, or so that you can have spikes to use in winter arrangements, cut the stems when the flowers are fully open, usually at the end of July, bunch together and hang upside down in a warm place to dry quickly. I well remember seeing bunches hung up in the linen cupboard at home when I was a child.

Arranging These mauve spikes add outline and a touch of colour to a small vase of 'pinks' in midsummer, and are nice too for their fragrance.

Lavatera

'Mont Blanc', height 60 cm (2 ft). 'Silver Cup', height 90 cm (3 ft).

In the last few years I have found this a most interesting annual. The cup-shaped flowers, like a tree mallow, come in a good range of colours. 'Mont Blanc' is a glistening white and 'Silver Cup' a good pink. They last very well as a cut flower, and are still making a show in the garden well into September.

Cultivation Sow the seeds in March, planting out in the border in May/June.

Conditioning Place the ends of the stems in an inch of boiling water and then fill up the container to allow a deep drink overnight.

Arranging They last well in water and are good to mix with summer flowers, though they look well when arranged in a mass by themselves.

Leucojum

Summer Snowflake

After the snowdrops come the snowflakes, with hanging heads like a larger and more sturdy snowdrop, the attractive little bells tipped with green.

Cultivation Plant in September or October if possible, in any good soil. Lift the clumps and divide them after flowering if they become overcrowded and produce leaves but few flowers.

Arranging They look charming in groups in a moss garden and are very useful for adding to a green and white early spring arrangement.

Leucojum aestivum, height 60 cm (2 ft), planting distance 20 cm (8 in).

Leucothöe catesbaei

A peat-loving hardy flowering shrub, it has arching sprays of small leaves of lovely colour especially in autumn and winter when they become more bronze with the cold weather. The flowers, hanging under the leaves, are white and very insignificant.

Cultivation Grows well near azaleas, as they both enjoy the same conditions, a good peaty loam. Propagation is best by layering. You will have endless enjoyment from this plant, particularly in winter.

Conditioning Hammer the ends of the stems well and give a long drink.

Height 1–2 m (3–6 ft), spread 2.7 m (8 ft).

Ligustrum

Privet

One of the most useful evergreen shrubs in its own right, rather than for hedging as most of us think of it. I use golden privet all the year round, and find that it is a wonderful stand-by. I mention the common privet, *L. vulgare*, not because it is an ideal garden plant, unless you have lots of room, but because I do like to pick the delicate berried sprays in autumn. The smaller-leafed variety which is widely grown in America is also very effective, but as much disregarded there as ours is here – though for flower arrangement it really is *so* useful. I am now growing the cultivar *L.* 'Golden Wax' with waxy yellow leaves, which I have found to be equally invaluable.

Cultivation Tolerant of any soil conditions, in sun or shade, town or country, privet may be planted from October to April. No pruning is necessary beyond clipping to keep the shrub shapely and in bounds.

Conditioning Hammer the ends of the stems thoroughly before putting in deep water for an overnight drink. It is best to burn or boil the ends of the young growth. Although privets retain their leaves long after Christmas, it is best not to pick so late, for the foliage will not last well.

Arranging This is one plant that I find these days I can hardly live without. I use stems from 10 cm (4 in) long up to 1.2 m (4 ft) for large church groups, and find that it makes a good background for almost any flower arrangement. The delicate leaf form and light foliage of the golden privets are ideal. My sister has a large clump of golden privet, and is in favour with the cathedral flower arrangers, as they use it all the year round; and she is lucky too, since this constant heavy pruning is just what is needed to keep the golden colour.

Ligustrum lucidum 'Golden Wax', height and spread 2 m (6 ft); L. ovalifolium 'Aureum'; L. vulgare, height 1.5 m (5 ft), spread 1 m (3 ft).

Lilac see Syringa

83

Lilium

Lily

*Lilium candidum,
height 1.2 m (4 ft),
planting distance 30 cm
(12 in); L. regale, height
1–2 m (4–6 ft), planting
distance 30 cm (12 in);
L. martagon, height 1–
1.5 m (4–5 ft), planting
distance 20–25 cm (8–10
in); L. testaceum,
height 1.5–2 m (5–6 ft),
planting distance 15–20
cm (6–8 in); De Graaff
Hybrids, height 1–2 m
(3–6 ft), planting
distance 15–30 cm (6–12
in).*

L. candidum, the Madonna lily, is one of my favourites. A group makes a good show in the garden and the flowers enjoy the warmth of a south wall and they seem to flourish in many cottage gardens. *L. regale* is one of the most popular of all, lasting well and continuing to bloom year after year; the creamy flowers, backed with pink, are ideal in so many flower arrangements. *L. martagon*, white and purple, has a strange scent which makes it less popular, though I love it. All these are the standard lilies, but the American De Graaff hybrids have introduced a whole new colour range. From the yellow 'Limelight' to the pink of 'Pink Perfection' and the green and black of 'Black Magic' there is a wide choice. For reliability you cannot improve upon 'Enchantment' which I have grown for many years. 'Stargazer' is new and very dramatic.

Cultivation   Plant from October to March in well-drained good garden soil enriched with peat, well-rotted manure or garden compost. Lilies generally succeed in sun or partial shade, and will flower rather later in the shaded sites. *L. candidum* and *L. martagon* will put up with some lime in the soil. A free-draining soil is essential, and if the ground lies wet in winter plant your lilies in raised beds. A slightly sloping site is best. Plant the bulbs about 15 cm (6 in) deep. Give a mulch of manure, peat or compost in spring. Cut down the stems to the ground in late autumn.

Conditioning and preserving   Care in handling is very important as the petals bruise easily; cut the stems on a slant and place in warm water for several hours. The seed heads of *L. regale* dry well, though it is not very good for the bulbs to keep the seed heads on the stems. However, it is well worth trying one, as the stems have a candelabra-like seed head which will last all winter.

Arranging   All lilies have a quality, from the texture of that lovely trumpet to the way they hold their heads, that makes them superb for flower arranging. They seem to show up from a long distance better than any other flower, which makes them particularly valuable for church flower arrangements. Two lily heads make a focal point in the centre of the vase which is difficult to achieve in any other way. My favourite combination is to have lilies of any shade arranged with a background of stripped lime (branches of lime tree flowers with the leaves removed).

Lily of the Valley see Convallaria

Lobelia

Height 15 cm (6 in).

Half-hardy annuals, perhaps best known for their little blue or white flowers used as edging plants or for hanging baskets and tubs. It is a plant which in the past I did not hold in very high regard, but I have now changed my mind as it really is a joy all summer and, provided it is well watered, blooms for months on end.

Cultivation   The seeds need to be planted in a cold greenhouse and planted out not earlier than the latter part of May.

Conditioning   The stems are very short but I always try to give them a long deep drink before arranging, in a wine glass for example, so as to ensure the flower heads do not get under the water.

Arranging   These little stems add a touch of blue for a summer small arrangement. They are used quite a lot for miniatures where they represent a stem of delphinium.

Lonicera   Honeysuckle

The scent alone makes the honeysuckle worthy of a corner on the house wall or along a fence. There are so many varieties that it is hard to make a choice. *L. periclymenum*, our wild deciduous honeysuckle, has deliciously scented cream flowers, but I think that *L. periclymenum* 'Belgica', with fragrant deeper red flowers, is better for your garden. *L. japonica*, a striking evergreen Japanese honeysuckle which will climb 9 m (30 ft), has wonderfully fragrant pairs of flowers on long sprays, and scents the air on a July night. It has taken over in areas of the United States; it was a memorable experience to drive through parts of Maryland and Virginia on a warm night where for mile after mile the air was heavily laden with the perfume. *L. japonica* 'Aureo-reticulata' is a variegated form and has become a most popular plant for flower arranging. It climbs well and has long sprays of gold and green paired leaves, turning pinkish in autumn. It is reputed to flower only rarely, though mine, on a north wall, flowers well every year and is most fragrant. *L. sempervirens* has trumpets of scarlet and yellow, and is a most dramatic plant although scentless. It may be grown in a cool greenhouse but may reach 6 m or more. *L. Baggots Gold* is an excellent shrub with small leaves, the golden form of *Lonicera Nittida* for hedging. I now have a honeysuckle of one kind or another blooming for six months in the year.

Cultivation   Plant *L. periclymenum* from September to March, *L. japonica* in March or April, *L. sempervirens* in a greenhouse at any time. Honeysuckles are not fussy about soil, but they like a well-drained site, preferably in partial shade, but they will grow in full sun. Pruning consists of thinning out shoots after flowering, and trimming back over-vigorous growths in March.

Conditioning   Dip the stems into boiling water and then allow them to drink in cool water for an hour. This is especially important when you are using the variegated sprays, as without this treatment they may not last even for one day.

Arranging   They do not last well in water, but I use and replace daily, as there is generally enough to allow you to do this. Packed into a wooden box in which you have hidden your container, they look attractive, shed their petals on each other, and in this way seem to last better undisturbed. I use trailing sprays when copying arrangements in a Dutch or Flemish painting. The small-leafed 'Aureo-reticulata' provides graceful lines tumbling out of a vase of greens, or of apricot and creams when the leaves are turning colour.

L. japonica 'Aureo-reticulata', height 8 m (25 ft), spread 3.5–5 m (10–15 ft); L. periclymenum 'Belgica', height 4.5–6 m (15–20 ft), spread 3–4 m (10–12 ft); L. sempervirens, height 6 m (20 ft), or more.

Lunaria   Honesty

This is known as the money plant, because of its silver coin seed heads. It has purple flowers in spring, but is generally grown for its value as a dried flower. As you remove the outer bracts you reveal the shiny silver 'partition' and these stay like this for ever.

Cultivation   Grown as an annual, and planted in March in open ground. Once you have done this you have this plant for ever as it seeds freely – in fact, into everything in the garden, but the plants are easily pulled out or given away.

Conditioning and preserving   The seed heads take on lovely colours, and I like to hang these upside down, and use them for winter in these lovely colours, without removing the outer casing. It is possible to allow the seed heads to form on the plant, and let nature take its course and for the bracts to fall away, but there is a risk they will get damaged by wet and wind. I prefer to pick them as soon as they form their seeds and then hang them upside down to

Height 90 cm (3 ft), planting distance 30 cm (1 ft).

dry. When they are dry, place the seed heads in your hand and rub off the outer cover to reveal the satin part. The seed heads can be put in glycerine and water. They keep well with their silvery pink colours.

Arranging   These seed heads are useful in winter as the satiny bracts make an attractive light patch in a mixture of other dried materials. They are also effective in an arrangement of mixed green foliage.

Lupinus
Lupin

Lupinus arboreus, height around 1 m (3–4 ft), planting distance 90 cm (3 ft); L. polyphyllus varieties, height around 1 m (3–4 ft), planting distance 60 cm (2 ft).

Thanks to Mr George Russell, who spent his life hybridizing the familiar herbaceous lupin, we have a wonderful strain of these decorative plants with colours ranging from pink to deepest red and white, through yellows to apricot shades.

The tree lupin, *L. arboreus*, bears a mass of sweetly scented yellow flowers in mid-June and these last for 2 or 3 weeks.

Cultivation   Plant from October to March in full sun or partial shade, in any good garden soil, even in limy soils. Cut flower stems when flowers have faded, and cut the stems down to the ground in the autumn. Normally they do not require any support, but on rich soil in exposed positions a few pea sticks may be needed.

Conditioning and preserving   There are many theories about how best to keep lupins. I find that filling the hollow stem with water does help. Standing the stems in a weak starch solution will prevent them from shedding petals everywhere, and this water can be added to the water in which they are arranged. If left in a vase of water or starch water overnight before they are arranged, you will find that they take on strange curves which you can use in your arrangement, for they will not change back again.

Only the seed heads are worth preserving. Allow these to form on the plant, then pick the stems, remove all their leaves, tie in bunches and hang upside down to dry. You will have to use your discretion about doing this, since the good hybrids are best not allowed to set seed.

Arranging   With their fantastic colour range, lupins play a very important part in any of my flower arrangements in early June. I use the apricot shades with some apricot foxgloves and some early apricot roses, such as 'School Girl', in a copper container; white lupins in an all-white or green and white group; purple lupins with other blue and mauve flowers; pink lupins in a pink and grey arrangement, and so on. A small basket filled with tree lupins in a mass is heavenly and the scent penetrates every room in the house.

Macleaya

Macleaya cordata 'Coral Plume', height 1.5–2 m (5–8 ft), planting distance 1 m (3 ft).

Growing up to 2 m (7 ft) or more in height and inclined to spread (though easily checked) this hardy perennial assumes plumes of pinkish-buff coloured starry flowers, feathery in appearance. The large rounded lobed leaves are grey-backed or grey-green turning buff and golden, and the plant looks particularly effective placed in clumps among shrubs.

Cultivation   Plant from October to March in any fertile soil, in full sun but sheltered from prevailing winds. In exposed gardens some support of pea sticks may be needed. Cut stems down to the ground in the autumn.

Conditioning and preserving   Do not cut the flowers until they are fully open to the top of the stem. Then dip the stem ends in boiling water for a count of twenty, followed by a drink in deep cold water overnight. Individual leaves should be treated in the same way.

White hydrangeas, *Eryngium giganteum* 'Miss Willmott's Ghost' and *Lilium regale*. Hydrangeas need careful conditioning with Flowerlife to keep well. The eryngium is biennial but seeds freely.

Hosta tardiana 'Halcyon', *Helichrysum petulatum*, meadow rue, poppy seedheads, sedum. The flat oriental vase of a greeny blue colour compliments the Japanese influence of this arrangement. It is traditional, and rather nice, to have a little of the water showing through.

Dried flowers will last over the whole winter; the only real reason for throwing them out is if they start to look tired and dusty. Sprays of beechnuts and keys of hornbeam look particularly effective.

Perennial geranium 'Wargrave Pink', *Geranium armenum*, sweet william, pelargonium, 'The Fairy' floribunda rose, red tobacco flowers, petunia and fuchsia make a very feminine combination for a dressing table.

The flower stems form a lovely tracery effect once they shed their petals, and in this form they are well worth keeping for use as background material in dried or winter arrangements.

Arranging The coral flower plumes are a wonderful background for any apricot, buff or beige-toned arrangements, and I use the superb leaves frequently in large arrangements.

Magnolia

Magnificent shrubs and trees. Plant now – you haven't a day to lose! I just regret that I will never live to see the best of my magnolias, for I started too late. *M. grandiflora* must be one of the most beautiful trees in the world, with deep green glossy leaves and a burst of enormous creamy white flowers that scent the bedrooms of so many Georgian houses, against which it was often planted. *M. x soulangeana*: the cup-shaped flowers, cream suffused with pink, bloom in spring on bare black branches – a spectacular sight.

'Alba' is a form with pure white flowers; 'Lennei' has magnificent leaves and much larger, tulip-like flowers, rose-pink outside and white within; and 'Rustica Rubra' is a lovely form with the flowers stained a deeper purple. *M. liliiflora* 'Nigra' has large flowers that are deep purple outside, and paler within. *M. stellata* has grey mossy branches and a wealth of white star-like flowers bursting out of furry grey buds in March and April. *M. wilsonii* has nodding blooms with rich red stamens and purplish pistils.

Cultivation Plant from October to March in any good garden soil, in full sun or partial shade. If possible plant so that the magnolias are sheltered from north and east winds. *M. grandiflora* does best against a south- or west-facing wall. Pruning is not necessary except with *M. grandiflora* grown against a wall where forward-growing shoots must be cut back in spring.

Conditioning and preserving The ends of the stems should be well hammered before being given a long drink. Flowers of the *M. x soulangeana* varieties open well in water if picked when in bud. *M. grandiflora* flowers look spectacular, but do not last well when picked. However, the foliage is superb and lasts if given fresh water weekly.

To preserve the leaves of *M. grandiflora*, just pick up the fallen bronzy leaves and use them as they are, or coated with a layer of varnish. *M. grandiflora* is a good subject for glycerining: hammer the stems well and put into a solution for several weeks. The leaves will turn a glossy brown and last virtually for ever.

Arranging A marvellous oriental-type arrangement can be created with a stem of contorted hazel and some magnolia flower heads. Magnolias can be arranged alone, in a mass if you have enough, or one beautiful branch on a shallow dish or in a piece of alabaster.

Magnolia grandiflora, *height 3–4.5 m (10–15 ft), spread 2–3 m (6–10 ft)*; M. liliiflora 'Nigra', M. x soulangeana, *height 3–6 m (10–20 ft), spread 3–4.5 m (10–15 ft)*; M. stellata, *height and spread 2–3 m (8–10 ft)*; M. wilsonii, *height 3–4.5 m (10–15 ft), spread 4–4.5 m (12–15 ft)*.

Mahonia

One of the best evergreen shrubs, excellent for flower arranging and effective in the garden. The mahonia is sometimes confused with berberis, but is distinguished by its compound leaves and spineless stems. They have handsome pinnate leaves, often with good autumn colour, and yellow flowers. *M. x* 'Charity' and *M. japonica* both have erect racemes of bell flowers and those of *M. japonica* are very sweet-scented: as they start to appear in January, these are particularly welcome. *M. aquifolium*, the Oregon Grape, has good rusty foliage and a wealth of yellow flowers followed by clusters of blue-green berries.

Mahonia aquifolium, *height 1–1.5 m (3–5 ft), spread 1–2 m (4–6 ft)*; M. bealei, *height and spread around 2 m (6–8 ft)*; M. x 'Charity', *height 2–3 m (7–10 ft),*

87

*spread 2–3 m (6–9 ft);
M. japonica, height 2–3
m (6–10 ft), spread 1–2.5
m.*

Cultivation Plant in September or October, or in April or May. Mahonias thrive in sun or partial shade in any good well-drained garden soil. No pruning is normally needed.

Conditioning and preserving The woody stems need thorough hammering before being given a long drink. The flowers seem to last a little better if the stem ends are put into 1.3 cm (½ in) of boiling water, and then allowed a long drink.

The individual leaves of *M. japonica* and *M.* x 'Charity' take up glycerine well. Stand them in the solution, and sponge over each leaf with a piece of cotton wool soaked in the solution.

Arranging Mahonias are good for arranging in leaf, flower or berry stage. I use single leaves of *M. japonica* and *M.* x 'Charity' both at the green stage and, best of all perhaps, in autumn when coloured apricot to scarlet, when they look lovely with dahlias and tawny roses. The small racemes of sweetly scented yellow flowers added to a few *Iris unguicularis* and some early spring bits make delightful small arrangements.

Maple see *Acer*

Mexican Orange Blossom see *Choisya ternata*

Mock Orange see *Philadelphus*

Moluccella   Bells of Ireland

*Moluccella laevis,
height 60 cm, planting
distance 23 cm.*

Known as the Shell Flower and in Australia as Molucca Balm. Moluccella carries a spike of pale green bell-shaped bracts, and the flower is the small eye in the centre of the bell. The seeds are a little difficult to germinate without the help of a really hot summer, and artificial heat may be needed to start them off.

Cultivation Moluccella will grow in any reasonably fertile garden soil, and preferably in full sun. Sow the seed under glass in March, prick off the seedlings, and after hardening them off in a cold frame plant them out towards the end of May. Or sow the seed in late April in the open ground, and thin the seedlings gradually to leave them at their final distance.

Conditioning and preserving Remove the leaves, and the stems will last extremely well in water. They dry beautifully, either out of doors on the plant if the weather is really hot, or in an arrangement in water. They preserve best of all in a solution of glycerine and water. Leave the stems for four or five days and then remove them from the glycerine and hang upside down for a few days. In this way the stems stay quite firm and they turn a delightful parchment colour, with an oily feel. The glycerine treatment helps to ensure that the bells do not drop and makes the stems less brittle so that they are easier to arrange. In America, in order to retain the colour, a little green dye is added to the glycerine which results in an attractive, natural-looking green stem.

Arranging This plant is ideal for flower arranging in all stages of growth. The stems take on lovely natural curves and when the small leaves are removed they last so well that they will actually dry to a delightful cream colour while in an arrangement. They look good alone or with almost any colour combinations.

Monkshood see *Aconitum lycoctonum*

Muscari see *Hyacinthus*

Narcissus   Daffodil, Jonquil

Height up to 45–50 cm (18–20 in), planting distance 10–15 cm (4–6 in).

Heralds of spring and among our best-loved bulbs: what would any garden be without them? The yellow trumpet flowers of daffodils look their best when naturalized in grass or as underplanting for trees and shrubs; others, like the miniature species, are ideal for the rock garden. There are so many species and varieties that it is possible to have some in bloom over a period of almost three months.

Among the modern daffodils, I think the short trumpet varieties are the best for arranging, such as 'Polindra', 'Binkie', 'Green Island' and 'Fermoy'. 'Geranium' and 'Paper White' are both excellent for forcing early. White trumpet and unusual cultivars include: 'Mount Hood', 'Beersheba', 'Devon Loch'. Faintly pink ones are 'Mrs R.O. Backhouse' and 'Salmon Trout'. A good double white is 'Snowball' ('Shirley Temple'); 'Spellbinder' is a superb greenish colour; 'Cherie' carries three heads to a stem, and is cream-buff. For early flowering I would never be without 'February Gold' or 'March Sunshine'. The split corona or orchid daffodils, as they are sometimes called, are a wonderful addition to my daffodil collection. Their heads stand proud and make an excellent focal point for a cream or white arrangement.

For the rock garden the miniature species I would recommend are *N. bulbocodium* and *N. bulbocodium* 'Conspicuous' (hoop petticoat), *N. cyclamineus*, *N.* x *hawera*, *N. triandrus* 'Albus' (Angel's Tears). These look effective in the garden and arrange well, too.

Cultivation Plant in September or October for preference, or as soon after as possible. Narcissi succeed in any good garden soil, especially if it is fairly moisture retentive. They may be grown in full sun or light shade. See that they get plenty of water if the weather is dry between the time the flowers fade and the leaves begin to die down. Spraying the leaves with a foliar feed several times at 10-day intervals, from mid-April onwards, helps to encourage offset bulbs to grow to flowering size more quickly. Remove the dead heads as the flowers fade to prevent seed formation.

Arranging Daffodils and narcissi last better if arranged in shallow water, and I enjoy them best when they look as if they are growing naturally. So I often use a shallow container, cover the netting and mechanics with a layer of moss, and make the arrangement with one attractive branch of catkin or blossom and a group of daffodils. When they are plentiful and inexpensive, they also look delightful massed in a basket.

Nepeta

Nepeta x *faassenii* (*N. mussinii*), *height 45 cm (18 in), planting distance 30 cm (12 in).*

Known as catmint – and cats really do love it – this hardy perennial makes an excellent ground cover with very aromatic grey foliage and spires of mauve flowers. It flowers almost non-stop from June to October, but is at its best in July.

Cultivation Plant from October to April in full sun or partial shade, in any reasonable soil. Cut the plants down to the ground in November.

Conditioning   All these flowers need is a long drink in deep warm water as soon as picked.

Arranging   I first saw these flowers used in an arrangement many years ago, when they were placed round the edge of a shallow bowl and the centre filled with roses. I still think they look pretty used like this, but find now that they also make a good background for a small urn-type vase of mauve and blue flowers, and look particularly lovely with 'New Dawn' roses.

Nerine bowdenii

Height 60 cm (2 ft), planting distance 15 cm (6 in).

The hardiest of these decorative South African bulbs is *N. bowdenii*, with pale pink flowers borne in umbels on slender stems, its greatest asset being that it flowers in September and October. This nerine does well on a south wall, liking the shelter and warmth and increasing well after it has been established for a few years. I also have a white-flowered variety which is not quite so hardy.

Cultivation   Plant in spring or August, preferably in a border at the foot of a south-facing wall, in any good but well-drained soil. The bulbs tend to draw themselves on to the surface of the ground, and while they will withstand a normal winter, they may be killed in a very severe one. So it is worth while covering them with a foot of peat during the winter months.

Arranging   Nerines mix well with the last pieces of pink and blue out of the border, but also look good alone with a dramatic stem of lichen-covered branch. The flowers should be used with stems never shorter than 13 cm (5 in) to be sure of showing off their elegant form.

Nicotiana   Tobacco Plant

Nicotiana affinis (N. alata) 'Lime Green', height 60–90 cm (2–3 ft), planting distance 30 cm (12 in).

The green tobacco, growing to 60 cm (2 ft) high or more and wonderful lime-green in colour, is an annual I cannot wait for once the moluccella is over. The white form, which has a lovely perfume at night, is superb when planted near the house. Green tobacco is easily grown but it is difficult to buy in plant form, although the coloured varieties are easily obtainable.

Cultivation   Sow the seed in March in a heated greenhouse, harden off the seedlings, and plant out when danger of frost is past – end of May or early June. Plant in full sun or light shade in any reasonably fertile soil. Water well in dry spells.

Conditioning and preserving   Nicotiana lasts well in water with little more than a long drink of warm water for an hour or so after picking. Unfortunately there is no means of preserving other than by drying the individual flowers in silica gel.

Arranging   The lime colour harmonizes with any colour scheme from pinks and reds to white and cream and is invaluable for all sorts of arrangements.

Onopordum salteri

Height 3 m (10 ft), planting distance 1 m (3 ft).

A most handsome grey thistle, towering up to the sky, of statuesque beauty with prickly grey leaves and purple Scottish-thistle-like flowers – though I really much prefer the plant before these open. It needs quite a lot of space as it grows up to 3 m (10 ft), but makes the most wonderful silhouette against an evening sky or dark trees.

Cultivation   A biennial which may be sown in the open ground in spring in good soil.

Conditioning and preserving   Foliage stems and individual leaves all last better if the ends are dipped into boiling water until you count twenty, and given a deep drink in cold water overnight.

When the flowers are well open, they can be picked and hung up to dry, and sometimes retain a good purple colour.

Arranging   When fully grown, the large leaves make a wonderful base for a really big group. The small side shoots add good grey colour and lovely form to smaller arrangements. Just before the flowers break colour, I use a long stem of the grey buds and foliage with other greys, or as a background for blues or mixed greens.

Osmunda regalis

Worthy of its name, the Royal Fern, this is the largest and most handsome hardy fern. The fronds are copper-brown when they first unfurl, turning green as they lose their early pale-brown woolly covering, and taking on beautiful yellow-brown tints in autumn.

Height 1–1.5 m (4–5 ft), planting distance 1.2 m (4 ft).

Cultivation   Plant from October to March in sun or partial shade, in reasonably fertile soil – the richer the better. Work in compost or peat, and give a mulch in April. Cut the old stems down to the base in autumn.

Conditioning and preserving   Dip the ends of the stems into boiling water and leave for several minutes, and then submerge the whole leaf in a bath of cold water for as long as possible.

To preserve, take the fronds when either green or of good autumn colour, and press between sheets of newspaper under a carpet for several days. When dry the stems often need support, and I find it is best to place a really long piece of wire against the back of the stem and then twist fine wire round both at about three points up the stem.

Arranging   Avoid the temptation of picking in spring, for the fronds will not last well in water unless they are mature on the plant. Once they are green, you will need a vase large enough to take the handsome stems, and then you will find they make good background material, especially for an all-green arrangement. If used in autumn, there is the possibility that they may curl, so I find it better to use pressed leaves with autumn colourings, when again they make a marvellous outline.

Pachysandra terminalis

Undoubtedly one of the best ground-cover plants. *P. procumbens*, which is native to America, is widely grown in that country, yet rarely seen in Britain. The dark-green, close-growing serrated leaves of *P. terminalis* make a wonderful carpet beneath trees and shrubs. There is a variegated form which is also effective, though less rapid in growth.

Height 30 cm (12 in), planting distance 45 cm (18 in).

Cultivation   Plant in early autumn or March in any reasonably fertile soil that is moisture retentive but not liable to be waterlogged, preferably in partial or total shade. It does best in lime-free soil.

Conditioning and preserving   Give a deep drink in cold water for several hours.

Individual leaves press well for use in flower pictures. As the stems last for literally months in water, they need no additional preserving.

91

Arranging   The leaves of pachysandra will last for weeks in water, so much so that they will grow roots. They are very pleasing arranged alone; they make a good base or fill-in for spring flowers, and for this purpose the variegated form is especially good as it is lighter in appearance.

Paeonia

Peony

Shrub peonies: Paeonia delavayi *and hybrids, height and spread 2 m (6 ft);* P. lutea ludlowii *and hybrids, height and spread 1–2 m (4–6 ft);* P. suffruticosa *hybrids, height and spread 1.5–2 m (5–6 ft).*
Herbaceous peonies: P. lactiflora *hybrids, height 60 cm (2 ft), planting distance 75–90 cm (2½–3 ft).*

Choosing peonies is as difficult as choosing roses, for so much depends on your personal taste. I prefer the soft colours, and these with white would always be my first choice, but I also use some of the brilliant colours in mixed arrangements.

Shrub peonies grow to about 1.5 m (5 ft), and bear single blooms usually smaller in flower than those of the herbaceous varieties. *P. delavayi* has maroon single small flowers, but I have some Sarson hybrids with large and beautiful flowers *P. lutea ludlowii* has sweetly scented single yellow flowers, also rather small, and good seed heads. Hybrids of the tree peony, *P. suffruticosa*, are a 'must' for the garden, and given shelter from the wind they are lovely plants to grow. 'Hakugan' and 'Mrs William Kelway' both have superb single white flowers and lovely foliage which turns yellowy-bronze in autumn. 'Souvenir de la Reine Elizabeth' has enormous double pink flowers spanning 20–30 cm (9–12 in). 'Lord Selbourne' has flowers of a soft blush-pink with similar large heads opening in June. The red-tinted buds appearing from March onwards, and the good leaf colour make this an interesting plant all the year round. The *P. lutea* hybrid 'Souvenir de Maxime Cornu' bears huge pale-yellow flowers tinged with red that tend to hang their very heavy heads, and are better with support for their full beauty.

The herbaceous peonies, hybrids of *P. lactiflora*, are among the very best plants for the garden and can be grown in clumps among shrubs. 'Sarah Bernhardt' is still one of the most outstanding peonies of all time, with double sugar-pink heads flowering in July – rather later than the average time for this group – and producing an abundance of blooms once established. 'Solange' is one of my favourites, amber on creamy buff large heads of which I can never get enough. 'Kelway's Queen', blush-white tinted coral, is another outstanding peony. 'Duchesse de Nemours', sulphur-white incurved, and 'White Wings' are I think the best white singles. Others I would recommend are 'Beau Geste', semi-double flowers in brilliant glowing carmine; 'Lord Kitchener', single blooms of intense maroon-red; 'Dresden', a blush-white single; and 'Pink Delight', a good pink. If you are fortunate enough to be able to get some of the Sanders' hybrid peonies from North America, try the superb 'Janis', with a lovely apricot-coloured single flower appearing in May. Sylvia Sanders hybridized peonies for the greater part of her life.

Cultivation   Plant from October to March in any good garden soil enriched by digging in old manure or compost. Choose a sheltered site if possible, in full sun or partial shade.

Shrubby peony varieties are usually grafted on to a vigorous stock so the union where the graft was made should be buried 7.5–10 cm (3–4 in) below the surface to encourage rooting of the scion (the grafted variety). Conversely, the crowns of herbaceous peonies should not be covered more than 2.5 cm (1 in) deep with soil or they may fail to flower. It is important to remember this when applying mulches in subsequent years – do not cover the crown of the plant (where the growth buds are) more than 2.5 (1 in) deep. Mulch generously all peonies in April, give water in dry spells, and cut herbaceous peonies down to the ground in the autumn.

No pruning beyond cutting out dead wood is required on shrubby peonies.

Conditioning and preserving If you can bring yourself to do it, peonies last better if cut and laid on a cool stone floor overnight: then cut off the stem ends and put them in warm water. They can be kept in a really cold freezer room for several weeks if necessary, but the buds must be showing colour before the stems are picked, and they should be placed in airtight plastic bags and left until required. Again, you should cut the ends of the stems when they are taken out of the bags, and put into warm water for several hours. Though you may lose one or two, it is well worth trying this method for some very special occasion.

The seed heads of the shrubs such as *P. delavayi* last well if picked when green, and hung upside down to dry. The open flowers of the herbaceous peonies can be dried in flower-drying powder, but the temperature must be very high to allow them to dry off really quickly. They keep their colour beautifully if dried at a temperature never lower than 15° (65°F), which is not always easy in Britain, but I have seen the most lovely vases of them in America.

The leaves of tree peonies glycerine well, giving you an interesting leaf shape for a dried arrangement in winter. For glycerining, it is best to pick the leaves when they are still green.

Arranging Peonies are for me the highlight of the summer, making a spectacular centre for any group, whether it is in all-white, white and pinks, scarlets or an arrangement in pastel shades. Two single shrub peonies and a stem of walnut with its red-brown furry bark make a most pleasing arrangement. Both single and double blooms are beautiful: I used to be very fond of the double flowers but now feel that I almost prefer singles. As they can withstand intense cold and hot summers, they grow marvellously in North America.

Papaver   Poppy

Poppies not only provide so much colour in the garden, but can be cut and last surprisingly well in the house. The Orientals 'Perry's White' and 'Mrs Perry', the latter a soft pink, are to be recommended, as are the off-beat colours of the art shades, and though it is difficult to get seed of these, plants are still available. Shirley Poppies, *P. rhoeas*, come in a wide range of colours, white and pink-mauve to red, but though I do use them as cut flowers, I really grow them for their delightful seed heads, excellent for so many dried arrangements. The Iceland poppy, *P. nudicaule*, is one of my favourites, delicate transparent-looking little flowers in colours ranging from white to apricot, salmon-pink and clear orange. This poppy is listed as a perennial, but I find it better grown as an annual. The big blowsy peony-flowered annual poppy, *P. somniferum*, in soft shades of pink, mauve, white and deep red, is easily grown and seeds freely, but I do scatter some ripe seeds each year where I hope they will grow.

Cultivation Plant *P. orientale* and its varieties from October to March in any normal garden soil. Give support with twiggy sticks if necessary. Cut stems down to the ground in the autumn.

Sow *P. nudicaule* in May or June in the flowering site, and thin to the planting distance indicated – or transplant to this distance very carefully.

Sow the annual poppies in March or April, and thin the seedlings to the planting distance as indicated.

Conditioning and preserving All poppies should have their stem ends burnt, either in a gas flame or by putting them into 2.5 cm (1 in) of boiling water,

Papaver nudicaule (biennial), height 45–75 cm (1½–2½ ft), planting distance 30–45 cm (12–18 in); P. orientale 'Perry's White', 'Mrs Perry' (perennials), height 60–90 cm (2–3 ft), planting distance 60 cm (2 ft); P. rhoeas (annual), height 60 cm (2 ft), planting distance 30 cm (1 ft); P. somniferum (annual), height 75 cm (2½ ft), planting distance 30 cm (1 ft).

and they should then be allowed a really long drink in cold water for several hours. I like to cut the stems at different lengths, to avoid re-boiling after cutting: it is essential to re-boil or burn if you do cut the stems shorter before arranging.

Poppy seed heads preserve well and are a great asset for garlands, dried hanging balls, etc. The Oriental, opium and small Shirley poppies all produce heads that can be used in these ways. Let the seed dry on the plant, giving them some protection against birds who will otherwise peck the seeds as soon as they are ripe. Cut the stems, strip off the foliage, and hang them upside down until the heads are thoroughly dry.

Arranging   These are flowers that need careful preparation, and may be thought attractive by only a limited number of people; but if you are a keen arranger, then I think you will find the open-faced flowers of such a delightful colour range well worth the effort of growing and conditioning. I use the art shades in large arrangements, with Preston hybrid lilacs, pink cherry blossom and lupins, and they provide a wonderful focal point. The small Iceland poppies are beautiful if arranged with grasses, and in a delicate glass container, their hairy stems look pretty seen through the clear water.

Pasque Flower see Pulsatilla vulgaris

Pelargonium

Height 30 cm (12 in).

I have included the 'geraniums' one can grow from seed under Pelargonium to differentiate them from the hardy perennials, and they are most useful for window boxes, tubs and hanging baskets.

Cultivation   It has generally been customary to propagate pelargoniums by cuttings but these days they are being grown most successfully from seed. Unwins (of Histon, Cambridgeshire) have a wonderful range of geranium seeds.

Conditioning   I always try to put the cut ends in a little boiling water, and then give them a long drink overnight.

Arranging   These plants are most useful in flower arranging for their outstanding colour. Some of the fierce reds and puces are marvellous for brilliant red arrangements.

Penstemon

Penstemon fruticosus 'Cardwellii', height and planting distance 30 cm (1 ft); P. hartwegii 'Garnet', height 60 cm (2 ft), planting distance 30 cm (1 ft); P. laevigatus 'Digitalis', height 1 m (3–4 ft), planting distance 30 cm (1 ft).

One of the problems with penstemons is that they are not truly hardy perennials, but once established they flower continuously from June to September with spikes of bell-like flowers on stems of about 60 cm (2 ft). 'Garnet' is almost the hardiest, but the more striking blooms are those of *P. laevigatus* 'Digitalis', with flowers resembling a foxglove, as the name indicates. The blue *P. fruticosus* 'Cardwellii' is well worth growing, and provides that touch of blue so welcome for the flower arranger. It is advisable to take cuttings frequently, as it tends suddenly to die out.

Cultivation   Plant in March or April in full sun in any reasonably fertile soil provided it does not lie wet in winter. Cut the stems down to ground level and protect from severe frosts with a cloche or even some bracken or straw.

Conditioning   Conditioning is essential. Pick when the flower is well open,

94

Stark simplicity is always fascinating to me. Wild berries could easily be used instead of *Arum italicum* 'Pictum' with the variegated ivy.

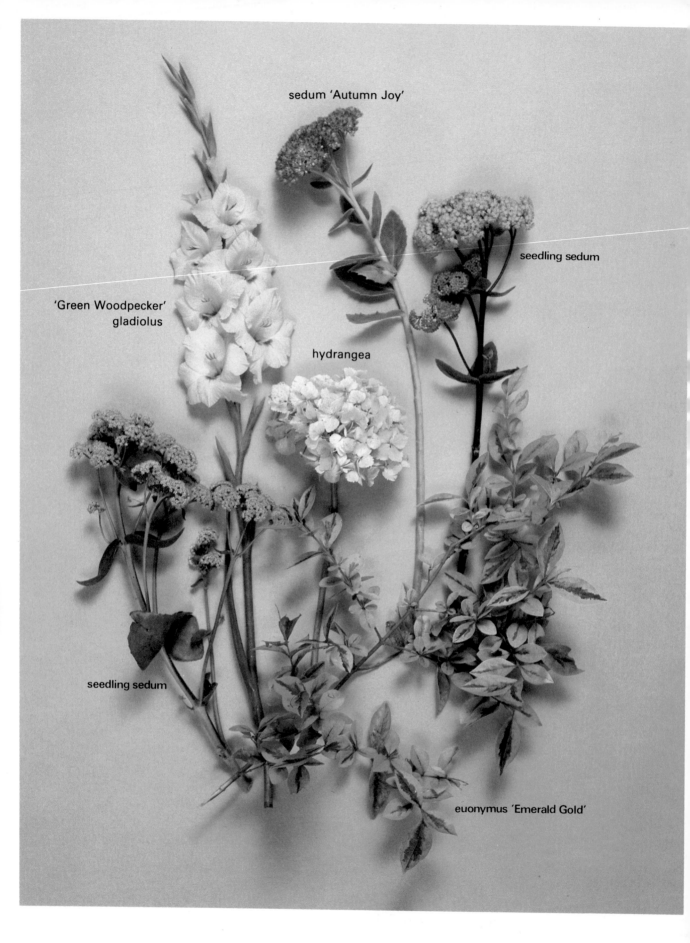

sedum 'Autumn Joy'

seedling sedum

'Green Woodpecker'
gladiolus

hydrangea

seedling sedum

euonymus 'Emerald Gold'

My favourite gladioli are 'Green Woodpecker'. They are tall and so useful in an arrangement to fill in an awkward corner such as here on a staircase.

The roses 'Rosemary Rose' and 'Just Joey', gladiolus and red dahlia. The use of unusual containers, like this marble pestle and mortar bowl, can be most effective.

remove as much foliage as possible, dip the stem ends into 2.5 cm (1 in) of boiling water, and then allow at least a night in deep water, but the longer the better.

Arranging   Penstemons are not entirely reliable as a cut flower, but they are so lovely in a mixed vase in summer that I take a chance, and replace any that wilt. They look superb used in a basket of summer flowers.

Peony see Paeonia

Pernettya

A South American evergreen shrub, a clumpy bush with small leaves and berries in a wonderful range of colours from white and pink to mauve and deep red. Those of P. mucronata 'Alba' are white, 'Lilacina' really lilac-coloured and 'Davis's Hybrids' have extra large berries in many colours. Of the heath family, they enjoy similar conditions.

Cultivation   Plant from October to April in a lime free soil. Pernettyas prefer a good rich loamy soil in full sun, although they will put up with light shade. Four or five plants should be planted in a group to ensure pollination and a set of berries. No pruning is normally required, but old leggy plants may be cut back hard in spring.

Conditioning   Put the ends of the stems into a little boiling water and then allow to drink in cool water for an hour or so.

Arranging   We have always managed to buy well-berried pernettya branches in London so I have had the opportunity of using them a lot. They look particularly attractive with gentians and autumn crocus, but can be used to add colour and form to any arrangement. Stems of 'Lilacina' are an excellent foil for some of the late mauve roses. If you are picking from your own garden, you may not be able to take long stems, but however short, they tuck into the front of a small vase most effectively.

P. mucronata 'Alba', 'Davis's Hybrids', 'Lilacina', height and spread 60–90 cm (2–3 ft).

Petasites

A perennial only to be grown by those who have a large piece of unwanted land. It is definitely not suitable for a spare corner, or under trees, or indeed anywhere in a small garden. P. fragrans grows wild in many areas, and is a joy to pick for its strange little fragrant pink flowers. P. japonicus 'Giganteus' has bright green flower spikes appearing well before the frill of enormous leaves. These large leaves and the plant's tendency to spread rapidly are the great problems, but it is none the less a magnificent plant for the waterside.

Cultivation   These plants need no cultivation! Plant from October to March in any waste land, and let the plant take it over. Do not, however, let it escape into any cultivated part of your property. It is a ground-cover plant *par excellence*.

Conditioning   The flower heads stand well with little special treatment, but I advise you to pick them a few days before you intend to use them, as the stems are so short that they are difficult to use when cut. If you can leave them in a vase of water, they grow quickly, making it much easier to use them effectively.

Arranging   The cone-shaped green flower head is wonderful in mid-February or early March, providing a solid centre for any vase of mixed green, and

Petasites fragrans, P. japonicus 'Giganteus', height 30 cm (1 ft), planting distance 1.2 m (4 ft).

looks enchanting with stems of green hellebore and catkins. And I find that arranged in a bowl on their own, these flowers of *P. japonicus* 'Giganteus' will make a talking point at any dinner party.

Petunia

Height 15–23 cm (6–9 in), planting distance 23 cm (9 in).

Half-hardy annual. The three best known kinds are the large-flowered grandiflora, the bedding or multiflora and the double-flowered. They have open cup-shaped flowers, and come in a good range of colours, purple-reds and pinks, a very good pure white and a soft yellow.

Cultivation They really must be grown from seed and need heat for germination. Plant out as soon as the frost has gone, usually at the end of May. Most useful for tubs and pots, hanging baskets and window boxes.

Conditioning Put the ends of the stems into boiling water for a few minutes and then give them a long drink. They last well as a cut flower.

Arranging All the attractive colours you can find in these plants make them very useful for small arrangements, they have a good face, as we call it, and make a good focal point in any small group. Arranging white petunias in clear glass is extremely effective and the same goes for the pinks and reds in cranberry-coloured glass, or a red lacquer box.

Philadelphus   Mock Orange

Philadelphus 'Beauclerk', height around 2 m (6–8 ft), spread 1.5–2 m (5–6 ft); P. 'Belle Etoile', height 2.5–3 m (8–10 ft), spread 3–4 m (9–12 ft); P. 'Burfordiensis', height 2.5–3 m (8–10 ft), spread 3–4 m (9–12 ft); P. 'Virginal', height 2–3 m (6–9 ft), spread around 2 m (6–8 ft); P. coronarius 'Aureus', height and spread around 2 m.

Often wrongly called syringa, this is a most rewarding deciduous shrub, doing well on poor soils and sending up stems of deliciously sweet-scented white flowers. 'Beauclerk' has large white single flowers with a zone of cerise round the stamens, while the flowers of 'Belle Etoile' are maroon at the centre. 'Burfordiensis' grows up to 3 m (10 ft) in height with straight stems, and is a really lovely single with large open white flowers and a mass of yellow stamens. 'Virginal' is still quoted by every nursery as the best double. One of the best shrubs for golden foliage in spring is *P. coronarius* 'Aureus', bringing a touch of sunlight to any corner of your garden.

Cultivation Plant from October to March in sun or partial shade, in any good well-drained garden soil. Pruning consists of cutting out old stems right to the ground after flowering to prevent the bushes from becoming congested.

Conditioning I would strongly recommend you to remove most or even all leaves before you start to condition. If you are using only a few pieces, dip the stem ends in boiling water and then allow a long drink; if you have many branches, plunge them into warm water for a long drink after the stems have been well hammered.

Arranging Stems of philadelphus are invaluable for wedding groups. Once I had the delight of using philadelphus, white delphiniums and white peonies for a wedding in the first week of July, and I feel the result was really ideal. Pieces of *P. coronarius* 'Aureus' make any spring arrangement.

Phlox

Phlox paniculata (P. decussata) hybrids:

Phlox form a patch of excellent colour from mid-July all through August, just when the garden is starting to become completely dependent on annuals, and are well worth growing on that account, in spite of being greedy feeders and lovers of moisture. I have chosen a few varieties for their colours: 'Admiral' is a very good white; 'Mother of Pearl' a soft pink; 'Sandringham' and 'Daily Sketch' both good pinks with a darker eye. There are many good reds, especially 'Vintage Wine', which suits its name perfectly, as does 'Star Fire'; and 'Prince of Orange' is an excellent orange. The mauves and lilacs are particularly good colours for mixed summer arrangements.

Cultivation   Plant from October to March in any ordinary garden soil, in full sun. Plant 15 cm (6 in) deep. Mulch every year with peat or compost in April as phlox roots tend to appear on the surface. They need plenty of water in dry spells. On established clumps reduce the shoots to about eight or ten in the spring. Cut off the top 5–7.5 cm (2 or 3 in) of some of these when they are about two-thirds of their final height, to encourage side growths that will flower later than the normal shoots. Cut stems to the ground in the autumn.

Conditioning   Though phlox last well with little special treatment, they benefit from a long drink in deep warm water before arranging. This should be done straight after picking, because if they are allowed to flag the flower stems will not recover. Remove some of the foliage before arranging, and always check each day to remove any dead flower heads: if they are left they make the whole stem look tired, and as the buds continue to open in water, it is particularly important to remove all dead heads.

Arranging   A mass of mixed coloured phlox in a large wooden bowl will scent the room on a midsummer's day. Like all arrangements using only one type of flower, this takes a lot of material and you may feel as loath as I do to pick so much all at one time. But phlox look just as well in one-colour groups, and a few stems of white phlox can make an ideal centre for a mixed white vase in July.

'Admiral', 'Daily Sketch', 'Mother of Pearl', 'Sandringham', 'Vintage Wine', etc., height 75–90 cm (2½–3 ft), planting distance 45 cm (18 in).

Photinia

This is an evergreen shrub that has now become quite widely known and I am delighted as it belongs to such an attractive family. 'Red Robin' has oval leaves and gorgeous dark plum-coloured foliage. It is a sun-lover and does very well in North America, so I am hoping very much that I can manage to keep it.

Cultivation   Plant in September or October, or in March or April, in fairly rich loamy soil, in full sun if possible. No pruning is normally required.

Conditioning   The ends of the stems should be put into boiling water and then allowed to have a long drink.

Arranging   The leaves, through their lovely glossy colour and shape, seem to look good with almost anything. A small piece makes a splendid foil for *Helleborus foetidus*.

P. serrulata 'Red Robin', height 2 m (6 ft), spread 1–1.5 m (4–5 ft).

Phytolacca americana   Virginian Poke Weed

A perennial plant standing from about 1–2 m (4 to 8 ft) high, with nondescript flowers, but excellent seed heads forming right up the stem, starting green and turning black by autumn.

Cultivation   Plant from October to April in sun or shade, in any good garden soil. In exposed gardens give the plants some support. Cut the stems down to ground level in the late autumn.

Conditioning and preserving   The flower stems of phytolacca should have their ends put into boiling water and then be given a long drink. Seed heads need little extra care, but remove the foliage as this fades very quickly. The only reason for drying is to save the seed, which is the best way to propagate the plant.

Height 1–2.5 m (4–8 ft), planting distance 1 m (3 ft).

Arranging If you use the seed heads as soon as they form, the long green spikes of close green seeds can be cut to any length according to where you wish to place them in the vase, either for an outline or for the centre of the arrangement. As they turn black they are ideal for a black and white arrangement, or with autumn-coloured material and berries. Care must be taken to see that the over-ripe seeds do not fall, as they can stain badly: understandable for they were used as a dye many years ago. The seeds are also poisonous.

Pinks see Dianthus

Polyanthus see Primula

Polygonatum   Solomon's Seal

Polygonatum multiflorum (P. hybridum), height 60–120 cm (2–4 ft), planting distance 30–45 cm (12–18 in).

A hardy perennial with arching stems clothed in pairs of green leaves and white pendent bell flowers. It grows well in shade and is found growing in woods in its natural state. In garden cultivation, the stems grow to 60 cm–1 m (2 or 4 ft), or rather less in shady situations.

Cultivation Plant from October to March in any good well-drained garden soil. The plant enjoys full sun, but should be planted so that its roots are shaded. It also appreciates a suitable mulch in April. Cut the stems down to the ground in November.

Conditioning and preserving No special treatment is required to make the stems last well in water. They take up glycerine very well and, though rather limp, remain a good golden brown.

Arranging Without doubt one of the most useful flowers to grow for flower arranging. I use the stems all summer: their graceful arching form is invaluable as outline and to give a natural curve to balance the base of a vase. When in the green stage, I find them perfect for an all-green group, and later, when they are turning gold in autumn, I feel they enhance any autumn arrangement.

Polygonum

Polygonum affine 'Donald Lowndes', height 23 cm (9 in), planting distance 45 cm (18 in); P. aubertii, height and spread 6 m (20 ft); P. bistorta 'Superbum', height 75–90 cm (2½–3 ft), planting distance 60 cm (2 ft); P. cuspidatum 'Variegatum', height 2.5 m (8 ft), planting distance 2 m.

A vast genus, but the perennials I have listed here are well worth growing. *P. bistorta* 'Superbum', growing to about 90 cm (3 ft), sends up small poker spikes of deep pink in May, and continues intermittently till autumn. *P. affine* 'Donald Lowndes' has short 20 cm (8 in) stems of deep pink flowers, which appear on and off all summer, turning a deeper colour as the winter approaches. These low spreading varieties provide good ground cover and are useful on a bank, especially since the foliage turns russet red in autumn. The tall shrub species, *P. cuspidatum*, should be mentioned, but it is a rapid spreader and therefore only useful in a spare corner. The variegated form, *P. cuspidatum* 'Variegatum' is not so rampant, and with good variegated leaves it mixes well in the shrub border. The pink-flowered climber *P. aubertii*, often confused with *P. baldschuanicum*, is widely grown in America, and dries well.

Cultivation Plant from October to March in good garden soil, in sun or partial shade; a moist situation is best. Trim flower stems to the base after flowering in the autumn. *P. aubertii* may be trimmed hard with shears in spring to keep it within bounds.

Conditioning and preserving   For the shrub type and taller varieties, dip the stem ends in boiling water and follow with a long drink.

The deep pink stems of 'Donald Lowndes' preserve well if the heads are hung upside down. To dry *P. aubertii*, strip off the leaves after picking the stems, then place them in a vase with a little water, or hang them upside down.

Arranging   Small pieces of *P. bistorta* 'Superbum' are good in mixed vases in May, and the odd stems that flower later are always useful. 'Donald Lowndes' can be used in small arrangements and their deeper shades later in the year are lovely in autumn-coloured arrangements.

Poppy see *Papaver*

Primrose see *Primula*

Primula

A vast family, in which I have included just a few of my favourite species and also the hardy auricula and the polyanthus.

The wild primrose, *P. vulgaris*, with its open small yellow or sometimes pink flowers on short stems is good for woodland underplanting to make a lovely show in spring. *P. rosea* 'Delight' is a mass of bright pink flowers in early spring, suitable for rock garden or scree. We have to grow *P. malacoides* as a greenhouse plant, but I have seen this primula with flowers in all shades of pink and mauve growing in great drifts of colour in California, looking superb beneath camellias.

I grow the deliciously scented hardy auriculas for their wonderfully subtle colour range. They are sometimes known as Dusty Millers, for their white flour-dusted foliage. The polyanthus needs no description, with its multi-headed primrose-like flower stem and excellent colour range of white, yellows, pinks, blue and orange.

Cultivation   Plant from October to March. Any good garden soil is suitable, preferably one that is moisture retentive. *P. rosea* particularly revels in moist, even boggy conditions. They enjoy full sun, but also thrive in partial shade. Work in plenty of compost or other organic manure before planting; mulch generously in April and give plenty of water during dry spells.

Conditioning   Primroses, if picked in quantity, are better bunched and kept in a polythene bag until arranged. Polyanthus flowers last longer in arrangements if the stems are pricked with a pin just under the head and then allowed a long drink of water. Auriculas last well with a long drink.

Arranging   I use 'wild' primroses in early spring, either in a little basket arranged on a bed of leaves, or individual bunches placed in a bed of moss. The rock species of primula, *P. rosea* or *P. denticulata*, with its rounded purple heads, mix well with small spring flowers, or in a moss garden. Polyanthus flowers can be used through the whole spring and summer, as they often bloom at strange times of year. A mass of polyanthuses in a wooden box looks so right and attractive, though stems of separate colours added to any spring vase are also an asset. The flowers of *P. malacoides* are rarely used as cut flowers, as they are too precious, but look lovely in a planted dish garden.

Primula auricula, height and planting distance 15 cm (6 in); P. denticulata, height and planting distance 30 cm (12 in); P. rosea 'Delight', height and planting distance 15–20 cm (6–8 in); P. vulgaris, height and planting distance 15 cm (6 in).

99

Privet see Ligustrum

Prunella grandiflora

Height 15–30 cm (6–12 in), planting distance 45 cm.

A hardy perennial with deep purple flowers on 23–30 cm (9–12 in) stems, making a good carpet of colour for the front of the border, or under roses.

Cultivation   Plant from October to March in any good garden soil, in sun or partial shade. On dry soils water in hot dry spells. Trim over flower stems as necessary.

Conditioning and preserving   The flowers last well with no special treatment.

The seed heads preserve excellently, and this is one of my reasons for growing the plant. The stems with seed heads can be hung upside down to dry, or allowed to dry in a vase with a little water.

Arranging   The solid purple flower spikes come in useful as infilling material for a mixed blue and purple arrangement in June or July.

Prunus

Prunus cerasifera 'Nigra', height and spread 6–8 m (20–25 ft); P. communis 'Pollardii' (now correctly known as P. dulcis), height and spread 6–8 m (20–25 ft); P. davidiana 'Alba', height 8–9 m (25–30 ft), spread 4–4.5 m (12–15 ft); P. laurocerasus, height 4.5–6 m (15–20 ft), spread 6–9 m (20–30 ft); P. lusitanica, height and spread 4.5–6 m (15–20 ft); P. padus 'Watereri' ('Grandiflora'), height 6–8 m (20–25 ft), spread 4.5–6 m (15–20 ft); P. persica 'Cardinal', 'Prince Charming', height and spread 4.5–8 m (15–25 ft); P. serrulata 'Ukon' ('Grandiflora'), P. serrulata 'Amanogawa' ('Erecta'), P. serrulata 'Shirotae' ('Kojima'), height 5–8 m (18–25 ft), spread 9–11 m (30–35 ft); P. subhirtella 'Autumnalis', 'Pendula Rosea', 'Autumnalis Rosea', height and spread 6–8 m (20–25 ft).

There are so many members of this huge family that I can only suggest a few of my own favourite decorative and fruiting varieties.

A variety of the common almond, *P. communis* 'Pollardii', might be a good one to grow as the flowers are larger than those of the type and of a deeper colour with crimson stamens. The almond is lovely for town gardens, giving a wealth of pink blossom in March, flowering before the leaves on coal black stems. It also forces well, making it a 'must' for the flower arranger.

The flowering peaches I would choose are *P. davidiana* 'Alba', which produces clusters of white flowers on leafless branches in February; *P. persica* 'Cardinal' with vivid double red flowers in April; and *P. persica* 'Prince Charming', with semi-double rosette-like flowers, appearing in April on upright stems.

Flowering plums are also useful for the arranger, especially those with red foliage. *P. cerasifera* 'Nigra' is the improved form of 'Atropurpurea', having darker ruby-red foliage and single pink flowers in March.

P. padus 'Watereri' ('Grandiflora'), the Bird Cherry, flowers later than the other flowering prunus, producing pendulous white racemes in May. This is a wonderful sight in the garden, though sadly short-lived, and is also attractive for arranging.

Among flowering cherries perhaps my favourite is *P. subhirtella* 'Autumnalis', which flowers off and on all winter, starting in November with semi-double white flowers which get pinker with age. I thought I was planting this, but in fact was sent 'Higan-Zakura' (*P. subhirtella* 'Autumnalis Rosea'). I have loved every minute of the deep rose-pink buds in March, which develop into single pink flowers, and it forces well in water. *P. subhirtella* 'Pendula Rosea' (Cheal's Weeping Cherry) has long branches sweeping to the ground which in April are covered with small pink flowers. All weeping trees are decorative, particularly in flower, but though suitable for a small garden, they need to be planted in a lawn, where their beauty can be really appreciated. The most wonderful specimen of 'Pendula Rosea' I have seen was in Portland, Oregon; 9 m (30 ft) high, it was smothered in cascading pink blossom.

Other good Japanese cherries are hybrids from *P. serrulata*: *P. serrulata* 'Amanogawa' ('Erecta'), Lombardy Poplar Cherry, with clusters of semi-double pale pink flowers, becoming a veritable pillar of flower, is ideal for the small garden. The widely planted 'Kanzan' (*P. serrulata* 'Sekiyama') I could well do without, as I think there are better ones to grow, such as 'Shirotae' ('Kojima'), with large pendulous flowers on beautifully shaped arching branches; or 'Ukon' (*P. serrulata* 'Grandiflora') with bronzy young foliage, and greenish flowers which turn creamy-buff after opening.

P. lusitanica, Portugal laurel, has bay-like leaves and pendulous white flowers in June. It is a good evergreen, even hardier than the common laurel, *P. laurocerasus*. The latter has good shiny oval leaves of pale green turning darker as they mature, white flowers and purple berries. It is a good shrub for sunless areas.

Cultivation Plant from October to March in any well-drained reasonably fertile garden soil, preferably in full sun or light shade. If the soil is slightly alkaline, this is an advantage. All the prunus family is rather shallow rooted, and the trees should be firmly staked for the first few years after planting.

No regular pruning is normally needed on the almonds, peaches, plums or cherries, but the ordinary laurel and the Portuguese laurel may be cut back with secateurs to keep them within bounds. Old specimens that have become bare at the base may be cut hard back to 30–60 cm (1–2 ft) above ground and they will make new growth.

Conditioning and preserving All woody stems need careful treatment. Either hammer the ends, stripping off the bark for about 7.5 cm (3 in) up the stem, or dip the stem ends in boiling water. In both cases follow by a long drink.

The only member of the prunus family that will preserve well is the common laurel. After picking, give the branches a drink of warm water, so that the leaves are really crisp. Then stand in 2.5 cm (1 in) of glycerine and hot water solution, and you will see the leaves gradually turning brown. To help them take up the solution more quickly, paint a little glycerine on to the leaves with cotton wool. Allow up to four weeks for this process.

Arranging Sprays of delicate pink almond blossoms on dark stems can be forced as early as February. A month later, it can be picked in the garden and used as background for a few blue iris and pink hyacinths or tulips, or added to a few bought flowers to make a delightful arrangement. *P. subhirtella* 'Autumnalis', flowering all winter, can be used with the first *Iris unguicularis*, or twigs placed to give height to a moss garden of crocus, snowdrops and aconites. The purple-leaved plums, though difficult to condition, are wonderful background material for a vase of pink rhododendrons and purple lilacs. 'Ukon', in the first stages of opening buds, looks good with greens, or in a vase of contrasting purples – dark tulips and early peonies. All these flowering trees must be picked with great care, but even the weeping varieties need a little pruning or shaping every now and then, so trim them when you want branches for forcing, or later when the trees are in flower, so that you can shape the tree and have material for flower arranging at the same time.

Leaves of the common and Portugal laurel make excellent backgrounds for large church groups, especially on a windowsill where you can have a problem screening the light so that it doesn't take all the colour. Stems of laurel also look well when the leaves are browned in glycerine, either in a vase of dried material, or with fresh evergreens, in both cases providing solid contrast of form. The fruits of any of the plum or peach families should be used on the branch, or for fruit and flower arrangements like those in early flower paintings.

101

Pulmonaria

Pulmonaria
angustifolia 'Azurea',
height and planting
distance 30 cm (12 in);
P. saccharata 'Pink
Dawn', height and
planting distance 30 cm
(12 in).

A good perennial for underplanting – early flowers stay in bloom for nearly two months. The earliest is *P. angustifolia* 'Azurea' with flowers that are at first pink and then a brilliant blue, so that you often get a couple of pink bells amongst the gentian-blue ones. 'Pink Dawn' has flowers of pale mauve-pink and lovely foliage, particularly desirable because it lasts well all summer.

Cultivation   Plant in any reasonably good soil from October to March. While pulmonarias will grow in full sun, they need plenty of water in dry spells, and are happier in partial shade, and they appreciate a good mulch of peat in April.

Conditioning   The small flower stems should be plunged into very deep warm water for several hours; the leaves require burning and overnight submerging. Take care to remove a small piece of the lower part of the leaf before arranging, as otherwise this may cause siphoning – water held by the hairs on the lower part of the leaf dripping over the side of the vase.

Arranging   The very early blooms make a lovely touch of colour in a moss garden, or in any small vase of spring flowers. The leaves of 'Pink Dawn' are effective but difficult to condition.

Pulsatilla vulgaris Pasque Flower

Height 30 cm (12 in),
planting distance 40 cm
(15 in).

The spring-flowering Pasque Flower is a beautiful plant with tufts of deeply cut leaves and nodding flowers in mauve, purple or white on short stems.

Cultivation   Plant from October to March in any well-drained fertile garden soil, in full sun.

Conditioning and preserving   The flowers last well without any particular treatment. They are followed by enchanting fluffy seed heads.

Arranging   Pulsatillas are a great asset in a vase of mixed small spring flowers.

Pyracantha Firethorn

Pyracantha
angustifolia, height 3 m
(10 ft), spread around 2
m (6–8 ft); P. crenulata
'Rogersiana', P.
crenulata 'Rogersiana
Flava', height 2.5–3 m
(8–10 ft), spread 3–4.5
m.

Handsome shrubs with masses of white flowers in spring and a profusion of orange or yellow berries in late summer. They are generally used for training against a wall or fence, and can reach up to around 2.5 m (8 or 9 ft) or more. The berries of *P. angustifolia* are particularly fine, and if not taken by the birds will last right into winter and may even still be there in spring. *P. crenulata* 'Rogersiana' has deeper red berries and can be trained to grow on a wall or as a bush in the open. 'Flava' is the variety I personally prefer, as the berries are a bright clear yellow.

Cultivation   Plant October to March in full sun or partial shade in any good garden soil; they will put up with some lime in the soil. They make excellent wall plants, but must be tied to wires or square-mesh wire panels until they can stand on their own. If grown as bushes in the open no pruning is required, but if grown against a wall or fence they should be trimmed in early summer.

Conditioning   Hammer the woody stems very hard and allow several hours in warm water before arranging.

Arranging   As the stems grow pretty tall, one can use berried branches around 1.5 m (4 or 5 ft) long, making them ideal for a church group or really large arrangements. The yellow-berried form tones in well with yellow flowers like dahlias, roses and gladioli, whereas the orange-berried branches make a marvellous background for apricot and orange flowers and any arrangement of

'Palace Purple' heuchera – leaf and flower. *Allium pulchellum*, a member of the onion family and very useful for drying, green beans, Khol-rabi, peppers and grapes. Impale fruits with a wire or a cocktail stick to stop them falling about. Edible fruits make economical table decorations when flowers are in short supply.

Helichrysum, dried poppy heads, hydrangeas, curry plant, sedum, clematis seedheads, dried box branches, thistle, hollyhock seedhead, *Alchemilla mollis* – this is very useful because it doesn't deteriorate. This arrangement is made on a small wire-netting mesh envelope which I filled with moss. It could be made with Oasis and covered in plastic.

Clematis macropetala seedheads, purple berberis, plums, dock seedheads, 'Palace Purple' heuchera, Cox's Orange Pippin apples and black grapes. Even when flowers are in short supply it is easy to make use of fruits and leaves from the garden.

Use as many shades of red as possible, from the blue reds through to the orange reds, to get the right effect. If you use all the same tones, the effect will be rather dull.

good autumnal colours. I once used the red-berried form in Santiago with *Strelitzia reginae* and a collection of succulents in deep russet colours, and even with all these tropical exotics, the Firethorn made a wonderful contribution to the arrangement.

Ranunculus

R. bulbosus 'Pleniflorus' grows to about 45 cm (18 in) and has double yellow flowers, often with green centres. *R. aconitifolius* 'Flore-pleno' (Fair Maids of France) produces perfect double white button flowers for 3 months from May. Both these herbaceous perennials enjoy moisture. The tuberous rooted Persian and Turban varieties of *R. asiaticus*, thriving in the warmth of Florida, California and Kenya, are grown in Britain as annuals – though never doing well for me – and are a popular cut flower. They have a wonderful range of colours in orange-reds, white and pinks; both the single and double forms are good for the flower arranger.

Cultivation Plant *R. aconitifolius* and *R. bulbosus* from October to March, *R. asiaticus* in late February or March in any good garden soil, in full sun.

   R. asiaticus is not reliably hardy. The tubers should be lifted when the foliage has died down, dried and kept in a frost-free place to re-plant in spring. Or they may be grown in a frame and covered with glass in the winter.

Conditioning Herbaceous ranunculus lasts better if the stem ends are dipped into 2.5 cm (1 in) of boiling water and then given a long drink. For *R. asiaticus* varieties, the ends should be cut and the stems left in deep water for several hours. Whether you buy them or are lucky enough to grow them, they improve in every way after a night in deep water.

Arranging The herbaceous varieties are useful throughout the summer, particularly a few white stems for a white and green arrangement, or the yellows for a lovely splash of pure yellow in any arrangement of mixed yellows. The Turban ranunculus gives a focal point to an arrangement.

Ranunculus aconitifolius 'Flore-pleno', height 60 cm (2 ft), planting distance 30–45 cm (12–18 in); R. asiaticus, height 30 cm (12 in), planting distance 15 cm (6 in); R. bulbosus 'Pleniflorus' (R. bulbosus 'Speciosus Plenus'), height 30 cm (12 in), planting distance 45 cm (18 in).

Red-hot Poker see Kniphofia

Rheum

Perennials for the large garden, members of the rhubarb family with enormous leaves that are wonderfully coloured in spring. *R. alexandrae* has never grown well for me, which is particularly sad as the leaves are not too large, fleshy and dark green, and in spring the stems carry paper-looking bracts on spikes 90 cm (3 ft) high, handsome and long-lasting. *R. palmatum* 'Rubrum' and 'Atrosanguineum' produce 1.8 m (6 ft) plumes of flower in pinkish reds and enormous handsome leaves, deep red to purple in April but fading to dull green after flowering.

Cultivation Plant from October to March in any good garden soil, in a sunny site. Water well in dry spells, and give a mulch of suitable material in April. Cut the flower spikes down to ground level in the autumn.

Conditioning and preserving The large new leaves should have their stem ends burnt or dipped in boiling water, and then the whole leaf should be submerged under water overnight. This treatment may need to be repeated after several days, though it depends very much on the maturity of the leaf.

Rheum alexandrae, height 75–90 cm (2½–3 ft), planting distance 60 cm (2 ft); R. palmatum 'Atrosanguineum', 'Rubrum', height 1.5–2 m (5–8 ft), planting distance 1 m (3 ft).

The flower stems should also have the ends boiled or burnt, followed by a long drink.

The seed heads dry well if picked after they have formed on the plant and hung upside down until thoroughly dry.

Arranging In spring the young leaves are an asset to any foliage arrangement or at the base of a vase of forsythia and white-backed daffodils. The tall flower plumes are useful for large arrangements in May, and bring height and delicacy to a vase of more solid flowers.

Rhododendron

'Christmas Cheer', 'Cunningham's White', 'Doncaster', 'Pink Pearl', height and spread 2–3 m; 'Praecox', 'Purple Splendour', height and spread around 1 m.

These familiar evergreen shrubs with large leaves and clustered flower heads range from small rock varieties to massive plants growing up to 9 m (30 ft), all equally attractive and effective in their own way. The hybrid rhododendrons have beautiful foliage, felty and brown backed, and some are sweet-scented with nodding bells. They can be grown from seed if you are patient, and it is also possible to move them at almost any age. I have chosen 'Doncaster' as a good red; 'Pink Pearl' as one of the handsomest of all with large heads of deep to paler pink flowers; 'Cunningham's White' as a good early white; 'Christmas Cheer' as a very early pink; and 'Praecox' as a very early delicate-flowered mauve. These last two early varieties are particularly helpful for the flower arranger, though also effective in the garden.

Cultivation These rhododendrons must have an acid soil. They will thrive in light shade and need shelter from north and east winds. They are very shallow rooted and need plenty of water on quick-draining soils in dry spells. Plant from October to March. No pruning is required but old gaunt specimens may be cut back hard. It is better, however, to replace such worn-out shrubs, or move them to a better place if they are too big for their present position.

Conditioning and preserving The ends of the stems should be hammered, or dipped in boiling water (I prefer this second method). Remove some of the foliage, not only to show the face, but because the flowers will last longer. I was once given a tip to add a little household bleach to the water – it seems to help keep flowers fresh.

The foliage of rhododendron glycerines well, going a good brown colour. The seed heads of some of the hybrids also dry well.

Rhus see Cotinus

Ribes   Flowering Currant

Ribes laurifolium, height and spread 30–45 cm (12–18 in); R. sanguineum 'Atrorubens', 'Brocklebank', 'Carneum', height 2–3 m (6–9 ft), spread 1.5–2.5 m (5–8 ft).

Flowering currants are good for both planting and arranging, whether the prostrate *R. laurifolium*, with masses of greenish-white flowers in February, or the better-known *R. sanguineum*. Here I would recommend 'Atrorubens', a North American variety with deepest red flowers, 'Brocklebank', worthy of a place for its golden foliage and pink flowers, and 'Carneum', flesh-pink flowers.

Cultivation Plant October to March in any good garden soil in an open sunny site, or even in light shade. No pruning is normally necessary, but old worn-out stems should be cut out at the base in spring.

Conditioning To force, pick branches as the buds are forming, hammer the stems well and place in warm water. If you can stand them in a dark place they seem to come out much more quickly. They need about five weeks to bloom, and the forced flowers are much paler than those grown out of doors, but are none the less attractive.

For branches picked when in blossom, dip the stem ends into boiling water and then allow a long drink before using.

Arranging   Currants can be forced easily. Early forced stems, mixed with a bunch of bought pale tulips or some lilies, bring a feeling of spring and blossom time very early in the year.

Rodgersia pinnata 'Superba'

Outstandingly handsome foliage plant with red-tinted five-finger leaves, which make a canopy colouring beautifully in autumn, and tall pinkish-red flower spikes appearing in July. It is water-loving and prefers partial shade.

Height around 1 m (3–4 ft), planting distance 60–90 cm (2–3 ft).

Cultivation   Plant in March or April in any good soil, preferably in a moist situation and in partial shade. Mulch in April, water well in dry spells. Cut down flower spikes to ground level in the autumn.

Conditioning and preserving   The flowers keep better if they are not picked until they are mature. Both flower stems and leaves should have their stem ends dipped in boiling water and then be allowed a long drink.

The flower seed heads dry well, but I really prefer to use them fresh in July.

Arranging   If I have only a few of these leaves, I prefer to save them until the autumn, when they turn such beautiful colours. They bring great distinction to any vase of autumnal colourings especially if arranged in a copper container. The flower panicles are excellent in large arrangements.

Rosa   Rose

It is extremely difficult to make suggestions for a collection of roses! Once again, I can only list a few of my favourites in each group, but for anyone trying to make their own selection I would recommend going to look at them in bloom first. The Rose Trial Grounds at St Albans are well worth a visit for this reason alone.

Shrub roses, height 1.5–2 m (5–6 ft), spread 1–2 m (4–6 ft); Hybrid tea roses, height around 1 m (3–4 ft), spread 60–90 cm (2–3 ft); Floribundas, height around 1 m (3–4 ft), spread 60–90 cm (2–3 ft); Climbing roses, height and spread normally 3–4.5 m (10–15 ft).

Perhaps the first point I must make about roses is that if you want to grow them well nowadays you really will have to spray to combat black spot. Since I wrote about roses originally this blight has become very much worse, but with a spray such as 'Nimrod' every ten days I can keep it in check.

Shrub roses   If you have enough space, shrub roses are rewarding to grow for their fantastic scents and old-fashioned charm, and though for arranging they are not to be compared with the modern Hybrid teas, they last quite well if displayed in a mass. I am not going to attempt to give full Latin names, but simply list my selection.

A pure white is 'Blanc Double de Coubert', flowering over a long period, even though individual flowers are short-lived.

In the purple to violet group: 'Charles de Mills', richest deep purple to mauve; 'Cardinal de Richelieu', deep violet; the striped 'Variegata di Bologna', purple and white.

'Tuscany' has maroon-coloured velvety petals with a cluster of yellow stamens. The semi-climber 'Madame Isaac Pereire' has heavily scented deep magenta pink flowers, and is a lovely rose for arrangements.

The largest group is of pink-flowered roses, from among the oldest to very recent introductions. A variety of the White Rose of Yorkshire is 'Great

Maiden's Blush', known since the fifteenth century and so vigorous that it is still found today. 'Celeste' is another member of the same family, with a wealth of soft pink blooms. 'Madame Lauriol de Barny' has flat heads of many-petalled pink flowers, and 'Fantin Latour' also has handsome foliage. 'Madame Pierre Oger' is better known as the Shell Rose, and has creamy pink flowers that deepen with age. 'Abraham Derby' is a superb modern shrub rose and has large many-petalled flat apricot pink flowers. 'Constance Spry' is another modern shrub rose, and I think one of the best of all, with large pink flowers, a musky scent and a wealth of bloom for two weeks or more. I find that it grows with great vigour if trained against a wall.

Crosses from 'Constance Spry', such as 'Chaucer', are also well worth trying and David Austin has continued to produce a great new collection. 'Graham Thomas' is an excellent yellow with lovely cupped flowers and glistening petals. 'Dame Prudence' – a small-growing, twiggy bush with pretty buds and delicate blush-pink flowers. 'Lord Oberon' – a large, deep, many-petalled flower, soft pink and very fragrant. 'Proud Titania' has glistening white flowers, it has a strong growth with smallish musk rose foliage – I fell in love with it at Chelsea. 'Tamara' is a short, bushy, upright plant good for a small garden, it has large, full-petalled, deeply-cut, peony-like flowers of an apricot colour. 'Charles Austin' is a strong grower with trusses of flat rose heads of apricot fading to cream.

Hybrid teas   White: 'Message', 'Pascali', 'Virgo', 'John F. Kennedy' if you can find it in Britain. It is a superb greenish-white.

The best cream rose is undoubtedly 'Elizabeth Harkness', and the new John Mattock rose 'Tynwald' is quite outstanding. It has vigorous growth, multi-headed ivory-cream blooms that are ideal as cut flowers.

Clear yellows: 'Sunblest', 'King's Ransom', 'Miss Harp', 'Golden Times'.

Apricot colourings: 'Whisky Mac', 'Bettina', 'Apricot Silk', 'Beauté', 'Vespa', 'Just Joey' and 'Blessings'.

Reds: 'Ena Harkness' and 'Josephine Bruce' for velvet red roses; 'Christian Dior', 'Super Star', 'Fragrant Cloud', 'Eroica', 'Sir Harry Pilkington'.

Pinks: 'Lady Helen', 'Anne Letts', 'Northern Lights' – and 'Ophelia' takes a lot of beating.

Mauve to purples: 'Blue Moon', 'Sterling Silver', 'Lilac Time'.

Off-beat colours: 'Helen Traubel', pinkish-apricot and one of the earliest to flower; 'Iced Ginger', light tan-coloured; 'Fantan', brownish; 'Amber', light golden brown and buff; 'Jocelyn', purple brown and most unusual. Lastly, 'Pink Chiffon', delicate pink buds with deeper pink centres, and 'Julia', an outstandingly attractive rose, especially for flower arranging, pretty copper and parchment coloured buds opening semi-double – beautiful at all stages.

Floribundas   'Iceberg' must be the top favourite, a pure white. 'Elizabeth of Glamis', 'Sir Lancelot' and 'Apricot Nectar' are good apricot shades. The latest very exciting (to me) addition, 'Sheila Macqueen', has green buds opening to apricot and yellow. 'Fashion' is deep salmon; 'Woburn Abbey' orange and gold – all these orangey colours perhaps even more useful in the autumn than in high summer. Good reds are 'Lilli Marlene', 'Topsy', 'Ginger Megg' and 'Rosemary Rose', though this last one suffers from mildew.

Climbing roses   I have included *Rosa filipes* 'Kifsgate' here for growing over an old apple or pear tree, or to smother an unsightly shed. It is at its peak in July, producing a mass of very sweetly scented white flower sprays with yellow stamens. 'Iceberg' is a marvellous sight seen growing over an arch at the Rose Trial Grounds – I can't wait to try one. Another lovely species rose is *R. banksiae* 'Lutea', with double rosette flowers of soft buttercup yellow, very sweet scented and needing little pruning. 'Mermaid' is particularly desirable for its superb glossy green foliage and because it flowers for such a long period, from June to November, producing its single yellow open flowers with amber stamens. 'Lawrence Johnston' is a lovely, vigorous yellow climber and makes a marvellous show on a fence or old apple tree. 'Paul's Lemon Pillar' is one of the earliest roses to come out and its creamy yellow flowers are doubly welcome for this reason. 'Climbing Allgold' is an excellent yellow with a long blooming period and good dark green foliage. 'Albertine' is not for the small garden and it needs a lot of attention to keep it in shape, but you are rewarded with a wealth of reddish buds opening to pale salmon pink, and with a perfume that wafts into every corner of the house on a warm June night. 'Bantry Bay' is a hardy, continuous flowering, showy, deep pink.

For reds there is nothing to beat 'Guinée' with dark rich colour and wonderful scent, or 'Etoile de Holland', not such a deep red but an old and popular rose still to be recommended. 'New Dawn' looks like an old rose but was actually hybridized in 1930 in New Jersey. It is excellent for climbing over an old tree, and its pale pink beautifully shaped flowers most useful for arranging.

Cultivation   Plant October to March. Roses prefer a sunny open site and will thrive in any good well-drained soil. On light soils work in plenty of peat or organic manure, and feed well with a soluble fertilizer every year.

Pruning of established roses: shrub roses need only shortening back of the main stems by a few inches, and any old worn-out stems cut out at ground level in March. Hybrid tea roses are pruned in December, or at any time when growth is dormant, up to March. Cut out weak and worn-out shoots. Cut main shoots back to leave about five or six buds or eyes. Cut to just above an outward pointing bud. Floribunda roses are also pruned from December to March, but more lightly pruned. Cut back weak shoots to leave three or four buds, but on strong growths leave five to seven buds. Climbing roses are pruned after flowering. If there are sufficient new growths to take their place, cut out completely the older stems. Bend the new growths over as nearly horizontal as possible to encourage the production of side shoots which will bear the flowers in the next year.

Conditioning and preserving   Dip the stem ends in boiling water for a minute, then follow with a long drink in cold water for several hours. Or hammer the ends of the stems and then give them a long drink in warm water.

It is possible to treat these flowers so that you can have them in bloom at Christmas: pick when the roses are in bud, wax the ends of the stems with paraffin wax and lay them in a long, closed cardboard box until Christmas. Then cut off the wax ends and place the stems in warm water: you will find that they open up very well.

Buds and even fully blown roses can be preserved in silica gel. Remove the stem and insert a florist's wire in its place (the stem would just break off when dry), then lay the rose face upwards on a bed of powder. Sprinkle with more powder, taking care to fill every crevice, until the bloom is completely covered. Leave for a few days before testing to see if the petals are perfectly dry and crisp.

Dried rose petals make wonderful potpourri. They should be spread on trays to dry out of doors, but not in full sun.

Arranging   I shall never cease to be amazed at the great gasp that goes up whenever I show a slide of a mass of pink roses during a lecture. Roses are one of the few flowers that most of us can arrange *en masse*, for it is usually possible to pick quite a lot at one time. On the other hand they are the ideal focal point and centre for so many arrangements, and I sometimes find myself wondering what to put into the middle of a vase when there are no roses in bloom, even being tempted to buy some, however expensive, to provide that final touch. Only the single blooms of climbing roses such as 'Mermaid' will not last well in arrangements. In mixed arrangements, I think roses can be used to best effect where they provide contrast in colour and form (such as a few white roses in a green and white arrangement, or roses for the white emphasis in a near-black and white arrangement) and where they are used as focal points in arrangements of many shades of one colour (such as mixed reds in high summer; or apricot colourings in autumn with turning leaves, apricot dahlias and gladioli).

Rudbeckia

Height 60–90 cm (2–3 ft), planting distance 60 cm (2 ft).

This dark-eyed, golden daisy perennial adds so much to the garden, flowering from July to October when its colour is welcome and always a good flower for picking. In America, where the rudbeckia grows wild in many areas, it may be felt that it is a strange choice for cultivation. However, we are not all so fortunate. I think that *R. fulgida* 'Deamii' is the only variety that I personally wish to grow, but there are many others that add late colour to the border.

Cultivation   Plant from October to March in full sun or partial shade, in any good garden soil. No staking is normally needed, except in exposed gardens. Cut down to ground level in the autumn.

Conditioning and preserving   Bruise the ends of the stems, or dip in a little boiling water, and then allow a long drink.

The single blooms dry well in any of the flower-drying powders and keep a very good colour.

Arranging   The small dark eye is the great attraction for me, and with some black privet or phytolacca berries you have the makings of an interesting arrangement.

Salix   Willow

Salix alba 'Chermesina' ('Britzensis'), height 9–12 m (30–40 ft), spread 4.5–8 m (15–25 ft); S. babylonica, height 6–8 m (20–25 ft), spread 6–9 m (20–30 ft); S. lanata, height 60 cm–1.2 m (2–4 ft), spread 30 cm–1.2 m (1–4 ft); S. matsudana 'Tortuosa', height 6–9 m (20–30 ft), spread 3–4.5 m (10–15 ft).

A vast range of plants from tiny shrubs suitable for a rock garden to large trees such as *S. babylonica*, the weeping willow. This is a very decorative tree, much taller than our native pussy willow, with very graceful hanging branches, bright yellow in spring. It looks particularly lovely underplanted with daffodils. But it is not a tree for the small garden, and is one that can be difficult, too, in built-up areas, as willows have a way of looking for water, and their roots can cause havoc while in pursuit of it. *S. lanata* is indigenous to Scotland, where I found mine, and makes a handsome small shrub of 60–90 cm (2–3 ft), with silver-grey fluffy down on the leaves, stems and golden yellow catkins. *S. matsudana* 'Tortuosa', the fan-tail willow, is wonderful for arrangements, with corkscrew-twisted red fasciated stems edged with silver catkins. *S.* 'Britzensis', to use its familiar name, has lovely red bark in winter, and when brought into the house the catkins open well in water. Also the fan-tail willow *S. sachalinensis* has wide, contorted branches ideal for modern flower arrangements. The red-barked willow, *S. Daphonoides*, is excellent for winter arrangements.

Cultivation   Plant from October to March in any soil. All willows love moist conditions, so the tall trees are not suitable for small gardens or dry soils. A fully-grown willow can transpire a ton of water a day and thus rob a large area of ground of moisture.

No pruning is required for the larger trees, but those grown for their coloured stems should be cut down almost to ground level in January or February every year.

Conditioning and preserving Hammer the ends of the stems and then put into warm water. For forcing, follow this procedure, but keep the branches in the dark for the first few days. Pussy willow stems will dry off in shallow water and can be used all winter.

Arranging The weeping willow is the only one that does not last well in water. I have used it for a wedding group, where the tumbling yellow stems were ideal, but it lived for just one day. All other willows last well and are a joy for winter and early spring as they develop in water. I use the 'Tortuosa' willow a great deal as it has such an excellent form for oriental-type arrangements. Small stems of native pussy willow (*S. caprea*) look well in spring arrangements with hellebores.

Salvia

S. nemorosa 'Superba' gives a lovely patch of colour to the border, and lives a long time, unlike *S. haematodes* which, for me anyway, seems to die out after a few years, though I think it quite the prettiest salvia, with pale lavender flower spikes on stems of about 60–90 cm (2–3 ft). *S. sclarea* 'Turkestanica' also dies out, but seems to seed freely so that once you have it, it will go on reproducing itself. For those of you who live in warm climates, try a brilliant patch of the scarlet *S. splendens*, often seen in our parks where it is treated as a half-hardy annual and used as a bedding-out plant. It grows on stems slightly shorter than the other varieties of salvia mentioned, and has more delicate pendulous flowers.

Salvia haematodes, height 90 cm (3 ft), planting distance 60 cm (2 ft); S. nemorosa 'Superba', height 60–90 cm (2–3 ft), planting distance 60 cm (2 ft); S. sclarea 'Turkestanica', height 75 cm (2½ ft), planting distance 30 cm (12 in); S. splendens, height 45 cm, planting distance 30 cm.

Cultivation The biennial species *S. sclarea* is sown very thickly in April in the final position where the plants are to grow. The seedlings are thinned out to leave them 30 cm (12 in) apart, or they may be carefully transplanted. *S. splendens* is a half-hardy annual which must be raised under glass and planted out at the end of May or early in June, when danger of frost is past. The other salvias are hardy perennials and may be planted in good soil from October to March in full sun or in light shade. Cut stems to the ground in November.

Conditioning All the salvias last better if the stem ends are put into 2.5 cm (1 in) of boiling water, and then given a long deep drink. *S. sclarea* 'Turkestanica' should be handled carefully as it has a very pungent smell that some people find unpleasant – though I find it disappears once the flower has been arranged in the vase.

Arranging Salvias are useful in mixed summer arrangements. The slim and delicate flower stems make a good background. Stems of the stronger-coloured flowers can be cut short (about 15 cm/6 in) and used as the centre of an arrangement, if this is the colour you particularly want to emphasize. The scarlet *S. splendens* is a wonderful help in clashing red arrangements as it has an outstandingly clear colour and lasts well in water.

Satin Flower see Sisyrinchium

Scabiosa   Scabious

Open-faced delightful perennials in shades of blue and also white, flowering on stems 60–90 cm (2–3 ft). I personally find them rather difficult to grow, and so have concentrated on having white ones only, as I am very attached to them and find they are not so easy to buy as the mauve ones.

Scabiosa caucasica 'Clive Greaves' and 'Miss Willmott', height 60–90 cm (2–3 ft), planting distance 45 cm (18 in).

Cultivation Plant from October to March in any good garden soil, in full sun. The site must be well drained, so on soils that tend to lie wet in winter plant in a raised bed – say 30 cm (12 in) above the soil level. Scabious appreciate a mulch in April. Cut the plants down to ground level in November.

Conditioning　A long drink in warm water is all they need to make them last very well. If you remember always to cut off the dead blooms on the growing plants, you will find that when arranged the buds will continue to open in water, though paler in colour.

Arranging　During my first-ever television programme, I showed viewers how to make an arrangement of four bunches of scabious in a silver bowl. The intention was to demonstrate that one could make a pretty vase at a very modest cost as they are quite inexpensive to buy. These flowers are ideal for arranging, making an excellent centre, and can be cut with different lengths of stems from 30 cm (1 ft) down to 15 cm (6 in). They can be used to give a recessed effect, which is so important especially if you are making an arrangement of scabious on their own with no unrelated foliage. The white-flowered varieties make a good centre for a mixed white vase or with green foliage.

Scrophularia nodosa 'Variegata'

Height 60–90 cm (2–3 ft), planting distance 45 cm (18 in).

The figwort is a wild plant, but this variegated form is highly recommended for the garden, statuesque in form and growing to about 90 cm (3 ft) in height, with leaves blotched and splashed with white.

Cultivation　Plant preferably in a moist spot in any ordinary garden soil, from October to March. Water copiously in dry spells on light quick-draining soil. Nip out the flower spikes as the flowers are insignificant and it is the foliage that is required. Cut down to ground level in November.

Conditioning　Stem ends should be dipped into boiling water for a few minutes, or singed in a gas flame, and then given a drink in deep water.

Arranging　It is advisable to wait until the foliage is mature before picking, and then small pieces can be used in mixed foliage arrangements. Like all variegated plants, it helps to add the necessary light touch for the centre of a foliage group. The small brown flowers are of no value, but after they have developed you can take longer stems of foliage of up to 60 cm (2 ft).

Sedum

Sedum aizoon, height and planting distance 30 cm (12 in); S. alboroseum 'Variegatum', height 30 cm (12 in), planting distance 60 cm (2 ft); S. x 'Autumn Joy', height and planting distance 60 cm (2 ft); S. maximum 'Atropurpureum', height and planting distance 60 cm (2 ft); S. 'Ruby Glow', height and planting distance 30 cm (12 in); S. spectabile 'Brilliant', height 30–45

One of the best perennials for flower arranging and for gardens large and small, growing with little trouble and easily propagated. In fact, when I was first given a piece of *S. maximum* 'Atropurpureum', I cut the stem just above a pair of leaves, removed the lower pair of leaves from each cutting and planted them in sandy soil. I was soon overjoyed to find I had two well-rooted plants which I still have 25 years later. Of course I have rooted many pieces in this way since, and have a fine collection of sedums; as they also seed freely I have many unusual crosses too. *S. maximum* 'Atropurpureum' is a handsome plant with deep red foliage, growing taller than most other sedums. The fleshy stems have pairs of leaves right up to a flat flower head of tiny stars, and stems, leaves and flowers all have this marvellous red-colour. *S. spectabile* 'Brilliant' is a Chinese plant, with glaucous fleshy foliage and attractive soft pink flower heads, making a very good patch of colour in the autumn. One of my favourites is *S. x* 'Autumn Joy' with a flowering period of nearly three months, the flowers starting pink and going a deep red colour, and useful for arranging at all stages. The variegated foliage of *S. alboroseum* 'Variegatum' is also lovely to use in arrangements and handsome in the border. I grow *S. aizoon* purely for the seed

Interesting fruits and nuts are in plentiful supply in the autumn. Using odd pieces of Oasis and chicken wire, it is easy to make the base for this impressive display of seasonal fare.

Brown and green-flowered sedums, crossed in my garden, Old Man's Beard, tree peony foliage, 'Palace Purple' heuchera, teasle heads and pine cones. The parasol mushrooms lasted extremely well.

head, though the yellow flowers are quite attractive. Among the smaller rock varieties, S. 'Ruby Glow', with dark maroon foliage and good deep pink flowers, looks well grown in pots, with its graceful fall.

Cultivation   Plant from October to April in any good garden soil, in full sun. Preferably give S. *maximum* a moist but not boggy spot. Unless the old flower stems and seed heads are used in arrangements, cut them or snap them off in March or April. The plants appreciate a mulch in April.

Conditioning and preserving   Sedums last well in water with no more treatment than the usual long drink. I always feel they ought to dry well, but in fact they do not, though if used in a vase in late autumn and left there, I find they will actually grow roots in the vase.

Arranging   Sedums are of great value. I start using 'Autumn Joy' in August in the green flowerbud stage, when it mixes with other green leaves; and then later use all sedum flowers as a centre in many arrangements – with the pinks and mauves of asters, for instance, or with apricot-coloured dahlias, gladioli and autumn-coloured foliage, or sprays of rose hips, cotoneaster berried branches and turning beetroot leaves.

cm (12–18 in), planting distance 45 cm (18 in).

Senecio

The grey-foliaged cinerarias are worth a corner, for they are useful to cut, and make a grey patch in the border, which creates a restful zone in any scheme of mixed planting. S. *cineraria*, with flannel-textured leaves of deeply cut furry grey, grows into quite a large plant, but then becomes woody and suddenly dies – so I take a few cuttings in July, tucking them into some sand by a stone on the rock garden, and in this way ensure that I always have young plants.

S. *laxifolius* is most useful for cutting and retains its good grey foliage all winter. It has rounded grey leaves with silver backs, grows to about 90 cm (3 ft) and has a mass of bright yellow daisy flowers in July. It tends to die out suddenly, and again it is important always to take a few cuttings.

Cultivation   S. *cineraria* is almost hardy but is usually treated as a half-hardy annual and planted out each year in spring. Plant S. *laxifolius* from October to March in sun or partial shade in any soil, no matter how poor. It will of course respond to feeding, a mulch in April, and water in dry spells. When the plant becomes leggy, cut it back hard, almost to ground level if necessary, and it will make copious new growth.

Conditioning   Dip the cut ends of the stems into boiling water, and then allow a long deep drink. With S. *cineraria*, it is particularly important to see that the hairy part of the leaf does not get into the water, either during conditioning or when arranging. The woody stems of S. *laxifolius* can be hammered before being given a long drink.

Arranging   I use the individual leaves of S. *cineraria* at the base of a vase, where they look so well with pale pink roses or garden pinks. Longer stems of S. *laxifolius* are ideal for the background to a winter foliage arrangement.

Senecio cineraria, S. maritima (now correctly S. bicolor), height 60 cm (2 ft), planting distance 30 cm (12 in); S. laxifolius, height and spread 1.2 m (4 ft).

Sisyrinchium striatum   Satin Flower

The satin flower, a hardy perennial, seeds itself everywhere, but makes splendid groups of grey-green iris-like leaves 30 cm (12 in) high. The flowers, appearing all down the stems of stiff spikes, are straw yellow and last for many weeks. Lovely black seed heads then form, and it is as much for these as for the flowers that I grow this plant.

Height 30–45 cm (12–18 in), planting distance 30 cm.

111

Cultivation   Plant from October to March in full sun, in a well-drained site which has been enriched with peat or leaf-mould. Cut down dead stems and foliage in autumn. Mulch in April.

Conditioning and preserving   Sadly there is no way to keep the little flowers open at night, but for just one day the spikes need no special treatment.

The seed heads dry well if hung upside down. If the stems are put into a glycerine solution, they go a wonderful colour, and like all things treated this way, they are not so brittle to use.

Arranging   The flowers close up at night, both in the garden and when cut, so I pick and use the spikes for only one day. They are useful outline material, and the flowers are a very pleasing soft yellow colour. I use the seed heads all the time, both in their earlier green state and then dried.

Smilacina racemosa

Height 60–90 cm (2–3 ft), planting distance 45 cm (18 in).

This hardy perennial is related to Solomon's Seal, and has a very similar growth habit, with pairs of leaves on arching stems, but the flower is a sweetly scented fluffy cream spike at the end. In its native North America it grows in the woods, and is a lover of shade and damp, but it also seems to grow well for me in the front of a fairly dry shrub border.

Cultivation   Plant from October to March in good garden soil enriched with compost or well-rotted manure. A moist, partially shaded site is best, and a mulch in April is helpful. Cut down to ground level in November or December.

Conditioning and preserving   Give a long drink in deep water.

The stems take up glycerine quite well: pick before they turn colour, and put the stem ends into a glycerine solution, and you will get a rather limp but well-coloured spray for winter use.

Arranging   These arching sprays add so much to any arrangement; I find them especially useful for giving form in a green group and in their lovely golden yellow autumnal colouring, stems add a downward sweep to a vase of yellows – roses, dahlias and gladioli in a brass pan or bowl.

Snapdragon see Antirrhinum

Snowberry see Symphoricarpus

Snowdrop see Galanthus

Solomon's Seal see Polygonatum

Spotted Laurel see Aucuba japonica

112

Stachys lanata   Lamb's Ears

A hardy perennial with good grey leaves densely covered in grey wool, and mauve flower spikes, which I personally like to preserve and use in dried arrangements. It provides excellent ground cover, though apt to spread almost too much. There is also a variety named 'Sheila Macqueen' but it has no flowers.

Height 30 cm (12 in), planting distance 30–45 cm.

Cultivation   Plant from October to March in any good garden soil, preferably well drained and in full sun. Plants may be grown in partial shade but may be less silvery. Trim the plants over in November or December.

Conditioning and preserving   It is best to burn the ends of the stems, either in a gas flame or putting the ends into boiling water for a count of twenty, and then give them a long drink, taking care to avoid submerging the hairy leaves, as this causes them to lose their grey colour. When the flower spikes are mature, remove any extra leaves and hang them upside down to dry.

Arranging   The leaves are particularly lovely used individually with pinks for a pink and grey arrangement. Later when the flower spikes form, their dense grey coating makes them ideal for mixing with a vase of old roses. The greys always look well in a silver container.

Statice

Mainly grown and used for everlasting flowers and adds colour to many dried arrangements through the winter. Tufted heads of good colours. A lovely pale yellow and new apricot are most attractive, though the colours most generally known are purple and puce.

Height 50 cm (1½ ft), planting distance 30 cm (1 ft).

Cultivation   Grown from seed under glass and then planted out in May. It is possible to plant the seeds in open ground and then thin out. As statice are not particularly pretty while growing and their value lies in cutting for winter, they are best grown in a cutting area.

Preserving   When the flower heads are fully open and showing colour, cut a bunch and hang upside down to dry. They dry quickly and are best placed in boxes until needed for winter arrangements.

Arranging   Statice last very well and keep their colour, so are ideal for the focal point to add colour to any dried arrangement. Use several stems of the same shade to concentrate the colour because a spotty effect is created if the colour is dotted through the arrangement.

Strawberry Tree see *Arbutus unedo*

Summer Snowflake see *Leucojum*

Sweet Pea see *Lathyrus odoratus*

Symphoricarpos — Snowberry

Symphoricarpos albus 'Laevigatus' (S. rivularis), height 1.5–2 m (5–7 ft), spread 2 m (7–8 ft).

Snowberries will grow in the shade, though I found that mine did much better in full sun, making 60–90 cm (2–3 ft) bushes of small-leaved plants with insignificant flowers followed by round white berries which are so pretty, and stay on the bush until after Christmas. There are pink-berried forms, and I have cut these in America but never used them in Britain.

Cultivation Plant October to March in any reasonably good soil, in sun or shade, even under the drip of trees. Birds seldom take the berries unless they are desperate. No pruning is normally needed but thinning out may be done during the autumn or winter.

Conditioning The stems need little treatment, but are better if left in deep water for some hours. They will last for weeks in water provided you remove any brown and dying berries, for once started the rot seems to spread very quickly.

Arranging If you can cut stems of about 15 cm (6 in) long, they fall gracefully from the centre of an arrangement. They are ideal with black privet berries, late-flowering 'Iceberg' roses and small white dahlias, to make an unusual arrangement.

Symphytum — Comfrey

Symphytum officinale variegata, height 80 cm (2½ ft), planting distance 1.3 m (4 ft).

One of the best variegated hardy perennials I know. It has large pointed leaves, green striped with cream. The flowers are unimportant but if you cut the stems down after flowering you get a marvellous second crop of leaves.

Cultivation Likes a moist spot, either in part shade or in the full sun.

Conditioning The ends of the leaves must be placed in 2.5 cm (1 in) of boiling water as soon as possible. Do not leave them in the water for longer than it takes to count up to ten, then plunge into cold water for several hours.

Arranging Comfrey leaves are the central point of any green arrangement and look well arranged with mixed summer flowers.

Syringa — Lilac

I can never bring myself to talk about lilac as syringa, which of course it is! With its beauty and scent it is undoubtedly a 'must' for every garden. The singles are my favourites, like the 'Primrose' lilac.

Conditioning It is best to remove much of the foliage, for the stems do not seem able to take up enough water for both the flower and foliage on the same branch. So remove most of the leaves and use a stem of green leaves separately. Peel off the bark to about 5 cm (2 in) up the stem, but be sure that all the white part of the stem is well under the water line or it will die. Then place the ends of the stems in boiling water and leave in deep water overnight for the best results.

Arranging Nothing looks more luscious and wonderful than a large vase of lilac which fills the house with scent. White lilac is a great asset for a large white group for a wedding, and the purples blend in with rhododendrons, mixed lupins and delphiniums for a glorious summer arrangement.

Tellima

An excellent ground cover. I particularly love the compact clumps of rounded hairy leaves of 'Purpurea', of a lovely rich colour good for picking all the year. The flowers of both forms of this plant have graceful stems of pale green bells. I grow mine in the front of the borders and find they spread well while remaining compact.

Cultivation Plant from October to March in any reasonably good garden soil, in sun or partial shade. This plant will tolerate dry shade. Cut down faded flower spikes.

Conditioning As the leaves grow on very short stems, it is best to burn the ends with a lighted match, or in a gas flame, then submerge in cold water for several hours.

Arranging The leaves act as undershadow at the base of any small arrangement.

Tellima grandiflora, T. grandiflora 'Purpurea', height 45–60 cm (18–24 in), planting distance 45 cm (18 in).

Thalictrum

Of the varieties of this hardy perennial *T. speciosissimum* (*T. glaucum*) is my first choice: with its grey-green columbine-like foliage and fluffy yellow flowers, it is excellent for the back of the border, the leaf colour setting off any plant grown in front of it. *T. delavayi* (usually listed as *T. dipterocarpum*) has delightful nodding heads of mauve flower sprays; it never grows well for me.

Cultivation Plant from October to March in full sun or partial shade, in any good garden soil preferably enriched with compost or manure. Mulch in April, and give an occasional feed of soluble fertilizer. Some support of canes will be needed. Cut the plants down to the ground in November or December.

Conditioning The ends of the foliage stems should be dipped into boiling water and then given a long deep drink, but avoid submerging any leaves as this will reduce the grey effect, particularly of *T. speciosissimum*. A long drink is always recommended.

Arranging I like to use the individual leaf sprays, for they are so pretty mixed with roses or delicate pink flowers. I find the flower heads do not last well, but when these are over, the long foliage spikes, of up to 1.2 m (4 ft), are ideal for a large group in July to October. I often use the leaves of *T. delavayi* with columbines, and they look particularly lovely in a glass vase.

Thalictrum delavayi, height 1–1.5 m (4–5 ft), planting distance 45 cm (18 in); T. speciosissimum, height 1–1.5 m (4–5 ft), planting distance 60 cm (2 ft).

Tiarella cordifolia

I grow this perennial herb mostly as ground cover, though naturally every plant for me has to be useful for arrangements. The small dense clumps of heart-shaped well-marked leaves spread easily, and the leaves turn reddish-bronze in autumn. The masses of white bottle-brush flowers are pretty, but they do not last very well in water.

Cultivation Plant from October to April in any good garden soil enriched with compost or peat. A moist site is preferable, but if this cannot be provided regular watering should be given in dry spells. Mulch in April. Tidy up the plants in late autumn.

Conditioning Submerge the leaves overnight in water.

Arranging The design and balance of small arrangements are much improved by the addition of these well-marked little leaves at the base.

Height and planting distance 30 cm (12 in).

115

Tobacco Plant see Nicotiana

Trollius chinensis   Globe Flower

Height 75 cm (2½ ft), planting distance 30–45 cm.

A perennial. The yellows and oranges contrasted with the blue of forget-me-nots and bluebells make a good combination in the garden. The rounded heads are rather like big double buttercups. The only one I would grow is *T. chinensis*, usually listed as *T. ledebouri*, as the soft yellow of its flowers is a wonderful blending colour for arrangements.

Cultivation   Plant from October to March in any reasonably good garden soil, in sun or partial shade, in a moist position if possible. In sun, or a dry position, water generously in dry spells, and mulch every April. If the flower stems are cut back after flowering, a second crop may be produced.

Conditioning   Dip the ends of the stems into boiling water before putting them up to their necks in cold water for a long drink.

Arranging   I love to use these flowers with the first opening buds of *Acer pseudoplatanus* 'Brilliantissimum', some tellima leaves and a few heads of lime-green hellebores or spurge.

Tulipa   Tulip

Late or Cottage, Darwin, Parrot, Doubles, Tulipa viridiflora, height 60–75 cm (2–2½ ft), planting distance 15 cm.

Cottage tulips flower in late spring and are good for both bedding out and cutting. There are numerous varieties of the popular Darwin tulips, which are also excellent for bedding out and cutting. One tulip I would never be without is the early flowering 'Apricot Beauty'. The delicate lily-flowered tulips are lovely to arrange, for they have the most graceful lines. Among the early Doubles 'Tea Rose' is a delightful cream blushed pink; from the late Doubles I would single out the May-flowering 'Mount Tacoma' (white), 'Eros' (pink), and 'Lilac Time' (mauve). These give a marvellous focal point to any large group. The green tulips, *T. viridiflora*, are splendid for arranging and 'Artist', which has apricot stripes, adds an unusual touch of interest to any vase. Parrot tulips with their strange markings look strikingly original in arrangements. The early tulips for the rock garden add a bright splash of colour in the winter days both in the garden and in the house; *T. hageri* is orange striped with green and *T. linifolia* is coloured a remarkable red and grey.

Cultivation   Plant tulips from September to December in any good well-drained garden soil in full sun. Some varieties will remain in the ground and flower for years, others dwindle away. If they are to be grown mainly for cutting, they may be planted in a patch in the vegetable plot or 'cutting garden', and left to grow for several years. Or they may be lifted after flowering, laid in the ground in a shallow trench, and the bulbs lifted when the leaves and stems have died down. Dry the bulbs off and store in a cool shed until planting time.

Conditioning   Cut off the white ends of the stems, wrap the bunch in newspaper with all the heads tightly together and put in deep warm water for several hours. I have found that pricking with a pin right under the head and through the stem releases the air bubble and allows the tulip to drink more easily and has the effect of making it last much longer.

Arranging   Tulips arrange well on their own or when mixed with unrelated foliage, such as hornbeam catkins or willow, as background. They blend with any colour scheme through having such a wide range of colours. A few double whites will make an outstanding centre in a large group for a white wedding in May.

116

Veratrum nigrum

A rare and extremely handsome hardy perennial. The leaves, which unfurl like a fan out of the ground, are pale green with a most unusual pleated effect. The flower spike grows to about 90 cm (3 ft), rising out of the centre of the leaf clump, and producing a thick mass of almost black star-like flowers on about the top 23 cm (9 in) of stem. It is worth growing for the leaves alone – at least that is what I tell myself to hide the real disappointment of not getting a flower, as my plant refuses to bloom every year. The veratrum needs sun, but shaded roots, and hates disturbance.

Height 1 m (3–4 ft), planting distance 45 cm (18 in).

Cultivation   Plant from October to April, preferably in a moist, semi-shaded site, in any reasonably friable soil. Water in dry spells, and mulch in April. Cut down to the ground in November or December.

Conditioning and preserving   The ends of the stems must be dipped into boiling water for a few minutes and then allowed a long deep drink. Never pick until the flower is open right up the stem, or you will find that the top of the stem droops, and will never recover. Pick the leaves only after the flower has formed, so that you do not risk taking the growing flower stalk. The foliage is decorative in autumn arranged with gourds and berries, but as the slugs love it, it is often difficult to get a perfect leaf.

The slender flower and seed heads dry well. Once the seed is set, pick the stems and stand them in a little water, and they will then dry off quite quickly.

Arranging   These tall handsome precious spikes must be arranged so that they show off their spectacular beauty. Never cut the stems shorter than 60 cm (2 ft), and then, used with stems of black phytolacca seeds, lilies and rounded heads of agapanthus, they are a real joy.

Verbascum bombyciferum

V. bombyciferum, often listed as *V.* 'Broussa', is a wonderful perennial herb for use in arrangements, and in the garden for its spectacularly beautiful grey hairy rosettes of leaves in winter, as good as any flower. In spring the leaves become more silvery, and covered in woolly down. The flower spike, heavily fleeced with white wool and then studded with small yellow flowers all the way up its branching length, can grow as tall as 3.5 m (12 ft). 'C.L. Adams' is one of the best verbascum cultivars, with deep yellow flowers; but my own favourite is 'Gainsborough', with silvery foliage and the most charming long stems of pale yellow clustered flowers. All verbascums enjoy the sun, and are rewarding because they remain in bloom for about three months.

Height 1–2 m (4–6 ft), planting distance 60 cm (2 ft).

Cultivation   Plant from October to April in any good well-drained garden soil. Verbascums love full sun, but they make large plants and appreciate plenty of water in dry spells and a mulch in April. Stake the plants in windy gardens, and cut them down to the ground in November or December.

Conditioning and preserving   Stems of the individual leaves should be put into boiling water, and then given a long drink, but avoid submerging the leaf as this will result in destroying the grey effect. The tall young flower stems should be treated in the same way.

The seed heads dry well. When they are set on the plant, pick the stems and hang them upside down to dry. They dry to the most lovely grey colour and are useful as tall stems in a winter flower arrangement.

Arranging   As these are tall erect flowers, they play a background part in any arrangement, and are useful as tall spikes in a summer group. The leaves of the

117

lovely grey *V. bombyciferum* make a base of distinction to a vase at any time of year.

Viburnum

Viburnum x bodnantense, *height around 3 m (9–10 ft), spread 2.5–4 m (8–12 ft);* V. x burkwoodii, *height around 2 m (7–8 ft), spread 2–4 m (8–12 ft);* V. carlesii, *height and spread 1–1.5 m (4–5 ft);* V. fragrans, *height and spread 3–4 m (9–12 ft);* V. opulus 'Sterile', *height and spread 4.5 m (15 ft);* V. tinus, *height 2–3 m (6–10 ft), spread around 2 m;* V. tomentosum, *height 2–3 m, spread 3–4.5 m.*

A varied and extensive family, from which I have selected just a few. *V. x burkwoodii* is a very attractive evergreen shrub growing to about 1.5 m (5 ft) with rounded clusters of pink flowers, sweetly scented, appearing from January to April. The deciduous *V. carlesii* is rather similar in appearance, but with looser heads of flowers, pink in bud and opening to white in April and May. *V. fragrans* is one of my favourite deciduous shrubs because I can pick its scented pink blossoms from autumn through to next spring. *V. opulus* 'Sterile', the deciduous Guelder Rose or Snowball Tree, has round hanging globes of bright green flowers, turning white as they develop, and leaves with good autumn colouring. *V. tinus*, evergreen and growing up to 3 m (10 ft), exists in many varieties and is another useful winter-flowering plant, by March covered in pinky-white blossom. The wide-spreading horizontal branches of *V. tomentosum* give this beautiful oriental shrub its characteristic appearance, flowering along the top of the branches and with beautiful deeply-veined leaves. The deciduous *V. x bodnantense* is another I cannot leave out, as the deep pink flowers in winter are a joy both to look at in the garden and to arrange.

Cultivation   Plant October to March in any good garden soil, preferably not too sandy or quick draining. Viburnums do best in an open sunny site. They do not need much pruning beyond thinning out old worn-out shoots and generally keeping the plants shapely.

Conditioning and preserving   All the sweet-scented varieties should have their stems dipped in boiling water and be given a few hours in deep water. The flowers of *V. carlesii* do not last well, but I love their scent so much that I pick one piece at a time and replace daily if necessary. The stems of *V. opulus* 'Sterile' should be hammered.

The deeply veined leaves of *V. tomentosum* take up glycerine extremely well.

Arranging   As these are all shrubs of merit, you will have to pick with care, and the length of stem will be determined by your tree. I cannot resist taking little pieces of all the sweetly-scented ones and using them for small arrangements. You can cut more lavishly from *V. opulus* 'Sterile' as heavy pruning seems to improve it. When the leaves are removed the lime-green snowball flowers are revealed, and it is at this stage that I like them best, especially for an arrangement copying a Flemish flower painting, with striped tulips and lilac. After the leaves of this viburnum have turned colour, I use them a great deal, as I find they last better than any other autumn-tinted foliage.

Vinca major

'Variegata', *height 30 cm (12 in), planting distance 60 cm.*

V. major 'Variegata' is the only periwinkle I grow, as it is the most useful for the flower arranger, with arching stems of cream and green leaves. All vincas make excellent ground cover below trees.

Cultivation   Plant from October to April, preferably in semi-shade in any good garden soil. Once established they grow luxuriantly, but they appreciate a mulch in April, and plenty of water in dry spells.

Conditioning   The stem ends must be either burnt or boiled, and then soaked in really deep water overnight.

Arranging   I find that I use these leaves more in winter than in summer, for they go so well in mixed green arrangements, and there are not so many attractive variegated plants that will hang gracefully for a winter group.

Vine see Vitis

Virginia Creeper see Vitis

Virginia Poke Weed see Phytolacca americana

Vitis
Ampelopsis

Vine
Virginia Creeper

Under this heading I have grouped one true vine, *V. vinifera* 'Purpurea', and one Virginia Creeper, *Ampelopsis aconitifolia*, because they both have superb autumn colour and are useful for the flower arranger. The large leaves of *A. aconitifolia* are most ornamental in autumn, changing from pink to glowing scarlet. The leaves of *V. vinifera* 'Purpurea' are a good purple colour all year, but deepen in autumn, and this plant produces the most lovely bunches of maroon-coloured grapes, which makes it doubly useful.

Cultivation   Plant from October to March in any reasonably good soil. A west- or south-facing aspect against a wall is best, especially for the vine if grapes are to be produced. The ampelopsis needs no pruning. The vitis may need to have surplus growths removed in early spring and some lush shoots pinched back in early summer.

Conditioning and preserving   The stems of both subjects last better if dipped in boiling water and then submerged overnight, or at least for a few hours. Both leaves may be given the wax treatment: iron with a cool iron between wax paper, then add false stems made with florist's wire.

Arranging   The large leaves of *A. aconitifolia* do not last long once they have changed colour, but they are wonderful to use for some special occasion. Sprays can give a big group of autumn colour a special touch of drama that is hard to beat. I use individual leaves for fruit and flower groups.

Small bunches of purple grapes from *V. vinifera* 'Purpurea' and a few trails of its maroon leaves are quite lovely with some full-blown red roses.

Vitis vinifera, V. vinifera *'Purpurea', height 6 m (20 ft), spread 3–4.5 m (10–15 ft);* Ampelopsis aconitifolia, *height 6 m (20 ft), spread 3–4.5 m (10–15 ft);* Ampelopsis brevipedunculata maximowiczii, *height approx 3 m (9 ft), spread approx 2 m (6 ft).*

Willow see Salix

Winter Aconite see Eranthis hyemalis

Winter Sweet see Chimonanthus praecox

119

Wistaria

Wistaria sinensis, W. sinensis 'Alba', height 24–50 m.

Quite the best and most popular wistaria is *W. sinensis*, and a wall smothered with the long mauve racemes of sweet-scented flowers looks magnificent – though since visiting the gardens at Bodnant I confess I have bitterly regretted not planting the white variety, *W. sinensis* 'Alba'. It is one of the most beautiful sights I have ever seen.

Cultivation   Plant from October to March in any good garden soil. Wistarias will ramble up over trees; they can be trained against a wall or over a porch or pergola; or they can be grown as a free-standing bush. They prefer a sunny aspect.

When grown against a wall or as a free-standing bush all new shoots must be pinched back when they have made four leaves in summer. Then in winter these shoots should be pruned back to leave only two buds.

Cultivation   I always wrap the flower trusses in tissue paper, then dip the stem ends in boiling water for a count of twenty, followed by the usual long drink in deep water. The tissue paper protects the tender blooms from the steam. In Japan I gather that they keep a bottle of pure spirit and allow the stems to drink that for a few hours.

Arranging   Wistarias are not long-lived in water, but nevertheless are worth picking as you will usually have plenty, and each stem can therefore be replaced easily. Just a branch of twisted willow (*Salix matsudana* 'Tortuosa') and a stem of wistaria take a lot of beating: so simple but very effective. One of the prettiest arrangements I ever made was a vase of pale pink peonies, 'Nelly Moser' clematis and mauve wistaria, which added a luscious touch.

Witch Hazel see Hamamelis

Yarrow see Achillea

Yucca filamentosa   Adam's Needle

Height 60–75 cm (2–2½ ft), spread around 1 m (3–4 ft).

Though many yuccas flower only once in seven years, I would recommend this shrub, for you are pretty certain to have at least one bloom every year; at its best planted in isolation, when you can really appreciate its statuesque appearance. It grows up to 1.5 m (5 ft) tall, and produces its dramatic tall flower spikes of pendulous ivory bells in July and August. The yucca is a native of California, so needs lots of sun and well-drained soil.

Cultivation   Plant from October to March in any garden soil, in full sun. This is an uncomplaining plant that will grow in even poor soils, but it does not like to lie wet in winter.

Conditioning   The ends of the stems should be put into boiling water for 5 cm (2 in) up the stem, left in it until the water gets cold, and then given a long deep drink overnight, or even longer if possible since the stems are so woody. Remove any drooping bells as they fade, and in this way you can keep them going a very long time.

Arranging   The tall spikes must be used so that their full height and beauty can be seen. This means a really large group for a really important occasion – I have used them in the Albert Hall where they looked superb. Nevertheless, they could look well in your own home if arranged in a very large shallow container, so that you can see the flower stems in all their glory.

Zantedeschia aethiopica   Arum or Calla Lily

I have managed to keep my arum lilies alive and healthy on a south wall now for three winters and look on this as a real triumph. This handsome plant is worth growing just for the magnificent dark-green spade-shaped leaves, though the white arum flower with its yellow central spadix is wonderful in the garden and in the house.

Height 60–90 cm (2–3 ft), planting distance 45–60 cm (18–24 in).

Cultivation Zantedeschias are hardy in the warm counties of Britain. They seem to thrive best in the deep mud of a pool margin, although they may be grown in a sunny border and covered with straw or bracken in really severe weather. The variety 'Crowborough' seems to be the hardiest. Plant in spring.

Conditioning The flowers last very well with no special treatment, but the leaves need to be submerged in water overnight. I have found that a weak solution of starch added to the water helps to stiffen them very effectively.

Arranging Arum lilies are marvellous for a modern arrangement with only line in mind. Using a shallow container, you can make a perfect long-lasting arrangement using a well-shaped background branch, three lilies, each shorter than the last, and two of their own leaves. But I think that the very best use for these lilies is in church decorations, as they show up so well from a great distance in simple altar vases or in a large group. Five lilies will make the centre of any church arrangement. When I was in Kenya once, I was able to use them in armfuls, so I cut them short and made a formal mass arrangement with no stems showing, just lily heads, in a raised black shallow urn. It looked lovely, but I don't suppose I will ever be able to do it again.

Zinnia

If you find zinnias do well in your garden, the colours will be superb and you must, of course, grow these annuals. I find them difficult but 'Envy' flourishes and adds colour to the border. As sunlovers, zinnias need full sun and like a well-drained soil.

Zinnia elegans, 'Envy', height 60–75 cm (2–2½ ft), planting distance 30 cm (12 in).

Cultivation Sow the seeds under glass in March, prick out and harden off the seedlings, and plant them out at the end of May or early June when danger of frost is past. Or seed may be sown direct in a well-prepared seed bed in mid to late May, and the seedlings thinned out gradually to their final distance. Zinnias enjoy good fertile soil and plenty of water in dry weather.

Conditioning and preserving The ends of the stems should be placed in boiling water and then allowed a long drink. If the stems are brittle, it is advisable to put a firm florist's wire right up the stem. (Very often when zinnias arrive in the market this has already been done.)

You can preserve zinnias beautifully by removing the stems completely and replacing them with florist's wire; the flowers should be laid in a box of preserving powder. They keep their colour very well and are ideal in winter arrangements.

Arranging 'Envy' makes a wonderful centre to any green arrangement, and if you grow other varieties as well they are excellent in mixed arrangements for late summer and the autumn.

INDEX

Acanthus mollis, 33, 36
 spinosus, 33
Acer ginnala, 33
 griseum, 33
 negundo, 'Aureum' 33
 pennsylvanicum, 33
 platanoides, 33–4
  'Drummondii', 33–4
 pseudoplatanus 'Brilliantissimum', 33–4, 43, 116; 'Nizetti', 33
 rubrum 'Schlesingerii', 33, 34
Achillea, 21, 29, 32, 34
 filipendulina 'Gold Plate', 34
 'Moonshine', 34
Aconite, 20
 winter, 101
Aconitum lycoctonum, 34–5
Acrolinium, 13, 30, 32, 35
Adam's Needle, 120–1
Agapanthus, 33, 35–6, 117
 Headbourne hybrids, 35
Air drying, 29–30
Alchemilla mollis, 9, 10, 22, 26, 36, 38
Alder, 37
Allium, 21, 36–7
 caeruleum, 36
 giganteum, 36
 ostrowskianum, 36
 rosenbachianum, 36
 roseum 'Grandiflorum', 37
 siculum, 36
Almond, 100
Alnus incana 'Aurea', 37
Alstroemeria ligtu hybrids, 3, 9, 10, 37–8
Alyssum, 14
Amaranthus caudatus viridis, 38
Ampelopsis aconitifolia, 119
Anaphalis margaritacea, 38
 nubigena, 38
Anemone elegans, 39
 japonica, 39
  'September Charm', 'White Giant'
Angelica archangelica, 39
Angel's Tears, 89
Antirrhinum, 10, 14, 39–40
 'Butterfly', 'Penstemon Flowered', 39
Aralia elata, 40
 'Aureo-variegata'
Arbutus unedo, 40
Artemisia, 21, 35, 41
 absinthium 'Lambrook Silver', 41
 lactiflora, 41
Artichoke, 3, 9, 10, 17
 Globe, 58–9
Arum italicum 'Pictum', 10, 41
Astrantia major, 41–2
Atriplex, 10, 42

 hortensis, 42
Aubretia, 14
Aucuba, 11, 20
 japonica, 42, 70
Auricula, 78, 99
Autumn arrangements, 23, 45, 56, 66, 80, 98, 99
Azalea, 35, 42–3, 53
 Deciduous, 43
  'Bouquet de Flore', 'W. S. Churchill', 'Coccinea Speciosa', 'Fireglow', 'Persil'
 Evergreen, 43
  'Adonis', 'Blue Danube', 'Orange Beauty', 'Palestrina', 'Vuyk's Scarlet'
Baby's Breath, 23, 24
Ballota pseudo-dictamnus, 43
Beech, 14, 30–1, 32, 67–8
Beetroot, 23, 64, 101
Begonia
 rex, 49, 66
 semperflorens, 13, 44
  'Coco Ducolour', 'Dancia Scarlet', 'Rosanova', 'Venus Rose'
Bellis perennis, 13
Bells of Ireland, 10, 28, 49, 88
Berberis, 23, 44–5
 'Buccaneer', 44
 darwinii, 44
 linearifolia 'Orange King', 44
 thunbergii, 44
  'Atropurpurea', 'Aurea'
 verruculosa, 44
Bergenia, 9, 10, 11, 20, 45, 70
 cordifolia, 45
 crassifolia, 31, 45
 purpurascens 'Ballawley', 45
Betula, 45–6
 costata, 45
 papyrifera, 45
 pendula, 45
  'Obelisk', 'Youngii'
Birch, Silver, 10, 45–6, 58
Bird Cherry, 100
Bittersweet, 14, 49–50
Black snake-root, 51–2
Bleeding heart, 61
Bluebell, 13, 25
Bracken, 31
Briza maxima, 30, 31, 32, 72–3
Buddleia alternifolia, 46
 davidii, 46
  'Black Knight', 'Harlequin'
 fallowiana, 46
Bullrush, 14
Burning bush, 62

Calluna vulgaris, 'H. E. Beale', 64–5
Camellia, 13, 20, 26, 27, 47
 japonica, 47
  'Elegans', 'Mathotiana', 'Mercury'
 x williamsii, 47
  'Donation', 'J. C. Williams'
Campanula, 14, 48
 carpatica, 48
 glomerata, 48
 lactiflora, 48
  'Loddon Anna', 'Prichard's Variety'
 latifolia, 48
  'Alba', 'Gloaming'
 persicifolia, 48
 portenschlagiana, 48
Cardoon, 30
Carnation, 15, 61
Carpinus betulus, 31, 48–9
Carrot, 13
Cathedral Bells, 53
Catmint, 71, 89–90
Cedar, Blue, 49
Cedrus atlantica 'Glauca', 49
Celastrus orbiculatus, 49–50
Chimonanthus fragrans, 75
 praecox, 20, 50
Chionodoxa gigantea, 50
Choisya ternata, 50–1
 'Sun Dance', 50
Christmas Rose, 32, 75, 80, 81, 109
Chrysanthemum, 14, 15, 21, 22, 29, 46, 51, 57
 Korean varieties, 51
  'Wedding Day'
 maximum 'Esther Read', 51
Cimicifuga racemosa, 51–2
 racemosa purpurea, 51
Cineraria maritima, 111
Clematis, 14, 52–3
 'Duchess of Edinburgh', 'Hagley Hybrid', 'Madame le Coultre', 'Nelly Moser', 'W. E. Gladstone'
 armandii, 52
 macropetala, 52
 montana, 52
  'Rubens'
 orientalis 'Orange Peel', 52
 tangutica, 52
 wild, 31
Climbers, Choosing, 10–11
Cobaea scandens, 53
Colchicum, 53
 autumnali, 53
Colour, arranging for, 9, 22, 23
Comfrey, 114
Conditioning flowers, 23

Conifer, Miniature, 14
Containers, 14–15, 23, 24–7
Convallaria majalis, 26, 54
Cornus alba, 54–5
  'Sibirica Variegata', 'Spaethii'
  florida 'Rubra', 32, 54
  mas, 9, 54–5
  nuttallii, 54
  sanguinea, 54
Cortaderia selloana, 72
Corylopsis pauciflora, 55
  spicata, 55
Corylus, 55–6
  avellana 'Contorta', 55
  maxima 'Purpurea', 55
Cotinus coggygria, 56
  'Flame', 'Foliis Purpureis'
Cotoneaster, 56–7
  congesta, 12, 101, 111
  'Cornubia', 56
  horizontalis, 56
  wardii, 56
  watereri, 56
Cow parsley, 13, 14, 26
Cow parsnip, 13
Cowslip, 13
Cranesbill, 71
Crocosmia masonorum, 57
Crocus, Autumn, 53, 95
Crocus, 20, 26, 32, 57–8, 70, 80, 81, 101
  biflorus, 57
  chrysanthus, 57
    'E. A. Bowles', 'Golden Bunch',
      'Snow Bunting', 'Zwanenburg
      Bronze'
  sieberi, 57
  tomasinianus, 57
    'Whitwell Purple'
Crown Imperial, 69
Cups and saucers, 53
Currant, Flowering, 20, 104–5
Cyclamen coum, 58
  hardy, 101
  miniature, 26
  neapolitanum, 58
  repandum, 58
Cynara cardunculus, 58–9
  scolymus, 10, 58–9

Daffodil, 13, 15, 20, 25, 34, 37, 55, 63,
  89, 104
Dahlia, 14, 20, 22, 23, 31, 43, 57, 59,
  64, 67, 81, 88, 111, 112, 114
  'Angora', 'Apricot Waverley Pearl',
    'Baseball', 'Cherry Ripe',
    'Chorus Girl', 'Delicious', 'Doris
    Day', 'Gold Crown', 'Hawaii',
    'Hockley Maroon', 'Jerry Hoek',
    'Jescot Buttercup', 'Jescot Jim',
    'Lilac Time', 'Newby', 'New
    Church', 'Polar Beauty', 'Ponos',
    59

Daisy, Shasta, 51
dog, 13
Daphne cneorum, 60
  laureola, 60
  mezereum, 60
    'Alba'
  odora 'Aureo-marginata', 60
Delphinium, 10, 14, 29, 32, 60–1, 79, 82,
  96, 114
  Belladonna varieties, 60
    'Blue Bees', 'Peace'
  Pacific hybrids, 60–1
Dianthus, 26, 61, 82, 101
  'Mrs Sinkins', 61
  rock garden, 14
Dicentra spectabilis, 61–2
  alba, 62
Dictamnus albus, 62
  'Purpureus'
Digitalis grandiflora, 62–3, 86
  parviflora, 62–3
  purpurea 'Sutton's Apricot', 62–3
Dizygotheca, 40
Dock, 13
Dogwood, 32, 54–5
Dried flower arrangements, 21, 29, 35,
  38, 74
Dutchman's Pipe, 53

Elaeagnus pungens, 63
  'Maculata', 'Variegata'
Elymus arenaria, 72–3
Epimedium x *rubrum*, 63–4
Eranthis hyemalis, 64
Erica, 25, 64–5
  carnea, 64
    'Eileen Porter', 'Springwood Pink',
      'Springwood White'
  mediterranea, 64
    'Superba', 'W. T. Rackliff''
Eryngium giganteum, 31, 65
Erythronium dens-canis, 65
  'Kondo', 'Lilac Wonder', 'Pagoda'
Eucalyptus, 9, 65–6
  gunnii, 66
  parviflora, 66
Euonymus, 14, 20, 66
  europaeus, 66
  fortunei 'Silver Queen', 66
  japonicus, 66
    'Aureo-pictus', 'Ovatus Aureus',
      'Microphyllus Variegatus'
Euphorbia, 9, 10, 22, 67
  characias, 67
  fulgens, 67
  griffithii 'Fireglow', 67
  myrsinites, 67
  polychroma, 67
  pulcherrima, 67
  robbiae, 67
  veneta, 67

Fagus sylvatica, 30–1, 32, 58, 67–8
  'Heterophylla Laciniata', 67–8
  'Tricolor', 67–8
  purpurea 'Atropunicea', 67
Fair Maids of France, 103
Fern, Royal, 31, 91
Fertilizers, 14
Filipendula ulmaria 'Aurea', 68
Firethorn, 102–3
Flag, 79–80
Flower beds, 8, 9
Flowers, Choosing, 9
Foliage colour, 22, 23
Forget-me-not, 26, 32
Forsythia, 9, 10, 20, 68–9, 104
  x *intermedia*, 68–9
    'Lynwood', 'Primulina',
      'Spectabilis'
  suspensa 'Fortunei', 69
Foxglove, 62–3, 86
Freesia, 15, 26
Fritillaria, 13
Fritillaria caucasica, 69
  imperialis, 69
  meleagris, 69
Fuchsia, 11
  miniature, 14

Galanthus, 20, 25, 26, 27, 32, 69–70, 80,
  81, 101
Garden design, 7–9
Gardenia, 26
Garrya elliptica, 10, 20, 70
Gentian, 26, 53, 70–1, 95
  willow, 70–1
Gentiana acaulis, 70–1
  asclepiadea, 70
  sino-ornata, 70–1
Geranium, 10, 71, 78
  'Ballerina', 71
  x 'Johnson's Blue', 71
  sanguineum, 71
  'Wargrave Pink', 71
Geranium, Ivy-leaved, 12
Gladiolus, 46, 57, 67, 71–2, 101, 108,
  112
  'Comic', 72; 'Dancing Doll', 71;
    'Greenwich', 71; 'Green
    Woodpecker', 72; 'Obelisk', 72;
    'Tropical Sunset', 71; 'White
    City', 72
Globe Flower, 116
Glory of the Snow, 50
Glycerine, Preservation in, 30–1
Grape hyacinth, 69, 78
Grapes, 23, 26, 47, 119
Grasses, 30, 31, 32, 72–3
Green arrangements, 20, 21, 22–3, 47,
  51, 63, 67, 70, 74, 91
Ground cover plants, 45, 54, 63, 64,
  76, 89, 91, 95, 98, 113, 115, 118
Guelder rose, 118

Gypsophila, 14, 22, 24

Hamamelis mollis, 19, 73
   'Pallida', 73
   virginiana, 73
Hanging baskets, 12–13, 94
Hawthorn berries, 14
Hazel, 13, 15, 20, 55–6
Heather, 64–5
Hedera, 10, 22, 31, 73–4
   canariensis 'Variegata', 73
   colchica, 'Dentata Variegata', 73
   helix, 73
      'Buttercup', 'Gold Heart'
Helichrysum, 31, 74
   petulatum, 74
Helleborus, 75, 80, 81, 109
   'Ballard's Black', 75
   corsicus, 75
   foetidus, 9, 10, 21, 75, 96, 97, 116
   lividus, 75
   niger, 75
   nigicorus, 75
   orientalis hybrids, 75
Hemerocallis, 76
Hemlock, 13
Herbaceous borders, 39
Hermodactylus tuberosa, 69
Heuchera, 76
   Bressingham hybrids, 76
   'Bridget Bloom', 'Greenfinch',
      'Palace Purple', 'Scintillation'
Hollyhock, 30
Honesty, 25, 85–6
Honeysuckle, 85
Hoop petticoat, 89
Hornbeam, 31, 48–9
Hosta, 9, 10, 30, 48, 77–8
   albo-marginata, 77
   crispula, 77
   fortunei, 77–8
      'Albo-picta', 'Aureomarginata'
      'Frances Williams', 77
      'Gold Standard', 77
   sieboldiana 'Elegans', 77
   x 'Thomas Hogg', 77
   'Wogan's Gold', 77
Hyacinthus, 13, 69, 78, 101
Hydrangea, 12, 14, 21, 30, 32, 33, 78–9
   arborescens, 78–9
   macrophylla hortensis, 78–9
   paniculata, 79
   quercifolia, 79
   sargentiana, 79

Iris, 22, 79–80, 101
   'Blue Admiral', 'Canary Bird',
      'Golden Planet', 'Magic Hills',
      'My Smoky', 'Prairie Sunset',
      'Tuscan', 'White City', 79
   foetidissima, 79–80
   histrioides, 79–80

pallida 'Argenteo-variegata', 79–80
pseudacorus 'Variegata', 79–80
reticulata, 80
sibirica, 79–80
stylosa, 80
unguicularis, 75, 79–80, 88, 101
Ivy, 10, 22, 31, 73–4

Jasmine, Summer, 25, 80–1
   Winter, 26, 75, 80–1
Jasminum, 25, 26, 75, 80–1
   nudiflorum, 25, 75, 80–1
   officinale 'Affine', 25, 80–1
Jonquil, 89
Juniperus communis compressa, 8

Kale, 14
Kniphofia, 81
   'Bee's Sunset', 'Brimstone', 'Earliest
      of All', 'Jenny Bloom', 'Maid of
      Orleans'
   uvaria, 81

Lagurus ovatus, 72–3
Lamb's Ears, 113
Larkspur, 32, 79
Lathyrus odoratus, 82
   'Jet Set'
Laurel, 8, 30, 31, 32
   Portugal, 100–1
   preserving, 30
   Spotted, 11, 42
Lavandula spica, 82
   'Hidcote'
   vera, 82
Lavatera, 82
   'Mont Blanc', 'Silver Cup'
Lavender, 82
Lawns, 11
Leucojum aestivum, 83
Leucothöe, 9
   catesbaei, 83
Ligustrum lucidum 'Golden Wax', 83
   ovalifolium 'Aureum', 83
   vulgare, 83
Lilac, 94, 101, 114, 118
Lilium, 12, 13, 84, 104
   auratum, 12
   candidum, 84
   De Graaff hybrids, 84
   'Black Magic', 'Enchantment',
      'Limelight', 'Pink Perfection'
   martagon, 84
   regale, 68, 84
   'Stargazer', 84
   testaceum, 84
Lily, 12, 13, 84
   Arum, 121
   Calla, 121
   Day, 76
   Madonna, 84

Lily of the valley, 13, 26, 54
Lime, 31, 84
Lion's Mouth, 39
Lobelia 'Blue Cascade', 12, 14, 84
Lonicera, 22, 25, 85
   japonica 'Aureo-reticulata', 85
   periclymenum, 'Belgica', 85
   sempervirens, 85
Love-lies-Bleeding, 38
Lunaria, 85–6
Lupin, 23, 30, 86, 94, 114
Lupinus arboreus, 86
   polyphyllus, 86

Macleaya cordata 'Coral Plume', 86–7
Magnolia, 87
   grandiflora, 31, 87
   liliiflora 'Nigra', 87
   x *soulangeana*, 87
      'Alba', 'Lennei', 'Rustica Rubra'
   stellata, 87
   wilsonii, 87
Mahonia, 30, 32, 87–8
   aquifolium, 87
   bealei, 87
   x 'Charity', 87–8
   japonica, 87–8
Maple, 33–4
Marigold, 14, 25, 26, 31
Mexican Orange Blossom, 50–1
Milkweed, 14
Miniature arrangements, 27–8
Miss Wilmott's Ghost, 31, 65
Mock Orange, 96
Moluccella, 10, 30, 49, 88
   laevis, 29, 31, 88
Money plant, 85
Monkshood, 34–5
Moss garden, 20, 50, 58, 60, 64, 69, 70,
   75, 78, 83, 101
Mountain ash, 14
Muscari, 78

Narcissus, 89
   'Beersheba', 'Binkie', 'Cherie',
      'Devon Loch', 'February Gold',
      Fermoy', 'Geranium', 'Green
      Island', 'March Sunshine',
      'Mount Hood', 'Mrs R. O.
      Backhouse', 'Paper White',
      'Polindra', 'Salmon Trout',
      'Snowball', 'Spellbinder'
   bulbocodium 'Conspicuous', 89
   cyclamineus, 89
   x *hawera*, 89
   triandrus 'Albus', 89
Nasturtium, 25, 26
Nepeta x *faassenii*, 89–90
Nerine, 26, 53, 60, 90
   bowdenii, 90
Nicotiana, 13, 26, 90
   affinis 'Lime Green', 49, 90

Oasis, 21, 26, 27
Old Man's Beard, 14, 22, 23, 26, 31
Onopordum salteri, 90–1
Orchid, 13
Orchis, 13
Oregon Grape, 87
Osmunda regalis, 31, 91

Pachysandra procumbens, 91–2
  terminalis, 91–2
Paeonia, 92–3
  delavayi, 92–3
  lactiflora, 92
    'Beau Geste', 'Dresden', 'Duchesse
      de Nemours', 'Kelway's Queen',
      'Lord Kitchener', 'Pink Delight'
  lutea ludlowii, 92
    'Souvenir de Maxime-Cornu'
  suffruticosa, 92
    'Hakugan', 'Lord Selbourne', 'Mrs
      William Kelway', Souvenir de la
      Reine Elizabeth'
Pampas Grass, 72–3
Pansy, 26
Papaver, 93–4
  nudicaule, 93
  orientale, 93
    'Mrs Perry', 'Perry's White'
  rhoeas, 93
  somniferum, 93
Parsley, 13
Pasque Flower, 102
Paths, 7, 8
Patio gardens, 11–14
Paved areas, 8
Peach, Flowering, 100–1
Pelargonium, 94
Penstemon, 94–5
  fruticosus 'Cardwellii', 94
  hartwegii 'Garnet', 94
  laevigatus 'Digitalis', 94
Peony, 10, 61, 78, 92–3, 96, 101, 120
Pernettya mucronata, 95
  'Alba', 'Davis's Hybrids', 'Lilacina'
Petasites fragrans, 95
  japonicus 'Giganteus', 95–6
Petunia, 10, 12, 13, 14, 24, 96
Philadelphus, 96
  'Beauclerk', 'Belle Etoile',
    'Burfordiensis', 'Virginal'
  coronarius 'Aureus', 96
Phlox, 96–7
  alpine, 11
  hybrids, 97
    'Admiral', 'Daily Sketch', 'Mother
      of Pearl', 'Prince of Orange',
      'Sandringham', 'Vintage Wine'
  paniculata, 96–7
Photinia serrulata 'Red Robin', 97
Phytolacca americana, 10, 14, 97–8, 108,
  117
Pin-holders, 21

Pinks, 14, 26, 61, 82, 101
Planning the garden, 7–10
Plum, Flowering, 100–1
Poinsettia, 67
Poke-weed, Virginian, 97–8
Polyanthus, 10, 26, 99
Polygonatum multiflorum, 22, 98
Polygonum affine 'Donald Lowndes', 98
  aubertii, 98–9
  bistorta 'Superbum', 98–9
  cuspidatum 'Variegatum', 98
Poppy, annual, 23, 93–4
  Oriental, 92–3
  perennial, 4, 10
  Shirley, 93
Portugal laurel, 100–1
Pressing flowers, 31
Primrose, 13, 26, 32, 80, 99
Primula, 99
  denticulata, 99
  malacoides, 99
  rosea 'Delight', 99
  vulgaris, 99
Privet, 14, 83, 108, 114
Prunella grandiflora, 100
Prunus, 100–1
  cerasifera 'Nigra', 100
  communis, Pollardii', 100
  davidiana 'Alba', 100
  laurocerasus, 100–1
  lusitanica, 100–1
  padus 'Watereri', 100
  persica, 100
    'Cardinale', 'Prince Charming'
  serrulata, 100–1
    'Amanogawa', 'Kanzan',
      'Shirotae', 'Ukon'
  subhirtella, 20, 100–1
    'Autumnalis', 15, 100; 'Autumnalis
      Rosea', 100; 'Pendula Rosea',
      100
Pulmonaria angustifolia 'Azurea', 102
  saccharata 'Pink Dawn', 102
Pulsatilla vulgaris, 102
Pyracantha, 102–3
  angustifolia, 102
  crenulata, 102
    'Rogersiana', 'Rogersiana Flava'

Queen Anne's lace, 13

Ranunculus aconitifolius 'Flore-pleno',
  103
  asiaticus, 103
  bulbosus 'Pleniflorus', 103
Red-hot Poker, 81
Rheum alexandrae, 103–4
  palmatum, 103–4
    'Atrosanguineum', 'Rubrum'
Rhododendron, 9, 101, 104, 114
  'Christmas Cheer', 'Cunningham's
    White', 'Doncaster', 'Pink Pearl',
    'Praecox', 104

Rhus, 56
Ribes laurifolium, 104–5
  sanguineum, 104–5
    'Atrorubens', 'Brocklebank',
      'Carneum'
Rock gardens, 8, 14, 58, 60, 80, 108,
  111
Rodgersia pinnata 'Superba', 105
Rose hips, 14
Roses, 10, 13, 14, 20, 22, 23, 26, 31, 47,
  57, 61, 71, 79, 81, 86, 88, 90, 95,
  105–8, 112, 113, 114, 119
  Climbing, 106–7
  'Albertine', 'Bantry Bay', 'Climbing
    Allgold', 'Etoile de Holland',
    'Guinea', 'Iceberg', 'Lawrence
    Johnston', 'Mermaid', 'New
    Dawn', 'Paul's Lemon Pillar',
    Rosa banksiae 'Lutea', *Rosa filipes*
    'Kifsgate'
  Floribunda, 106
  'Apricot Nectar', 'Elizabeth of
    Glamis', 'Fashion', 'Ginger
    Megg', 'Iceberg', 'Lilli Marlene',
    'Rosemary Rose', 'Sheila
    Macqueen', 'Sir Lancelot',
    'Topsy', 'Woburn Abbey'
  Hybrid tea, 106
  'Amber', 'Anne Letts', 'Apricot Silk',
    'Beauté', 'Bettina', 'Blessings',
    'Blue Moon', 'Christian Dior',
    'Elizabeth Harkness', 'Ena
    Harkness', 'Eroica', 'Fantan',
    'Fragrant Cloud', 'Golden
    Times', 'Helen Traubel', 'Iced
    Ginger', 'Jocelyn', 'John F.
    Kennedy', 'Josephine Bruce',
    'Julia', 'Just Joey', 'King's
    Ransom', 'Lady Helen', 'Lilac
    Time', 'Message', 'Miss Harp',
    'Northern Lights', 'Ophelia',
    'Pascali', 'Pink Chiffon', 'Sir
    Harry Pilkington', 'Sterling
    Silver', 'Sunblest', 'Super Star',
    'Tynwald', 'Vespa', 'Virgo',
    'Whisky Mac'
  Shrub, 105–6
  'Abraham Darby', 'Blanc Double de
    Coubert', 'Cardinal de
    Richelieu', 'Celeste', 'Charles
    Austin', 'Charles de Mills',
    'Chaucer', 'Constance Spry',
    'Dame Prudence', 'Fantin
    Latour', 'Great Maiden's Blush',
    'Lord Oberon', 'Madame Isaac
    Pereire', 'Madame Lauriol de
    Barny', 'Madame Pierre Oger',
    'Proud Titania', 'Tamara',
    'Tuscany', 'Variegata di
    Bologna'
Roses, wild, 14
Rudbeckia fulgida 'Deamii', 108

Salix, 108–9
  alba 'Chermesina', 108
  babylonica, 108
  caprea, 108–9
  lanata, 108
  matsudana 'Tortuosa', 20, 108–9, 120
  sachalinensis, 108
Salvia haematodes, 109
  nemorosa 'Superba', 109
  sclarea 'Turkestanica', 109
  splendens, 109
Satin Flower, 111–12
Scabiosa caucasica, 109–10
  'Clive Greaves', 'Miss Willmott'
Scrophularia nodosa 'Variegata', 110
Sedum, 10, 30, 110–11
  aizoon, 110–11
  alboroseum 'Variegatum', 110
  x 'Autumn Joy', 13, 110–11
  maximum 'Atropurpureum', 110
  'Ruby Glow', 110–11
  spectabile 'Brilliant', 110
Seed heads, 29
Sempervivum, 14
Senecio, 22, 111
  bicolor, 111
  cineraria, 111
  laxifolius, 111
Shell Flower, 88
Shrubs, choosing, 10–11
Silica gel, preserving in, 107
Sink gardens, 8, 14, 80
Sisyrinchium striatum, 111–12
Size of arrangements, 22
Smilacina racemosa, 112
Smoke bush, 56
Snapdragon, 10, 14, 39–40
Snowball tree, 118
Snowberry, 114
Snowdrop, 13, 20, 25, 26, 27, 32, 69–70, 80, 81, 101
Soil for patio plants, 14
Solanum capsicastrum, 14
Solomon's Seal, 17, 98, 112

Sorrel, 13
Spindle tree, 66
Spring arrangements, 23–4, 50, 73, 78, 96
Stachys lanata, 113
  'Sheila Macqueen'
Statice, 30, 31, 32, 113
Stem arranging, 22
Stock, 10
Strawberry tree, 40
Straw Flowers, 74
Summer arrangements, 20, 37, 38, 40, 109
Summer Snowflake, 83
Sweet Pea, 20, 24, 25, 82
Swimming pools, 12
Symphoricarpos albus 'Laevigatus', 114
Symphytum officinale variegata, 114
Syringa vulgaris, 114, 118

Teasle, 14
Tellima, 9, 69, 116
  grandiflora, 115
  'Purpurea'
Thalictrum delavayi, 115
  speciosissimum, 115
Tiarella cordifolia, 115
Tobacco plant, 13, 26, 49, 90
Tree lupin, 86
Tree peony, 92
Trees, choosing, 11
Trollius chinensis, 116
Tubs, 12–14, 94
Tulip, 13, 27, 34, 43, 55, 62, 69, 101, 104, 116, 118
  'Apricot Beauty', 43, 116; 'Eros', 116; 'Lilac Time', 116; 'Murillo', 13; 'Peach Blossom', 13; 'Mount Tacoma', 43, 116; 'Tea Rose', 116
Tulipa hageri, 116
  linifolia, 116
  viridiflora, 116
  'Artist'

Vases, 22, 23, 24–5
Veratrum nigrum, 117
Verbascum bombyciferum, 117–18
  'C. L. Adams', 'Gainsborough'
Verbena, 10
Viburnum, 26
  x *bodnantense*, 118
  x *burkwoodii*, 118
  carlesii, 118
  fragrans, 20, 25, 118
  opulus 'Sterile', 118
  tinus 'Evelyn Price', 118
  tomentosum, 118
Vinca major 'Variegata', 118
Vine, 119
Violet, 26, 32
  Dog's Tooth, 65
Virginia Creeper, 119
Vitis vinifera, 119
  'Purpurea'

Wallflower, 13, 25
Water, drying in, 30
Willow, 108–9
Willow herb, 13, 14
Window boxes, 12
Winter Aconite, 64
Winter arrangements, 20, 25, 49, 66, 117, 119
Winter cherry, 14
Winter Sweet, 20, 50
Wire netting, 21
Wistaria sinensis, 21
  'Alba'
Witch hazel, 73

Yarrow, 21, 29, 31, 32, 34
Yucca filamentosa, 120–1

Zantedeschia aethiopica, 47
  'Crowborough', 120
Zinnia, 22, 31, 49, 121
  elegans 'Envy', 121